ADVANCE PRAISE
FOR **RAILROADER**

"Hunter Harrison was a colorful man with a zest for life and a passion for railroading. He was certainly the greatest modern manager of these massive networks of commerce that undergird industrial society. *Railroader* is the story of an interesting life and the intricacies of complex managerial challenges, woven into an enjoyable and highly informative book."

FREDERICK W. SMITH, chairman and CEO, FedEx Corporation

"*Railroader* presents both a fascinating business story with global resonance and a very personal tale of a life fully lived in a 'no-holds barred' fashion to the very end. It is a brilliant profile of an enigmatic, somewhat obsessed, railroad mercenary, who turned his industry on its head, with new benchmarks for future generations of leaders. Lots of juicy learnings throughout."

CALIN ROVINESCU, president and CEO, Air Canada

"Precision railroading was his vision and unbending will his advantage. In this tightly written account of Hunter Harrison's fifty years of extraordinary achievement, Howard Green has captured the essence of the man. A valuable history and, as well, a great read."

BILL DOWNE, former president and CEO, BMO Financial Group

"A great read. *Railroader* offers a balanced view of Hunter Harrison's complex personality. Hunter Harrison, like Steve Jobs, is proof that a strong, knowledgeable leader with a vision can make a huge difference."

JIM KEOHANE, president and CEO, Healthcare of Ontario Pension Plan

"A riveting, up-close profile of one of the most successful and controversial CEOs of the modern era. *Railroader* is a master class in sharp-elbowed management in a fabled industry. Part hard ass, part mentor, part preacher, Hunter Harrison goes from one railroad to another to another to another, turning them all around and creating conflict everywhere he went. You won't be able to put this book down."

ALI VELSHI, anchor, MSNBC and business correspondent, NBC News

"Howard Green infuses his narrative with the passion and snap that epitomized Hunter Harrison's consummate success running four different North American railroads. *Railroader* is an affectionate but blunt portrayal that is a lively, compelling read, giving vibrant, human texture to an exceptional business career."

DEREK BURNEY, former Canadian ambassador to the United States

"This book energized me to approach business and life just a little more like Hunter Harrison... Howard Green masterfully puts you up close and personal with a man who's both utterly straightforward yet complicated, all while giving a great perspective on what was happening in business at the time... This is one of the best books I've ever read."

NICOLE VERKINDT, founder and CEO, OMX

"Revered and reviled, Hunter Harrison was a CEO like no other. He transformed North American railroads. He repriced executive compensation. He ignited debates about safety and competitiveness, and left us all debating the price of precision... In *Railroader,* Howard Green captures the man in full, with an intimate yet nuanced portrait of an uncompromising, compulsive executive whose legacy both endures and confounds."

JOHN STACKHOUSE, senior vice-president, RBC, and former editor-in-chief, the *Globe and Mail*

RAILROADER

RAIL

HOWARD GREEN

Finalist for the National Business Book Award

ROADER

THE **UNFILTERED GENIUS** AND **CONTROVERSY** OF **FOUR-TIME** CEO **HUNTER HARRISON**

PAGE
TWO
BOOKS

ISBN 978-1-98902-504-8 (hardcover)
ISBN 978-1989025-24-6 (ebook)

Produced by Page Two Books
www.pagetwobooks.com

Cover and interior design by Taysia Louie
Cover photos by Dermot Cleary | dermotcleary.com
Printed and bound in Canada by Friesens
Distributed in Canada by Raincoast Books
Distributed in the US and internationally by Publishers Group West

The author has made every attempt to locate the copyright holders(s)
of all photographs reproduced in this book. All photos courtesy of
the Harrison family unless otherwise credited.

18 19 20 21   5 4 3 2 1

www.howardgreen.com

For my parents

Action is eloquence
CORIOLANUS, ACT 3, SC. II

CONTENTS

INTRODUCTION

HUNTER HARRISON LIVED for telling stories. Not only did he love to entertain and charm, which he could do for hours, but as a CEO he was purposely sending a message with his tales. He seemed to have an endless supply of fables, and few people could string one out better than he could. With a Tennessee drawl that oozed from his very pores and the timing of a cranky comedian, Harrison knew how to play for maximum effect, often finding a way to weave in one of his trademark expressions, like "I'm gonna ring his head like a church bell."

One story that he liked to retell was about Robert Crandall, the former CEO of American Airlines. Crandall was traveling around the airline's network, checking station expenses. Four times he went back to the same station, cutting costs each time. On one visit, he noticed a dog.

"What's that for?" Crandall asked.

"Security," an employee said. "He barks."

"Get a recording," the CEO said.

It's easy to see why that one made Harrison chuckle. He was an unsentimental efficiency wizard who'd risen to the top by lopping expenses, maximizing the use of assets, and creating enormous value for shareholders. He reshaped an industry by literally making the trains run on time. While Sir Richard Branson advised executives to focus on employees first, customers second, and investors third, Harrison reversed the priorities: investors came first. For him the game was capitalism, pure and simple. You either played it or you didn't.

Individuals like Hunter Harrison are rare. They are singular in their talents, possessing laser-like focus and an atomic-level understanding of their businesses. By dint of starting at the bottom, questioning the status quo, and enduring backbreaking effort, they can slide into a niche that few others occupy. As a result, they represent extraordinary value to their companies and are compensated handsomely, while making tens of billions for shareholders. But they're never satisfied. Even though Harrison had won the game for decades, contentment was elusive for him, as it often is for elite performers. Competitive to the core, they live by scorecards such as higher stock prices and one more championship ring. They also love it. It's who they are and what they know. Try telling Mick Jagger not to perform.

The term "legend" is tossed around freely these days, but in Hunter Harrison's case, it fits. Starting out as a laborer in a Memphis rail yard when he was nineteen in the early 1960s, Harrison rocketed upward to CEO. He held that position four times over an almost twenty-five-year span, turning around three major railroads: Illinois Central (IC), Canadian National (CN), and Canadian Pacific (CP). In the last year of his life, while his shelves groaned with awards and his bank account bulged, he was hell bent on fixing a fourth railroad, CSX Corp. Only nine months into that last assignment as CEO, he died, but he had already increased the value of the American railroad by billions of dollars. In the view of many, the fourth turnaround was well underway, in record time.

It's hard to over-emphasize the impact railroads have had in the United States and Canada. In the US, they opened up the west and connected the huge population centers of the east, providing a transportation network to service the world's largest economy. Canadian Pacific Railway helped forge a nation, not only tying it together but encouraging settlement in the western provinces, the burgeoning population creating a protective barrier against invaders from the south. Without the railroad, British Columbia would not be part of Canada, since the construction of the CPR to the Pacific was a condition of the province joining Confederation. Its completion meant people could travel coast to coast in a matter of days. Goods, particularly grain, could be shipped along the CPR and what became CN. Telegraph lines would span the nation, running alongside tracks and, in CN's case, ultimately leading to the creation of the Canadian Broadcasting Corporation. CN would also spawn a national airline, Air Canada. The construction of the CPR led to the discovery of base metals—copper and nickel—in northern Ontario. The original surveyor of the Canadian Pacific route, Sir Sandford Fleming, invented Standard Time. Prior to Fleming's invention, there was no regulation of time zones. The US had one hundred of them, with twenty-seven time zones in Michigan alone. The impact of the railroad boom of the late 1800s was akin to the internet blossoming in the 2000s.

In spite of the human toll it took to build North American railroads in the nineteenth century (in Canada alone, 600 Chinese workers died constructing the railway and Indigenous communities ceded control of land, an issue that still reverberates today), the continent's economy now depends on all manner of freight shipped by rail: automobiles, lumber, agricultural products, and general merchandise. Some of what's shipped is hazardous material and, in the case of oil, highly controversial. It was one thing to construct railroads; it is quite another to run them profitably in today's hyper-competitive and publicly sensitive business environment. For decades, Hunter Harrison, an American from working class Memphis, would repeatedly show people how to do it better than anyone else.

FROM LAGUARDIA AIRPORT, it's a short drive to one of Harrison's estates in the luxuriant rolling hills of Connecticut. A horse farm sits amidst this storybook New England tableau of clapboard churches and cemeteries dating back centuries. Multiple barns dot the manicured landscape. Between facilities in Connecticut and two in Florida, at its height, Harrison's Double H Farm boasted somewhere between fifty and sixty horses, including retirees. They have been highly competitive on the global show jumping circuit—winners at the Olympics, World Cup, and major Grand Prix. Hunter Harrison didn't do anything by half measure.

On May 24, 2016, Harrison's wife of more than fifty years answered the door. Wearing canvas sneakers, Jeannie Harrison has an easy, youthful charm and a welcoming way. Through the main entrance of the home, there's a great room with a commanding stone fireplace and a vaulted ceiling with thick beams. When I visited that day, Hunter Harrison, then still the CEO of CP Rail, looked gaunt, wearing a blue cardigan, a sports shirt, black casual pants, and loafers without socks. We sat in front of the unlit fireplace, along with Mark Wallace, his chief of staff and vice president of corporate affairs, whose connection to Harrison dated back to his days running CN and who figured prominently in the railroader's odyssey at multiple companies. I asked Harrison how he was doing. The implication of the question was clear—how was his health, given the scare he'd had a year before that had required a vascular procedure on both legs up to his groin and hospitalization for shortness of breath, forcing him to miss CP's quarterly earnings call. As was often the case, though, he'd bounced back and was soon on the golf course, knocking the ball 250 yards while polishing off two cigars over eighteen holes.

But now he indicated he wasn't so good. A couple of weeks beforehand in New York City, Harrison had been admitted to hospital again. He'd had a bad cough and was short of breath after a meeting with investors. He'd used oxygen in his limo and asked his driver to put the heat on full blast, even though it was May. The previous year's diagnosis, which pointed to pneumonia, had turned out to be wrong. While he said the Mayo Clinic had called him its poster boy because of his amazing recovery, health issues lingered.

For a man who'd begun his career by squirting oil into railcar axles and who ultimately amassed great wealth—his Connecticut estate was on the market for USD $55 million—Harrison seemed profoundly dissatisfied. Perhaps it was the overhang of his health issues, but he also talked about CEOs not leaving their jobs with a smile anymore, citing his own unhappy departure from CN Rail in 2009. With just a year left on his contract, he was foreshadowing a similar exit from CP.

He was also frustrated and angry at his peers in the railroad industry, going so far as to say they may have helped stymie CP's growth plans—a brief and unsuccessful merger discussion with CSX, followed by unsuccessful hostile bids for Norfolk Southern. How ironic, he said, given that their companies were all products of consolidation. Good enough for them, but not for others, he complained.

How could someone with such achievements feel so aggrieved? He had been paid enormous sums, was the recipient of countless awards, and possessed several fat scrapbooks celebrating his work. Perhaps toiling day and night and weekend after weekend building businesses and financial security only took a person so far down a path to a satisfying life. Perhaps it was the prospect of retirement again, which he'd "failed" the first time after leaving CN at sixty-five, discovering that, for him, a life without work was a void. During that interlude, he had been anxious to get back into railroading, and he had made a dramatic comeback two years later. Or perhaps it was the realization that time was not on his side. After four years at CP, Harrison was tired. He'd done it again—increased shareholder value by making the railroad more efficient—but now seemed like a spent force, soon to be eclipsed by younger, healthier leaders.

"I worked my ass off all my life so I could afford to drink a good bottle of wine, and now I can't drink it," he said. He could no longer play hard, unable to enjoy the rewards that had always been there for his considerable efforts.

Still, Harrison believed in a key message: *The transportation infrastructure of North America is vital to the well-being of the continent.* Without freight railroads, the economy would be crippled, so why not make them the best? He was all about being the best. Why couldn't everybody else be?

After three hours of talking, he was weary. But in the fourth hour, the adrenalin kicked in and the old Hunter Harrison reappeared. An extra store of energy is one of the defining characteristics of the CEO. They can go fourteen hours a day, seven days a week for months on end, with calendars that would induce anxiety attacks in the rest of us. But Harrison was in a league of his own, even when physically unwell. The reason? There was only one version of Hunter Harrison. Many people have multiple personae they present to the world, depending on the situation or person with whom they're interacting. But Harrison was the same with everyone. He didn't waste precious energy playing roles. He just was. That meant his battery pack always had a bit more juice.

I first spoke with Harrison around 2004 while he was running CN. At the time, I hosted an interview program on Canada's business television network, BNN. Harrison became a fairly regular guest. I tried to ask informed questions and challenged him, which I think he appreciated. On one occasion, when CN had a strong year and the amount of

Harrison's particularly enormous compensation became public, he was in front of a camera in Montreal when I asked what he was going to do with all the money. He thought I was asking about what the railroad would do with its profits and began giving a fairly standard answer. I quickly butted in and said, "Not *that* money, *your* money!" He laughed and told me about his interest in horses, and I think that episode created a relationship, of sorts. When he was about to leave CN, I invited him to Toronto to do a full-show exit interview, which he did. It was something he reminisced about a number of times in later years. Bit by bit, I was getting to know Harrison's story, and we stayed in touch. He'd always take my call, often on a Sunday afternoon. Clearly, when he came back to run CP after CN, his story only got richer and rougher.

I'd heard reports that Harrison was a "mean guy," given that he took no prisoners at CN and cut so many positions when he arrived at CP. You don't turn around capital-intensive businesses with legacy costs and thousands of employees, making them the most efficient major railroads in North America, without leaving some "blood on the tracks." Without a doubt, Harrison was tough. As an employee, if you didn't get with the program, you were gone. You got a chance to mend your ways, but only one. If you were dragging down the team, he believed, the consequences for the company could be a disastrous spiral that would be bad for everybody. But this was a man for whom an efficiently operating railroad was like the performance of a Mozart symphony by one of the world's great orchestras. It's what he loved and what accounted for his peerless skills. That love, however, made him vulnerable to emotional wounds, as it frequently does to true believers who throw every ounce of their being into what they do.

The first time I asked him whether he was mean was during an interview on my television program during his CP chapter. He looked puzzled, smiled in an "aw shucks" way, and brushed off the question as unfair. Certainly, the label "culture of fear and discipline" bothered him, a description of CN under Harrison in a Government of Canada review of the Railway Safety Act in 2007. He preferred to call it a "culture of consequences." During the research for this book, I asked him the "mean guy" question again. He smiled. "I've been watchin' these talk shows [business channels] for three years now and I ain't heard anybody ask anybody else if you're mean." He referred to the litany of business leaders who would also be candidates for the question, but whom he hadn't heard it asked of. "What the fuck? Why they askin' me, 'Am I mean'?" The answer is yeah, he said, probably in some peoples' eyes. Even his daughters, who loved him beyond measure, had heard him on the phone and asked him why he was so harsh. "Let me tell you something," he had explained to them. "I'm savin' someone's life."

"But why do you have to holler?" they had asked.

"They won't listen if I don't holler."

Harrison yelled at people and fired many. But he also cared deeply, lending a helping hand to many in personal distress. He coached countless employees, drastically altering their lives, and could be generous to a fault, inspiring decades of loyalty from many. And while he didn't seem to work solely for the money, he was unquestionably motivated by what he could earn by being the master of his craft.

That he could improve a business with so many pieces—thousands of employees, locomotives, railcars, and miles of track—demonstrated that Harrison was a compound of innovator, field general, motivational preacher, efficiency expert, and virtuoso of railroad minutiae. After more than a half century in an industry where he had started at track level and worked his way to the executive suite, he knew how a railroad worked in such molecular detail that he could envision how inefficient scenarios would play out and how to avoid them. He became a piece of very high-end, pricey human software with the nose of a bloodhound. There's a now-famous story of him checking into a Vancouver hotel room that happened to be equipped with binoculars and had a view of a CN rail yard. Harrison spied a locomotive—number 5867—sitting idle. A half hour later, it was still there. He made a call and asked what was happening with 5867. The worker was startled. How did Harrison know about *one damn car* sitting there? The incident reverberated through the company.

The flip side of the railroad genius was dismissiveness and distaste for corporate protocol. Harrison had little patience for boards. Put simply, they were a pain, a waste of time and money. They didn't increase shareholder value or improve the operating ratio (OR), the key metric for a railroad that's constantly scrutinized by investors. Boards at publicly traded companies essentially have two jobs—hiring and firing the CEO, and oversight. No wonder they drove an action-oriented CEO like Hunter Harrison up the wall. *It ain't railroadin'*. The public fuss about compensation and executive jets—both obsessions of corporate governance watchdogs—was an acute irritation to him. Just more *boolshit*, when you're makin' billions of dollars for shareholders. This was not a man who lost sleep over optics.

The overbearing, one-man-show approach certainly appealed to the press and many investors as a gripping story. But to get away with it these days, you have to produce superstar results, which he did. Harrison would say that he actually *built* teams and knew how to put great people in the right positions at the right time to get the job done. It's hard to argue with that. But he also intimidated people, and it was only a small group that would tell a boss like Harrison that he was wrong about something. He was not exactly wired for an era that embraced "soft skills."

Harrison commissioned me to write his biography, but he did not dictate what I should write, nor did he read any draft or portion of the manuscript. Our agreement was that the book would be "unauthorized" and I would have final say over content. Given his serious health concerns, the only instruction he ever gave me was "write fast." But why me? I never asked, but I assume it was the relationship we'd developed, which included testy exchanges. My guess is that he wanted someone who'd written books, could interview him at length, would give him a fair shake, and would write about his remarkable journey, warts and all. He had a knack for sizing people up quickly and he must have decided that I "got" him. Not only did he want to run railroads, but he also desperately wanted to be understood.

Hunter Harrison had both a substantial ego and a desire to be remembered as one of the greatest, if not *the* greatest, railroaders ever. While he knew his family, and certain close colleagues loved him, Harrison was unsure about others. Many readily called Harrison a railroading genius, revolutionary, and mentor; others called him mean, ruthless, and a bully. But all labels—good and bad—can be simplistic and easily applied. Harrison was a complex human being. This book tells the story of his life, extraordinary career, and accomplishments in an attempt to paint him, not just in broad brushstrokes, but also in the nuances—a portrait of the man as he truly was. Given his stormy upbringing and turbulent adolescence, it's unlikely anyone could have predicted who he would become.

1 MEMPHIS BOY

EWING HUNTER HARRISON Jr. had enough trouble. The last thing he needed was a troublemaking son. After being wounded overseas during the Second World War, he returned to Memphis. Soon after, on November 7, 1944, Ewing Hunter Harrison III was born, the same day Franklin Delano Roosevelt was elected to a fourth term as president. For several years of his youth, that son—the Hunter Harrison who would go on to transform the railroad industry—did not live up to his dad's expectations. The father was known as "Tank" because of both his assignment as a tank driver and his intimidating size—six-foot-one, 270 pounds—and his son was appropriately known as "Little Tank." Ewing was an old family name, but Harrison's mother, Dorothy, insisted that the boy go by Hunter.

Tank and Dorothy Harrison's son was effectively an only child for the next six years until a string of four sisters came along—Mary, Sydney, Diane, and Helen. Their arrival was a shock to Hunter. Until then, he had been treated as the center of the universe by his father, his mother, and his grandparents, with whom the young family lived. But now, the favorite son had to compete for attention.

Young Hunter also had to adjust to an enigmatic man who'd clearly experienced emotional distress in his early life and during the war. Tank Harrison had been a gifted athlete who had left home at sixteen after signing with the Memphis Chicks, later a farm club of the Chicago White Sox. While he was equally at home on a football field, all indications were that Tank would become a major-league pitcher. When he returned home after his first year with the team, however, he discovered his family no longer had a place for him. Tank's parents had given his room to his sister. He was on his own.

"It cut him to the core," Harrison said in late 2016, some forty years after his father's death. Harrison's sister, Mary Couey, added that their father "joined the army so he could have a place to sleep."

While serving overseas, something happened to Tank. Harrison couldn't say for sure what befell his father during the war, but a surgical scar pointed to the strong possibility that Tank took a bullet in the shoulder, his pitching arm.

"I think it was a shot, but it was a shoulder injury," Harrison said. "When I asked him, he didn't want to talk about it."

Whatever it was put an end to Tank's professional baseball career. He was lost. Other than baseball, "he had no real—to my knowledge—ambition," Harrison said. Tank worked for several years as a driver for a funeral home until he found a fit as a cop in the Memphis Police Department. It was there he found direction, and even recognition as Policeman of the Year in 1960, as well as Lawman of the Year in Tennessee and Mississippi. But frustration lingered. Soon enough, his only son became the focus of his unfulfilled dreams.

Harrison, like his father, was a good athlete. But Tank saw a son not taking advantage of his talents. "He, to some degree, was trying to live his life through me and it didn't work," Harrison said.

Mary told me her brother felt the burden of being a policeman's son—he was expected to be a saint. By the time he was a teenager, he wanted to break out of the chrysalis constructed by others. Anything his father did or wanted him to do, he did the opposite. His group at school was "the rat pack," named for the 1960s Las Vegas boys club of Frank Sinatra, Dean Martin, Peter Lawford, Joey Bishop, and Sammy Davis Jr.

According to Mary, "If anything happened at school, they were involved somehow."

During those years, there were glimmers of Harrison's potential. Mary remembered he was charismatic from the get-go and that he always had a sense of fashion. With his booming voice and sharp wit, other kids looked to him as a leader. But there was no denying he was a troublemaker. On one occasion while walking down the hall with a friend, his high school math teacher said to the other boy, "You know, you're judged by the company you keep." The next day, Tank confronted the teacher and made her apologize. Even so, with a sizeable chip on his shoulder, Harrison took the path of embarrassing his father.

"If there ever was a juvenile delinquent, I was one."

Tank's emotional state was precarious. Working on the vice squad, where he was only in contact with hookers, drug dealers, and other miscreants, he almost ended up in an institution. He would come home from work and load up on medication. A favorite was the over-the-counter painkiller BC Powder. "He would take them like they were lollipops," Harrison recalled. "He had no release valve."

After his stressful time on the vice squad, Tank moved on to head up a newly created juvenile division. To his frustration, he soon found that his own son was on police radar because of a propensity for fights and misdemeanors. This was a major humiliation for Tank in the department and the community at large.

Besides the brawls, Harrison could be a bully. If his father got wind of an incident, he'd take up the cause of the bullied party and his son would pay the price. Young Hunter could also be a prankster and would go too far. In one incident, during a night game in the Tennessee state softball championships, he decided to pull the power switch, creating chaos at the stadium. Four or five days later, driving the family car, he dropped his father off at the zoo. There, his dad ran into one of the park police, who told Tank that his son was a prime suspect in the ballpark caper. When Harrison returned to pick up his father, he was asked point blank: "Did you turn those lights off?"

"Me?"

Tank grabbed his son by the collar.

"You lie to me?"

The boy trembled. "Yessir, I did it." His father's fury was enough of a lesson.

Tank wasn't the only one to have trouble with the young man's cocky ways. Buddy Lewis, a scout for the St. Louis Cardinals, put his finger on it. Harrison was a talented catcher, but he had attitude. Lewis, who'd played in the majors, let the boy have it, telling him to get rid of his "rabbit ears and red ass." That was scout lingo for someone who heard every slight or criticism from the stands and blew a fuse. Harrison ultimately squandered all his opportunities in sport and even stopped participating as part of his rebellion against his father. In his senior year, he was deemed ineligible to play because he'd done so poorly in school as a junior, failing every class except physical education.

During his teens, Harrison chummed around with a young man nine years older than him. His name was Elvis Presley. Although there was a big difference in ages, Harrison knew Elvis—at least a little. After Presley hit it big, he bought his parents a house. Harrison said everyone in Memphis thought it was a mansion, but today it would be considered run of the mill. The house lay between Harrison's parents' and grandparents' houses. On Sundays, the family would visit the grandparents and drive along the road where the singer's folks lived. The first time Harrison met Elvis, the entertainer was in the yard. His parents stopped the car and Harrison's mother encouraged him to go and say hello to the star, along with another dozen young people. Presley gave them each a cookie and, in Harrison's words, *"boolshit"* with them.

Harrison had other brushes with the singer. A friend who lived across the street went to karate school with some of Elvis's bodyguards and hangers-on, and Harrison became part of the roving group. Periodically, Presley rented the Memphian Theatre so he could watch movies surrounded by his intimate circle and undisturbed by screaming fans. Because of his connection to the Elvis entourage, Harrison would go to the theater along with ten or twelve others.

"About halfway through [a movie], he'd say 'Cut! Seen enough of this shit,'" Harrison said. "'What's the next one?'"

Elvis would also rent the local fairgrounds for a select crowd of forty or fifty people. At the time, Presley was seeing a young woman named Anita Wood who was co-host on *Top 10 Dance Party*, a local *American Bandstand*–style show that featured different schools each week. Harrison's school had been on the program so Wood knew him. One evening at the fairgrounds, Wood wandered over to Harrison and his friend to say hello. They made some small talk about the show and then she said she had to go.

"Gotta get back to E!"

A few minutes later, one of Elvis's bodyguards came over to see Harrison.

"The man doesn't like that," the tough said.

Apparently, Elvis the Pelvis didn't like anyone talking to his girl. It then became a big joke that the famous singer was jealous of teenage boys. Harrison allowed that he was never much of a fan of the King. Years later, while at CN in Montreal, his fellow executives were all aflutter because they heard he knew Elvis, with stories circulating about a young Harrison frolicking in Presley's swimming pool. While others might exaggerate their brushes with celebrity, Harrison said that aside from these few encounters, he never really knew Presley. "You go from shakin' his hand to bein' second cousins."

Call it a moment of introspection, but in his senior year, there was a flicker of the smarts that would flourish and distinguish Harrison in his career. He applied himself and got straight A's in the first half of the year, an honor student. The principal even toured him around to show the kind of improvement that was possible. But come the second semester, school was dull again. Harrison went to class, laid his head on his books, and went to sleep. He was back to F's, another embarrassment to his father, who knew the teachers, administrators, and principal. Slaps quickly turned to punches.

"It wasn't child abuse, but he'd bust your ass. It was common, kind of, in those days," Harrison explained. This happened more than once, a couple of times with pretty hard punches, in one case bloodying the boy's lip. Harrison said, "I thought, well he shouldn't hit me that hard. But that's a whole lot different than the traumatic scars that stayed with *him* for years." Harrison had a need to talk about what today would be considered child abuse but would then downplay its impact.

Harrison's father once said of him, "He's not worth the gunpowder it would take to blow him up." "He didn't mean it cruelly," Mary said, "but he meant it." Tank never hit Mary and her sisters, she clarified, adding that he was indifferent to his daughters. But "he was harder on him [Harrison]." Normally, she said, the girls didn't see what went on, either because it didn't happen in front of them or "I guess you block out things as you get a little older." During one incident, however, when Harrison wouldn't get out of bed, Tank got a mop out of the closet to wake him up. Just as he took a swing with it, his son rolled over and the mop caught him square in the face and mouth, drawing blood.

"My dad was mortified that it happened," Mary said, believing him to be both shamed and embarrassed. But her brother used the injury as if to say, "look what you did to me," expressing the injustice to their father. Their mother, Mary said, was the buffer. She knew her husband was right to expect more from their son, but the father "went to an extreme." Their mother, according to the girls, favored Harrison. They jokingly called him "the chosen one."

Years later, when their sister Sydney died, Harrison and Mary had a long conversation that included discussion of Sydney's interest in genealogy. One of their other sisters had been going through Sydney's personal effects and discovered the deed to the old family home at 4795 Durbin Avenue in Memphis. They asked their brother if he wanted it. He said no.

"I don't have any fond memories of Durbin."

Despite their collisions, Harrison referred to his father as "a helluva guy" and came to revere him. When Harrison bashed up the family car, Tank was only concerned that his boy wasn't hurt. "There was no doubt [our father] loved him deeply," Mary said. In another mishap when Harrison was fourteen, he crashed his moped while collecting for his paper route and required sixty-seven stitches in his leg. Tank was too emotional to even be in the emergency room. Still, Harrison's fractious and volatile relationship with his father continued through his teens. Harrison's tendency to act out was also perhaps partly ignited by the unexpected and untimely death of his grandmother, Mary Lee Stewart, who doted on him. The family woke up one morning and found she was dead at just fifty. Harrison was eleven or twelve when she died. Until then, he had been quiet and well-mannered, but after that, he decided he could do anything he wanted. Again, no one really talked about what had happened or the emotional impact of it. It just wasn't done.

"That was God's plan," he received as explanation for his grandmother's sudden death. "There's a reason for everything." For Harrison, these kinds of comments didn't add up. "*God doesn't have a plan,*" he thought. A questioning mind was beginning to form, one that looked for flaws in an argument or situation, asked why, and then began to construct creative solutions to problems. Mary Lee Stewart's husband had abandoned her and her daughter, Harrison's mother. Harrison only knew because he asked a question—a behavior that would become a trademark. He saw a document that showed her maiden name, Nethercott, and piped up, adding he might have gone to his grave not knowing about the desertion.

He learned that after the abandonment, his mother and grandmother went to live with his great-grandfather, Richard Nethercott. Nethercott was a railroader. He worked for Illinois Central, where by 1993 Hunter Harrison would be CEO. In 1998, Illinois Central was purchased by Canadian National, and Harrison eventually became CEO of CN. Upon Harrison's retirement, the company named a yard in Memphis after him, the very yard that his great-grandfather had worked in during the 1930s.

"Big Daddy" Nethercott, as he was known to the family, was a workaholic, grinding away seven days a week, twelve hours a day. Nethercott would come home every day and ask, "Have you got my drink ready?" Bourbon and simple syrup was his preferred concoction. He'd have two, eat dinner, and pack it in for the night. One day he came home livid.

"They're going to make us take a day off," he said. "What do they think I'm going to do?"

Although Hunter Harrison would have other interests as an adult—family, horses, and golf—that plaintive cry would be echoed as his own obsession with railroads took hold.

In what would become Harrison yard, Nethercott was run over one day while walking with his back to a train. A railcar hit him in the shoulder, spinning him around, and the train ran over his thigh. Bleeding and alone, he applied a tourniquet and lay there for four hours. When they found him, Nethercott was rolling a cigarette. He lost his leg in the accident. With the aid of a prosthesis, he returned to work and was eventually trainmaster, a key position his great-grandson would one day hold that would establish him as someone with an uncommon ability to move boxcars. But Harrison's great-grandfather died before he was born, so their only career connection was an eerie coincidence.

When Harrison was fifteen, Tank got him a construction job. It didn't take the boy long to realize that being a supervisor was a better place to be on the ladder. His first day, they gave him a shovel and said, "Get in that ditch and dig!" He jumped in with the rest of the workers. There was a man standing on top yelling at the group to hurry up.

"I'm diggin'. I'm sweatin'," Harrison told a group years later. "He's drinkin' lemonade by the jar with ice in it and I'm sayin', 'That's the job I want right there.'" Other people, he observed, would rather dig than accept the responsibility of telling others to dig. It was an epiphany for the young Harrison.

AT THE END of 1963, word went out that Frisco—a railroad that had hired very few people from 1946 until then because of veterans returning from war—was looking for help. Frisco—the St. Louis–San Francisco Railway, which dated to 1876—plied the routes of the southcentral United States and the Midwest. It is now part of Burlington Northern Santa Fe (BNSF), owned by Warren Buffett's Berkshire Hathaway. Little more than a year after graduating from high school, Harrison got his first railroad job there, though he'd tried and failed the mechanical aptitude test to work as a summer laborer at the Louisville and Nashville Railroad (the L&N is now part of CSX) when he was sixteen. He said he was only the first or second person hired in his department at Frisco since the end of the Second World War. Harrison had turned nineteen in November 1963, and when he started at the railroad in December, his pay suddenly quadrupled to just over two dollars an hour from the fifty cents an hour he was making slinging loaves at Hart's Bakery. His job was carman oiler, pouring oil into "journal boxes" on railcars. The journal was an extension of the axle. Journal boxes protruded outside the wheels and carried the weight of the car. The box contained a mop-like material that required oil to keep the axle bearings lubricated. When he came home from work, Harrison's overalls were so fouled by oil that he had to strip off before entering the house.

"When he went to work for the railway, he found himself," Mary said. "Up to then, he didn't really have purpose."

In addition to pouring oil, Harrison did safety inspections, saying he was "scared to death" there might be a derailment. To complete the inspection, there was a requirement for one person to be on each side of the train. One night, he was paired with an old-timer named Zoomer, "one of the sorriest human beings that ever walked on the face of the earth." Harrison checked his side of the train but never saw Zoomer, until he went back to the shanty and found him fast asleep.

"What are you doing?" Harrison asked him. "You're going to get us in trouble."

"Kid, relax. Hey, did you do all your side?"

"Yessir."

"Is your side going to get to Amory, Mississippi?"

"Yessir."

"If your side gets there, my side will get there. I've never seen half a car get there yet."

"It all pays the same," was the quote that stuck. "Good job. Bad job. Up. Down. Sweepin' or drivin'. It all pays the same." Harrison, the new railroad employee, was struck by the complacency of his fellow workers. But over time, his confusion and his questioning mind would have a profound impact on his views about leadership and direction.

He also learned consequences on the jobsite. Harrison had a bit of a habit of being late for work and one day it caught up with him. "I can remember being one minute late and jumping through the boxcars trying to hide," Harrison said. It was summer, he was in gym shorts, and he said he probably broke some rules about getting between cars. He was about to punch in when a hand reached over his shoulder and grabbed his timecard. It was his supervisor, "Wild" Bill Longston, a dedicated railroader. Longston told Harrison to go home. "What do you mean go home? I need to work," Harrison pleaded.

"Well, if you need to work, you come on time," Longston told him. "Shit, that had an effect on my behavior," Harrison said. "If it hadn't been for him, I might have got fired." The concept of consequence would come to figure prominently in Harrison's approach to management. Longston also started an informal apprenticeship at the railroad. Even though Harrison needed supervision, his boss thought he was worth the trouble. This in-house education program helped cover for the fact that taking business courses at Memphis State (now University of Memphis) was not working for him. After two years on and off of part-time night classes, Harrison "flunked out, quit."

JEANNIE DAY WAS two years younger than Harrison and had gone to the rival school, also attended by Johnny Cash. An alluring majorette, she caught Harrison's eye at a dance at the YMCA in 1960. According to her, he was his own person who made a bit of mischief and was a good dancer who could do the Bop. Was it love at first sight?

"Fred Astaire," he wisecracked, throwing his arms open wide. "Whaddya gonna do?"

It actually took time for the relationship to take flight, but they were married in 1963. By his own admission, aside from the railway, Jeannie was the only direction Harrison had. Soon, she was pregnant, and in February 1964, when Harrison was nineteen, their first child, Elizabeth, was born. He was fond of the nickname Libby, but the little girl got her name, in part, because Harrison liked the voluptuous actress Elizabeth Taylor. Libby's birth changed his life.

"It's one thing to embarrass yourself, but if you've got a child, they shouldn't be subjected, and so my value system totally made a significant change. It's not just you. You're responsible for a child now. I kind of really manned up."

Not only did they have a child, they soon had their first new car, a 1964 red Corvair convertible—four on the floor—sticker price $2,500. "It was loaded up," he said, grinning. They bought it with their first loan. Money was often tight, and in one instance Harrison told Jeannie they had five dollars for the week. At the time, he was also walking the dogs that raced at the local track. Ever enterprising, Harrison studied the track sheets as though he was studying for the LSAT. Based on his spadework, he bet the couple's last five dollars on two dogs.

"I'll be damned if those two dogs didn't come in," said Libby's husband, Earl. Harrison won eighty-seven dollars, enough for groceries and gasoline to get them through the week. Earl called Harrison his second father and best friend and knew him for more than thirty years. He also claimed to have heard the dog story fifty times.

Around the same time at Frisco, Harrison's superiors asked him to do some extra work as foreman. When his supervisor was absent, he would fill in and receive the supervisor's level of pay for those weeks. Like certain kids take to the violin, Hunter Harrison took to the railroad. During those periods when he was acting-supervisor, seven boxcars were repaired instead of the usual five. It might be small beer for railroaders today, but at the time it got him noticed. Here was this kid getting things done that people senior to him couldn't or didn't do. Leadership traits and boxcar moving skills would one day coalesce into Precision Scheduled Railroading, the operating philosophy that would become his calling card worldwide. The extra work he took on paid off, and within a few years he was asked to enter a management training program. But there was a condition: he'd have to relocate. Harrison went home to tell Jeannie. Except for a brief trip to Florida, where it was one hundred degrees Fahrenheit, neither of them had ever been a hundred miles out of Memphis.

"We were raw kids," he said. But they discussed it and said, "Let's do it." That decision to move began to knit together a career path.

In 1968, they moved to Springfield, Missouri, where they didn't know a soul. Still, they were relieved to be out of Memphis. The Reverend Dr. Martin Luther King Jr. was murdered there in April of that year, and the young couple felt it was good to get away from a poisonous atmosphere. Harrison settled in for a year and a half, which included the management training program.

It would be the first of many relocations, but necessary to succeed in this industry. During one eleven-month period, they lived in three cities—and one of them twice. He'd gotten the railroading bug.

"Finally, I think I had a grasp on something. I had my head on straight. I could complete it and be recognized for it. This was an opportunity to bring it all together."

2 THE MAKING OF A RAILROADER

WHILE HUNTER HARRISON flourished, his young wife withered. Although Jeannie looked after Libby and was a bookkeeper at a car dealership, she didn't have the all-consuming purpose he now had. Having lived in the same city all her life, she now found herself in a place with no friends and a young child. A night out at a bar with her husband and his boss during an earlier visit to Springfield underlined her sense of isolation. The Harrisons were used to the Memphis way—a brown bag town. You brought your own bottle and bought your mix and your ice. Now they were in Missouri—virtually a foreign land—at an open bar. Not only that, Jeannie was underage and not a drinker. The boss offered to order for her.

"She'll have a Go Cadillac," he said.

A martini glass arrived filled with green liquid and a bit of foam on top. Jeannie took a small sip and Harrison saw a "godawful look on her face."

"I said, 'What's it like?'"

"It's the worst thing I ever tasted."

"Drink every drop," he commanded. Appearances were paramount, but the marriage was strained.

"I've got my railroad and she had nuthin'," he said, looking back on the imbalance in their relationship at the time. They grew apart, separated, and then divorced in 1969. But it was an amicable settlement. Jeannie stayed in Springfield, and Harrison would spend the next six months to a year in Mobile, Alabama, where Frisco had transferred him.

But after the divorce he was once again in a self-destructive spiral, as in his teen years. "I was not a good citizen," Harrison confessed. "Messin' with women I shouldn't have been messin' with, altercations." The night before he left Springfield could have been his last. After a bar room brawl outside a local watering hole called The Alibi—Harrison said it was referred to as The Knife and Gun Club, as many dives were known—he was pummeled by three guys and left for dead. Harrison said he managed to crawl to his car, open the door, and get in the back seat, where he passed out. He came to at three in the morning, drove home, and fell into bed fully clothed, waking up a few hours later in a pool of blood. His liver had ruptured.

Libby, who was only five or six years old, recalled visiting her father in Mobile with her grandparents. They asked her if she wanted to stay with him. "I can't stay," she said. "There's crackers, crumbs in the bed." Her laughter while recounting the episode, though, was tearful. To this day, she is torn about the separation. "Why didn't I stay with my dad?"

He was saved by a call from Jeannie. At that point, she was working for General Electric but had been told the company was cutting back and she'd lose her job. "Just move down here," he said. "We're going to get remarried."

He took off for Springfield, got a U-Haul, packed her belongings, and brought her and Libby to Mobile, where they got a condo and settled into family life. They remarried in Memphis on July 10, 1970, the anniversary they would celebrate. He cried that day, as did Libby.

In Mobile, he was the "chief of everything" for Frisco's operations, looking after the Alabama part of the railroad and managing thirty people. Jeannie recalled that period as a great time together. When he wasn't working, they went to the beach or played tennis. While there, his career began to take off, an upward slope for the next ten to twelve years. But the glow of Mobile would not last long. From 1971 to 1982, the Harrisons moved eighteen times.

In the meantime, Jeannie had developed her own career. She worked in auto dealerships for a company that had several locations throughout the southeast. Eventually, she became business manager and was promised a percentage from all the business units. Harrison pooh-poohed the promotion and the promise of a cut, telling her "that'll be about five hundred dollars." He was wrong. For the first month under her new deal, Jeannie made more than ten thousand dollars. At one point in the 1970s, she was making more than $70,000 a year.[1] Her husband was making about half that.

"I'll do Mr. Mom," he joked.

"No," came the firm answer. Jeannie Harrison did not enjoy her work like her husband enjoyed his. The stress took a toll on her. They would follow his career.

While he was working in the yard in Memphis, the so-called tower had caught his eye. Much like air traffic control at an airport, it was where the action was. Instead of directing aircraft, it directed rail-cars. More often than not, trains coming in had to be broken up so that certain cars on train A could be inserted into train B for travel to desti-nation C. It required a person who was decisive, could find solutions on the fly, and could move boxcars the most efficiently. The tower and the person running it—the trainmaster—controlled everything in the yard.

"There were cars everywhere, ground speakers everywhere," he said. "Those voices sounded like they were right below God. The guy in the tower, he was *the guy*. I was fascinated with the whole logistics chal-lenge of trying to move stuff, to problem solve. I thought, 'If I could ever be that guy.'"

It wasn't long before he was. In 1972, at age twenty-eight, Harrison became a trainmaster, the turning point that would imprint heavily on his future. Somehow he had a knack for moving cars efficiently, and moving cars was the game. If they sat in the yard, they weren't making money. Freight trains needed to be deconstructed, reassembled, and put on the right track to their next destination. It was like playing checkers, only with big clunky railcars and multiple tracks. The faster and more efficiently you did it, the faster boxcars got to where customers needed them to go. If you needed to get two green cars between two red cars with the fewest moves, Hunter Harrison was your man.

His life became twelve-hour days in the tower, and he came to work with his own medical kit—Maalox, BC Powder, Tylenol, and Rolaids. It was a defining period for him. He was now one of nine or ten in that

---

1   Based on inflation, $70,000 would be equivalent to $277,885 in 2018.

position at the company. But as always with Harrison, it wasn't long before he was in conflict. Only now it wasn't with his teachers or his father; it was with his colleagues. They wanted to know what kind of a trainmaster he'd be—one who would continue to let underlings behave badly and drink on the job, or one who would be a taskmaster.

"I chose the second." He told them he was there to do a job; the company was paying him to do it, and he was going to fulfill the contract.

"Anything else would be cheating the company."

He didn't win any friends, at least at first. Within about a year, he found himself tutoring his older peers, having the uncomfortable experience of relieving one who had been an early coach and sponsor.

"My stature went up several notches. [I] might not have been the best CEO in the world, the best general manager, the best COO," Harrison said. "But there ain't no sumbitch who could be a trainmaster like I could. I made my spurs there. That's when I became effectively the fair-haired boy with Thompson."

Thompson was William F. Thompson—a.k.a. "Pisser Bill"—who came to Frisco as senior vice president of operations in 1973, multiple levels above trainmaster. If Hunter Harrison ever had a mentor, it was Pisser, who'd previously run the St. Louis Terminal Railroad, an operation owned by all the railroads that went through St. Louis, much like the Belt Railway in Chicago. Thompson got the nickname because apparently if he had to "go," out it came, no matter where. He was a six-foot-three or -four, 230-pound, broad-shouldered "specimen" from Texas. A yeller and a screamer, he'd been hired by Frisco's president, Dick Grayson, who wanted to shake up the family atmosphere at the company, which was allegedly rife with nepotism.

Grayson loved the employees but felt they'd become sloppy, apathetic. Enter Thompson, a "kick ass, take names, culture-of-fear kind of guy," as Harrison described him. Thompson knew nobody at the railroad and didn't owe anybody anything. Lyle Reed, who worked at Frisco then, recalled that Thompson's reputation alone was enough to get results.

"Mr. Grayson felt that was something we needed, kind of [a] kick in the ass, significant emotional event," Harrison said. "[Thompson] came in there like Sherman came into Atlanta." He was an imposing, intimidating presence with the forbidding mien of John Wayne. As Thompson settled into Frisco, the lore about him grew thicker by the day. There was a story that he'd kicked a four-hundred-pound keg of spikes over a fence in Birmingham and that he'd ripped the doors off boxcars. The forty-eight-year-old Thompson had learned railroading from the ground up, but he was about to run into another imposing character who'd also risen from the bottom and was just thirty years old.

"I've reached the cocky stage," Harrison described himself at the time. "I'm just waitin' for the president's job to come up." Harrison had heard the stories about Pisser Bill "and I'm thinkin', *boolshit.*"

Their first encounter was like an electrical storm. Harrison climbed onto the business car of the train that had brought Thompson to Memphis. Luxuriously outfitted for railroad executives, it had a parlor, dining room, and four or five bedrooms. When he got to the top of the steps, Harrison heard his boss and Thompson screaming at each other. Pisser had been in Memphis for only ten minutes. He spun around and faced Harrison.

"I'm Bill Thompson," he said, sticking his finger out, poking it into the end of Harrison's nose. "I've heard about your ass. I'm gonna tell you something. You delay one more of my transcontinental trains, I'm gonna run your ass so far off this railroad you'll never find your way back."

"Well, that's a good start," Harrison wisecracked. He pushed back to the point where his own boss was kicking him hard in the shins.

In spite of the sparks, Thompson saw potential in Harrison, or perhaps something of himself. He also liked that Harrison didn't resist his changes or approach. The next year, Thompson put Harrison on the road, moving him multiple times—from Memphis to Springfield to Kansas City and back to Memphis—in eleven months. Upon his return, Harrison became superintendent and took the risky step of going above his superiors to deal directly with Thompson, who was several levels above him on the org chart. It angered them, but Pisser Bill talked directly to Harrison, so what could they do? One day, Thompson's administrative chief called and announced that Thompson would be picking Harrison up at five o'clock to go to Kansas City. Harrison had no idea why.

"Fix this place," Thompson told Harrison once they were in KC. Harrison replied that, among other things, they needed two trainmasters and two Chevrolet Impalas. No problem, Thompson said. Soon, Harrison was calling up the general manager running Kansas City, telling him what they needed to do.

"Where'd you get the authority to come to Kansas City?" the man shot back at Harrison, who was still just a superintendent in Memphis. "We've been running this place for ten years and you want to buy two company cars and furniture?"

Harrison began, "Well, Thompson said . . ."

"What colors do you want?" came the instant reply. Hearing Thompson's name was enough.

"He was by far the best railroader I'd ever been around. He was a Patton," Harrison recalled. "You got a war, you want Thompson." Hunter Harrison would also be likened to Second World War General George Patton—memorialized in a 1970 film starring George C. Scott—decades later. Within two or three meetings, Harrison developed respect for the gunslinger from Fort Worth. It turned out it was mutual, and they worked together for twelve years. Harrison could have written a book about Pisser Bill and the lessons he learned from him. On one occasion, Thompson came into the tower in Memphis (Harrison was back there from 1971 to 1977 in various roles) and saw the yard crammed wall to wall with cars. As Harrison described it, there were so many railcars jammed together you could walk across the top.

"Yard's full, huh?"

"Yessir."

"Whaddya see out there?"

"Darn good, Mr. Thompson."

"What's good about it? Freight business is down 7 percent in this quarter."

"How the hell do you think I know business is down 7 percent?" Harrison shot back. "Nobody tells us anything."

"You don't get the T1 report?"

"I don't know what you're talking about," Harrison said.

Thompson got on the phone to Springfield and got the data. He then laid it out for Harrison, who was under the impression that if the yard was full, business was good. Thompson, meanwhile, saw a yard full of cars and immediately concluded there were delays. It was an object lesson for Harrison.

"If you want to be successful in the yard or the railroad, keep the car inventory down" to avoid congestion, Thompson advised.

Soon after Thompson arrived, Frisco started turning around and Harrison's career "hit the fast track." In 1977, he was promoted and sent back to operating headquarters in Springfield, even though there was no job for him there. It didn't matter. Thompson created one for him. Harrison would run the railroad at night while others ran it during the day. Harrison asked Thompson when he was expected to work.

"You work when you need to work."

Harrison didn't understand. "What's my hours?"

"I told you you're responsible from 6 pm to 6 am," Thompson said. "If I gotta tell you when to work and what hours, you got the wrong man."

"I'd get up at four in the afternoon and I'd call the railroad and say, 'How's the railroad?'" If the answer was "everything's on time," Harrison would have dinner with his family, "watch *Gunsmoke*," and go in at eight or nine and work till six the next morning. If he called at four in the afternoon and things were awry, he'd go in immediately and be there until perhaps noon the next day.

Thompson was giving Harrison authority along with a helping of accountability. He was gruffly mentoring Harrison, but for many, Thompson's modus operandi was repugnant. There were, Harrison recalled, numerous threats on Thompson's life, and a few times would-be assailants, brandishing pistols, got past security to his office. One day while Thompson was on the company plane, an anonymous caller said that when Thompson landed, he was a dead man. Railroad security met the plane and told Thompson about the threat.

"Take me to the house," he said. Thompson grabbed his .38 and shoulder holster. "Let's go."

Thompson took it to the limit, doing things that could get a manager arrested today. At one point, Harrison was working for a man named Earl who he said was scared skinny of Thompson. Earl was huge but Harrison claimed he got the shakes at the mention of Thompson's name. Normally, Thompson would knock off at 5 pm, citing cocktail hour. But on this particular evening, he summoned the two of them.

"What do you think he wants?" Earl asked Harrison.

"Shit, Earl, I don't know what he wants."

They walked into Thompson's office, which Harrison described as slightly smaller than a gymnasium.

"Sit down," Thompson yelled. From his body language, you knew "he ain't happy."

Thompson started in on Harrison, and Earl looked over as if to say "I told you so." At that point, Thompson reached down and pulled out his pistol.

"[It] looks like a fuckin' bazooka," Harrison recalled. Thompson spun the gun around on his desk. Harrison said, "I ain't gettin' shot over a late train." Earl was "shakin' like a leaf." They sat there in silence for the next fifteen seconds until Thompson started laughing. He told them he'd had a hard day and just needed a laugh, making them promise not to tell anyone about the episode.

"I didn't see the humor in that," Earl said as he and Harrison walked down the hall. "I'm not sure that man's sane."

People tiptoed around when Thompson was in the building. He would throw a fit at the office and people would tremble and say, "Oh shit, he's going to have a *big one* someday." Harrison knew differently. "He's around the corner laughing," he said, calling Thompson a great actor.

Did he model himself on Thompson? No, Harrison said. But he did model his approach on Thompson's principles. Yes, Harrison was loud like Thompson, but he was loud before Thompson came along. In 2008, when Harrison wrote the second volume of his railroading bible at CN, *Change, Leadership, Mud and Why: How We Work and Why*, he said Thompson was a perpetual teacher when it came to management principles.

"Hunter," Thompson said, "you're a hell of a car mover, but I'm not sure how good a leader you are." Thompson asked him how much time he spent developing people.

"About 10 percent of my time," Harrison said.

"You've got it all backwards. You should be spending 80 percent of your time coaching and teaching and 20 percent on all the other stuff. If you spend your time developing people, you won't have to be running everywhere."

When it came to people, Hunter Harrison was only interested in merit. He didn't give anyone a pass, even family. In the late 1970s, his sister Mary was looking for a job that paid better than her secretarial position. When he was about to leave for Springfield again, she applied to be a clerk at Frisco (he said he did not lobby for her to be hired). Mary started working for the railroad in 1977. A year later, her brother was transferred back to Memphis as superintendent. For a moment, she thought life would be good for her at the railroad, but then she came to the realization he'd be harder on her than anybody else. To anyone who needled her, predicting she'd be on easy street with her sibling in charge, she said, "You obviously don't know my brother very well." She didn't even know what to call him at work. Hunter? Mr. Harrison? Buddy? On one occasion, he saw her wearing the same clothes she'd worn the previous day. "Have you been home?" he asked. "No," she said, telling him she'd been on duty for thirty-two hours and didn't know how she was going to stay awake.

"Just keep countin' the money. That'll keep you awake," he told her. "No nepotism in my family," she said and laughed.

Sometimes she had to take a lot of heat from fellow employees. "When you're talking about him as a superintendent, I don't agree with everything he does," she'd tell them. "But when you get personal, he's my brother." He expected her to make her own way on the railroad, but she said she didn't cut him any slack either.[2]

The other person who didn't cut Harrison any slack had been his father. Tank Harrison died on February 18, 1976, at the age of fifty-five. Hunter was just thirty-two, and his career was starting to gel. In spite of the beatings he'd taken and the tension between them for a number of years, he credited his father with teaching him how to lead from the pulpit, a skill that would distinguish him as he rose in the railway business. In an effort to balance the books, he also said that after marrying and having his first daughter, he and his father had a wonderful relationship for a number of years. "Nobody I admired more than him. He was a special guy." Both were good athletes, although the father was more of a carefree natural than the son; Hunter relied on his head. Both could speak, hold a room, and be the life of the party, with the son a natty dresser and the father caring little about what he wore. The son

---

2   Once Frisco merged with BN, Mary stayed with the company. She worked there for thirty-eight years, finishing her career as director of administration in BNSF's Texas region.

never stopped thinking about the father. A photo of Tank Harrison in a baseball uniform throwing a pitch sat on the bookshelf of Harrison's home office in Florida. Continuing to monitor Hunter's potential, not long before his death, Tank Harrison told his daughter Diane, "Bubba's going to be president of the railroad."

IN NOVEMBER 1980—the same year American railroads were deregulated by the Staggers Rail Act—Frisco became part of a bigger picture when it was acquired by Burlington Northern (BN).[3] Although BN was larger, the Frisco operating people were the stars and took over running the company that had swallowed their railroad. Frisco's Dick Grayson became CEO of BN and brought along Thompson and Harrison. At the time, Harrison was back in Memphis as superintendent, running operations for the city and surrounding area.

When the BN-Frisco deal hit, Harrison got a call from Thompson, who told him he was being transferred to Kansas City.

"What's my title?" Harrison asked.

"Don't worry about that," Thompson said.

"What's my salary?"

"Don't worry about that."

Harrison was dumbfounded.

"I can tell you one thing. You're in charge of Kansas City," Thompson said, "and no one's going to give you any trouble."

Kansas City was a common point for the two railways. As was the case with any merger, there was overlap in business and changes needed to be made. In 1982, while Harrison was in the throes of "doctoring" Kansas City, Thompson called again and told him to go to St. Paul. There, he would be interviewed for the assistant vice president's position for the Seattle region for BN—three levels above his position.

Harrison said to Thompson, "Boy, that's a big job. I sure appreciate it. You think I got a chance at it?"

"Well," Thompson said, "you're the only one they're interviewing, so don't blow it."

---

3   From 1887 until 1980, US railroads were heavily regulated by the Interstate Commerce Act. Among other things, the Staggers Rail Act of 1980—named for the congressman who sponsored it—allowed railroads to set any rate for their services, provided there was competition.

The interviewer knew Thompson was sponsoring Harrison and wasn't going to fight Pisser Bill, who was now executive vice president of operations at BN. Within a year or two, with bonuses, Harrison was making $150,000.

"Look, you keep moving boxcars, and I'll keep signing checks," Thompson told him.

When Harrison was superintendent in Memphis, he'd been making $40,000 to $45,000 a year. In 1979, Frisco employees got a bonus for the first time. Stock option grants were also handed out, and Harrison recalled that several people gave them back.

"They said, 'You don't get anything for nuthin'. I kept mine." It was the beginning of almost four decades of Harrison benefiting from stock-based compensation that would make him a very wealthy man. Stock options continued at BN, and Harrison used his extra income to benefit his family as well. Andy Reardon, a tax lawyer at the railroad who Harrison knew from Frisco days and who would work with him again decades later as chairman of Canadian Pacific, recalled a conversation about what Harrison planned to do with one of his bonuses. "I'm going to buy a car for my mom," he said. "She's been driving a piece of crap for I don't know how many years."

The Seattle posting, like the others, did not last long. Thompson needed him somewhere else. At 5 am one Sunday morning, the phone rang at the Harrisons' home.

"We're going to have to move you to St. Paul," Thompson said. "If you're going to raise hell, raise hell now."

"What job?"

Thompson told him the terminals there were a mess, the service was bad, and Harrison needed to straighten them out.

"What do you want me to do?"

"*I want you to straighten them out!*"

"Let me talk to the family," Harrison told him.

"Fine," Thompson said. "Call me at nine o'clock and tell me."

Harrison didn't need four hours to decide. It was 1982 and he was now assistant vice president, Terminals. He ended up living at a Radisson hotel in St. Paul for a year and "commuted" by air everywhere he had to go. Hunter Harrison, at thirty-eight, was telling people how things should be done and as a result was helping set operating and financial records for the railroad. He was hitting his stride, and Thompson was on the phone again.

"I've got you in for VP."

Jeannie was about to move to St. Paul when Thompson and Walter Drexel, BN's president, came into Harrison's office. They told Harrison something no one else knew.

"We're moving out of St. Paul, probably to Kansas City. So, don't waste your time moving to St. Paul." It was back to KC for the Harrisons.

The number of moves had become dizzying. A few years earlier, Jeannie was in Kansas City hanging a picture in what became one of their many homes, in some cases newly built homes. "I wouldn't hammer that nail," her husband told her. Harrison's career was the priority. They were moving back to Memphis and Jeannie Harrison went with the flow. Libby said she never heard her mother complain about all the moving. But the daughter found the perpetual motion hard. When the Seattle transfer came up, Libby was a junior at an all-girls high school in Memphis. She begged to stay so she could finish the year. "You have to move," she was told. But a new school in Seattle wasn't appealing. "It was very difficult for me personally," she said, but allowed that being in yet another new environment prepared her for university.

Meanwhile, the numbers at BN had improved. Cash flow soared and a key measure of railroad performance, the operating ratio (OR), plummeted. A lower OR is better because it's an expression of expenses divided by revenue—BN was spending less to produce each dollar of revenue. Burlington Northern's low operating ratio caught everyone's attention.

A holding company contained the railroad and was run by executives who'd come from ARCO (Atlantic Richfield), an oil company. Harrison said the holding company's leadership didn't care whether you were a Frisco guy or a BN guy, but concluded that the Frisco boys—including Grayson, Thompson, and Harrison—knew how to run a railroad.

The halcyon days, however, would not last. The high-octane performance of the group that came from Frisco created animosity with those from the old BN, pre-acquisition. Thompson also had a heart attack, followed by heart surgery.[4] Grayson was still in charge, but his health

---

4   Thompson retired in 1984.

deteriorated as well. Harrison was by then VP of Transportation and VP of the Chicago region, but the Frisco ranks at BN were diminished.

"The team turned on us and all of a sudden we've got five or six guns turned on us," Harrison said. Thompson's replacement called Harrison into his office.

"Is there something wrong?" he asked.

"No," Harrison said.

"You just don't seem like you get along with the boys. You just don't fit. It just seems like you're mad all the time. Do you like 'em?"

"I said no."

"Do you respect them?"

"No."

"Why not?"

"They're lyin', no good, chicken-shit sons of bitches." That was the extent of Hunter Harrison's diplomatic skills, and it was the end of the meeting.

Prior to that, he'd found himself on the couch of a high-powered psychologist brought in by the company to analyze whether he and others should be promoted. The psychologist told him he needed to be honest with him—and that all the information would be confidential and he'd be shown the report when it was finished. Soon enough, Harrison's report came out, but it wasn't Harrison who saw it.

"Did you see this, by God?" Thompson asked him. "It's that goddam shrink's report."

"I thought I was going to see it," Harrison said. "You aren't going to see it," Thompson told him. "Here's what it says. Lean, mean, street fighter. That's the last thing we need attached to your name in this company." Lean, mean, street fighter was not the BN style, according to high-risk, high-reward Harrison.

Meantime, he was focusing on service, asset utilization, controlling costs, and safety, while coaching and motivating the right people for the right jobs. He knew that railroad market share in the freight business had fallen off a cliff. Trucking had usurped the rails, and he was determined to grab back share with a better product that included precise schedules and better pricing, underpinned by a more efficient operation. Satisfied customers could then lower their inventories and get rid of excess boxcars, saving costs.

It was during this period at BN that Harrison became intrigued by computers. As someone who later in life would be teased for his inability to use a cell phone or a PC, Harrison was acutely aware of the value of data. He just needed someone to mine it and shovel it onto his desk in a way that he could use it. That person was Sue Rathe. Rathe exemplified Harrison's canny ability to find people who were motivated to do a good job. She could get him what he needed.

Rathe had started as a key punch operator at BN in 1973 at age twenty-two and then became a yardmaster, rare for a woman.[5] Rail yards were typically male lairs and rough places. Her superintendent told her that she wouldn't survive—the men wouldn't listen to her. Rathe's husband worked in the military. At home, they would compare notes about their similar work environments, hierarchies in which subordinates were subjected to yelling and screaming. Like Harrison, Rathe moved to BN with the merger in 1980. At a certain point, she found herself compiling daily reports of train miles, carloads, and other statistics for Bill Thompson. These were called the DSOP—Daily Summary of Operating Performance. As she put together the reports for Thompson, she grew to dislike the man, finding him mean, rude, and scary. "He was a tyrant."

Word of a Thompson urination episode at a locomotive maintenance facility in Pasco, Washington, did not charm her further, nor employees at the shop. "He urinated right in their work area to let them know what he thought of their place." She said a wildcat strike resulted, with workers insisting Thompson "come and clean his mess up."

In 1983, Rathe heard that BN was getting a new VP of Transportation, Hunter Harrison. The mention of Harrison's name, like Thompson's name, "petrified" people. However, she discovered that the real Harrison was vastly different from the rumors. When he arrived, he spent an hour speaking one on one with each of his key people. When Rathe's turn came, she was told, "Hunter's set aside the whole morning to talk to you." In addition to performing data entry, she had been a programmer at the railroad for a couple of years. She knew the potential of the computer system at BN, and Harrison

---

5   In the days before computer programs were run directly, information was keyed into a card punch device, which translated it into holes in cards. Via a card reader, the information—e.g., waybill information or car status—was transmitted to a computer for processing.

wanted to learn more about it—particularly a system called COMPASS (Complete Operating Movement Processing and Service System), an online inventory tracker that told users, among other things, where all the railcars and trains were and whether they were on time.

"Teach me how to use this stuff," he said. According to Rathe, Harrison was a quick study and made astute queries. She would generate daily reports for him about anything that had happened on the railroad the previous day. Suddenly, Harrison had hard evidence about performance and was brandishing it around BN.

"Where in the hell is Hunter getting this data from?" his subordinates wondered after being berated by Harrison. Soon enough, every one of them had a COMPASS terminal so they could run queries and be ready for Harrison. Of course, it was never enough for him. He always thought everything could be better, perhaps because of the expectations put on him as a child.

"If you could work on anything you wanted, what would you want to work on?" he asked Rathe.

She told him she "had been thinking about a way to measure service performance, and his eyes lit up. I realized immediately that I'd hit one of his hot buttons."

"How long would it take you to put something like that together?" he wondered. Rathe told him four to six months, if that's all she did. Harrison then spoke to Rathe's direct boss, Phil Westine, and said, "Take everything off her plate. She only works on this." It was the birth of MCSM (Major Corridor Service Measurement), a system that tracked traffic patterns from origins to destinations, or O&DS. "From that day on," Westine said, "there became pressure to measure like that." The team would define an acceptable amount of time for a boxcar to get from origin to destination and then monitor it to see if it made it in the set time. If it didn't, the system showed them where a car lost time and why. "This is what you're really trying to do as a railroad, run cars. You're not trying to move trains." A train simply being on time didn't necessarily mean the individual cars were where they needed to be.

"He was the only one who actually understood what the data meant. He could look at the data and [know] exactly what that meant from an operating perspective," Rathe said. "He was absolutely amazing." Westine, who'd unsuccessfully tried to sell the notion of data analysis to the previous VP, agreed. "People looked at me like I was crazy. And he [Harrison] got it in about three minutes." Westine also reflected that Harrison had not graduated from college but was "smarter than anyone I knew on the railroad who went to college."

While they worked on MCSM in Harrison's office, the phone was ringing constantly. Rathe said that when Harrison took a call, he always put it on speakerphone so she could hear the conversation. It was his informal way of teaching her about the railroad and the multitude of decisions he had to make each day. She then had a better idea of what he needed and would then work it into the next version of the software.

"He's thinking in three dimensions and the rest of us are stuck in two," she said, and laughed.

In spite of what Rathe called his "horrible reputation for yelling at people and using foul language, he never acted that way around me." She said he "frequently called me ma'am," a reflection of the strict manners he'd learned as a child. "Hunter was calmer when I was in the room, so [the men] would frequently invite me to meetings." She also recalled that while everyone was taking notes "like crazy" in these meetings, she never saw Harrison take notes, and she believed that he had a photographic memory. Sue Rathe's "MCSM was the first baby step" toward Precision Scheduled Railroading, the philosophy for which Harrison would become renowned. For decades, freight trains did not run on schedules. They departed when a customer's load showed up for shipment. Harrison would eventually change that, providing more predictable service and shorter transit times for which he could charge premium prices, as opposed to the commodity-like pricing that railroads had accepted for years.

Soon he was scrutinizing the return on assets, capital spending, depreciation, cash flow, and revenue. He also wanted all of the regions on the railroad to be cognizant of these numbers.

"When regions start getting charged with depreciation and when they understand the real business impact of capital spending, they will be more selective in their capital spending," he told *Modern Railroads* in 1986. He was granting autonomy, but balancing it with accountability, just as Thompson had taught him.

It was also around this time that he received his first serious recognition from the industry. In 1987, while still a VP at BN, he was named

Railroad Man of the Year by the St. Louis Railway Club, the first non-CEO to win. Harrison was forty-three years old.

By 1988, he was named VP of Service Design at BN. Even though the position was perfectly synchronized with precision railroading, Harrison felt he'd been sidelined. It wasn't the "nitty gritty" of railroading, and he saw it as "a huge setback." But it was during this period when he reconnected with Sue Rathe, who had left the railroad in 1983. Harrison had to create a detailed service plan for the railroad so BN could be more effective selling it, and he wanted help computerizing it. He took Rathe to lunch.

"I wrote out on a napkin how I would design this system," she said. "And he goes, 'You're hired.'" Rathe was now part of the Service Design team. Harrison worked the group hard but treated them well. He took them to a beautiful historic hotel, The Eldridge in Lawrence, Kansas, for a three-day retreat. They'd put in a twelve-hour day trying to improve the railroad and then the next day go golfing—part relaxation, part team bonding. When they left, Rathe was flying back to Minnesota while Harrison was headed to Chicago.

"Well, I'll take you home," he told her.

"Hunter, I'm going to Minneapolis. You're going to Chicago." Harrison flew her home on a BN plane "and it was just the two of us." She said he wanted to talk about how she was going to make the system work. When they landed in Minneapolis, there was a limo waiting for her.

"I felt like royalty," she said. BN then found her an empty office in St. Paul and "I just programmed away like crazy for weeks on end." Harrison treated such people like stars, but he got loyal treatment in return. While some were afraid of him, the ones who thrived were those who gravitated toward his challenges and didn't want to disappoint him. Rathe began working furiously at devising a tool to make "trip plans" for each boxcar. "It was actually a trip planning algorithm," she said, a set of rules that a computer would follow when making calculations. Rathe created approximately fifty decision tables, real-world situations faced on the railroad that required a decision to get a boxcar from A to B. They all had to be mimicked by the algorithm.

Once completed, the algorithm could be run ahead of time or after the fact to see how a car ran and whether it followed its trip plan. This system had another acronym—SMS, which stood for Service

Measurement System. Hunter Harrison would drool over such data like a kid over a comic book. More precision was being built into the railroad's schedule, a step toward heaven for the obsessed, continuous learner and improver. "Every possible scenario had to be accounted for so it could be in the algorithm and the algorithm could figure out what was supposed to happen," Rathe said. Harrison, who was a white-knuckle flyer, would gather his team, hop on a company jet, and fly to the regions to see the railroad in action and find out how they could make it better.[6]

But despite the strides he made, Harrison's status at BN, either in his own mind or in reality, had become fragile. There was a new CEO, Gerald "Jerry" Grinstein, who had run Western Airlines and later went on to be CEO of Delta Airlines. He was not a railroader by background. Don Wood, who became executive vice president of operations at BN and also did a stint as BN's CFO, worked with Harrison for three or four years at BN in the 1980s. Wood said BN at that time didn't actually have many people who really understood railroads, with the exception of Harrison and a few others.

"The railroad guys [like Thompson, Grayson, and Harrison] at the Frisco kind of knew how it all worked," he said. "They couldn't afford to make a lot of mistakes and they didn't." Harrison, Wood said, "was the epitome of that," a scrappy character who'd come from a scrappy company and likely felt frustrated and thwarted at BN.

Lyle Reed, who'd worked with Harrison at Frisco since the late 60s, was also an executive at BN and worked closely with Grinstein. Reed recalled Grinstein "was a friend of labor," while "Hunter was hard charging, pushing the railway unions to be more productive." In Reed's view, it was only a matter of time before the hammer came down on him. Although Harrison said Grinstein was extremely nice and fair to him, "he effectively said, you're at the wrong place at the wrong time. We've got a job for you and an office for you. We just don't have anything for you to do." In an interview, Grinstein said such a conversation never took place. He maintained that he liked Harrison and believed he was destined to be a "breakout leader." Grinstein said he wanted to keep

---

6   Rathe rejoined Harrison at Illinois Central as chief information officer. Later, she got her PhD, and she is now a cancer researcher.

him and that he would never have put such an aggressive, ambitious executive on ice.

"I thought he was unusually gifted," Grinstein said.

He did allow, however, that Harrison may have *thought* that he had been sidelined. BN was slow to change, Grinstein said, and Harrison was impatient for change; he may have thought his only alternative at the company was an unchallenging role.

"I'm a much more aggressive individual than he is," Harrison said after hearing Grinstein's assessment decades later. "He's much more level headed, unemotional."

But Reed said that Harrison knew he wasn't getting any further at BN, and if he made a wrong move, he was certainly finished there. "He was already ahead of everybody else," Reed added. "He wasn't a part of the good ole boys club. He was part of the get results club." Wood said that if BN had any sense at the time, it would have let Harrison run the railroad's operations.

"It tells you more about Burlington Northern than it tells you about Hunter," he said.

For someone like Hunter Harrison, who needed the purpose of work, that period at BN was like a slow drowning. By his own admission, he was "not very good at sitting in an office twiddling my thumbs, reading the *Wall Street Journal.*"

Laird Pitz, a Vietnam veteran and former FBI agent who began working with Harrison at BN in 1986 as head of the railroad's police force, remained close to him over the next three decades and worked with him at two other companies.[7] The two men were born five days apart, and Pitz was astonished by how much they thought alike, both "very strong willed and very opinionated." He said he understood "the dichotomy" in Harrison's personality. People who knew Harrison professionally will tell you "he's a genius, he's got it all figured out, he's smarter than everybody else. He's a tough SOB, he's hard on people, he's demanding." One minute Harrison was all Southern charm, while the next minute people were running for the hills. What people didn't see, according to Pitz, was

---

7   Harrison was disqualified from service in Vietnam, he said, because of a knee injury sustained playing football. His father sent him back to the recruiting office, but he was disqualified a second time for the same reason. "They wouldn't take me."

the "loving father" who had "a heart of gold and cares about people." He described dinners they had when Harrison would complain about people at work not telling him the truth. "Well, they're scared shitless of you," Pitz would tell him. "How do you expect them to talk to you when they're afraid of you?" While they had disagreements over thirty years, respectful of the other's skills, Pitz said they never spoke a cross word. But Pitz knew Harrison "was not the favorite son" at BN and could see how Harrison had thought he'd been thrown into the penalty box.

"He was the strongest operating guy they had. But Hunter was Hunter. And you either loved him or you hated him. And the people at the top hated him." The plain-spoken Pitz described Harrison as "a threat" to the inner circle at BN—perhaps not to Grinstein, but to many of the other top executives at the railroad. Even Grinstein described those managers as not as aggressive as Harrison "and I think that frustrated him."

Fortunately, it was only a matter of months before a lifeboat came along.

3 AT THE HELM: ILLINOIS CENTRAL

THE LAST THING Jeannie Harrison wanted to do was move again. She was in the middle of finishing construction of the family's dream home alongside a golf course in Kansas City. But life with Hunter Harrison meant perpetual motion. A big job in Chicago with another railroad, Illinois Central, was now a possibility.

Darius Gaskins was a former president and CEO at BN, and he had previously chaired the Interstate Commerce Commission during the period the Staggers Rail Act was enacted. Gaskins had a wide array of connections in the transportation industry and happened to know of a private equity concern that was looking for someone who knew how to operate a railroad. Mostly financed with debt plus IC's cash, Prospect Group Inc. had bought Illinois Central Transportation Company in March 1989 for $440 million and assumed debts, taking it private while holding onto a 70.5 percent stake. The rest of the shares of IC went to management and another investment firm. A Washington law firm, presumably in Gaskins's orbit, called Harrison, told him he'd been recommended to Prospect, and asked whether he'd like to interview for the job.

"Well," Harrison said, deadpanning. "I'll take it under advisement." He then raised his arms and looked to the sky as if manna were falling from heaven.

Illinois Central had faltered badly during the 1970s and 80s. It had been under the umbrella of IC Industries, which in 1988 became the

Whitman Corporation, and had been enmeshed in the flavor of the era—the corporate conglomerate, a grouping of disparate businesses. In the early 1980s, a railroad executive named Edward Moyers, formerly of the Peoria and Pekin Union Railway, proposed to Prospect that it put together a few rail lines in Mississippi and Louisiana. That combination became MidSouth Rail, and Moyers ran it, making a tidy sum for those concerned. Prospect had invested approximately $16 million and eventually sold MidSouth to Kansas City Southern for $213.5 million. Now Prospect wanted to do it again with Illinois Central—a bigger outfit—and Moyers ended up running that too.

While Harrison had been working on early versions of Precision Scheduled Railroading at BN, Moyers had been thinking about something akin to it. Like Harrison, who claimed he'd been referred to by many traditionalists at BN as a "young nut," Moyers and his ideas had been dismissed as crazy by his previous bosses. However, the similarities ended there. Harrison described Moyers as a "Southern gentleman to a T... full three-piece suit, very rigid guy." A flashy dresser, Harrison went to Chicago to interview for VP and chief transportation officer. He sensed that Moyers was about to reject him.

"I said, 'Mr. Moyers, do you want me?' He said, 'I'm going to be honest with you. I didn't, but I'm changing my mind.'"

Harrison joined Illinois Central on May 1, 1989, but he knew it wouldn't go over well at home.

"I wasn't crazy about telling Jeannie, 'Forget that couch.'" Jeannie Harrison was not in favor of her husband's new job in Chicago. It was yet another move, IC was smaller than BN, and he'd essentially worked for the same company for almost twenty-six years. It was a gamble, she said, and she worried about her family's financial security. For the record, Harrison said almost three decades later, "That was not fun for me to leave BN. I didn't want to leave. It was embarrassing to me." Grinstein said he was surprised to see Harrison go and wanted to keep him, but Harrison's move to IC put him just steps from the corner office, closer than he would ever get at BN.

CHICAGO GREW AT a staggering rate. The population was just 200 in 1833 when it was first incorporated, but it would soon grow exponentially.

In 1848, the Illinois and Michigan Canal was completed, connecting the Great Lakes to the Mississippi River. In 1856, construction finished on Illinois Central—the first land grant railroad in the United States—making it the longest railway in the world at the time.[1] The IC ran down the center of the continent, from the Great Lakes and Chicago to New Orleans on the Gulf of Mexico and into the heartland across Iowa. Illinois Central once had Abraham Lincoln as its in-house lawyer and a steamboat operator named Samuel Clemens (a.k.a. Mark Twain). The rail baron E.H. Harriman—the other E.H.H. in railroading—had once controlled it, along with half a dozen others. Harriman was quoted as saying, "Cooperation means 'Do as I say, and do it damn quick.'" It would not be out of character for E. Hunter Harrison to say something similar.

Between the railroad, the Great Lakes, and the Mississippi, Chicago was destined to become a transportation hub. By 1860, its population had blossomed to 112,172. Ten years later, it was just shy of 300,000. By 1890, 1.1 million people lived there, and by 1940 the population was 3.4 million.

To this day, Chicago is still a nexus and choke point for all the major railroads in Canada and the United States. But being headquartered in a transportation hub didn't mean railroads like IC automatically made money. When Hunter Harrison arrived as VP, Illinois Central was heavily in debt. Interest rates were high, with the prime rate at 11 percent. He recalled IC almost missed making the payroll twice.

"It was a dog," said Gil Lamphere, who ran Prospect and became the chairman of IC. "It was the worst run railroad in the United States— major, Class 1."[2]

From the 1960s through the 1980s, Illinois Central was just another company among a portfolio of firms that were part of a conglomerate. Such holding companies were all the rage during that era but later fell out of fashion as major institutional investors like pension funds and mutual funds decided they would rather do their own diversifying than

---

1   The United States government granted almost three million acres so the IC could be built.

2   A Class 1 railroad is defined by revenue. Today, a Class 1 must generate $447,621,226 or more annually.

let conglomerates do it for them. During that period, IC was left to wither as the holding company dabbled in unrelated industries such as soft drink bottling, mufflers, aerospace equipment, and food products including evaporated milk and chocolate.

The railroad was basically worth "scrap value," Harrison said. The holding company wasn't focused on it. Throughout the 1960s and 70s, he said the owners wanted to sell it. At the time, no other Class 1 was interested in buying all of IC. So, bit by bit, the parent company generated cash by selling pieces of the physical railroad, eliminating thousands of miles of the route network. From the late 1970s onward, the railroad division also shrank dramatically, down from about 11,000 to 3,600 employees by the time Harrison got there.[3]

Illinois Central still operated, but it was at the brink. When Harrison arrived and got a look at the books, he claimed they were even worse than he'd imagined and wondered if he'd made the right decision to join the company. Morale was terrible. "Nobody wore a hat that said Illinois Central on it," he said.

He found employees were scared about whether the company would continue to exist. Their first question was whether they'd have jobs. Clearly, management had the upper hand. "The first quarter was, 'Were we going to make it?' I don't know," Harrison said. "I wish I could tell you." He said he told workers that a lot of the situation rested with them, meaning how hard they worked.

The second question was, "Are we going to buy locomotives?" Illinois Central hadn't purchased new ones in more than thirty years, a delay that was unheard of in the industry. Harrison soon bought about forty used locomotives from Burlington Northern for what he considered a steal, $243,000 each. He said IC employees thought these "new" engines, which were twenty years old, were the equivalent of Cadillacs. Their third question to him was, "Will you stop contracting out our work?"

"You work with me," he told them, "I'll work with you. I'm a fair guy." In fact, he was most definitely on their side on the last question.

---

3   The holding company was IC Industries, followed by Whitman Industries. In 1988, Whitman had 14,868 employees.

"I've never been a big advocate of contracting out. I think it shows a great weakness on your part. [It signals] you don't know how to run the business."

Harrison arrived at IC in May 1989 not knowing anything about the company. On July 4, he closed a hump yard in Chicago, a point where everything slowed down in the network. Humps are literally that, small hills that allow railcars to be moved around a yard with the help of gravity. The problem was, humps had outlived their usefulness. Railroads had moved to unit trains, consisting of the same type of cars carrying the same type of loads. Individual cars didn't need to be moved around as much as in the past. On August 3, Harrison called a meeting of his key personnel and told them he was about to close a second hump yard. Cutting out hump yards meant trains could move faster from A to B, which meant that suddenly IC was offering a more valuable product to customers, which could result in a premium price. Soon after, he called a scheduling meeting.

"This was four or five days of blood, sweat, and tears," he told a group years later. Harrison was astonished that the head of marketing for the railroad didn't want to attend. Why would the person responsible for selling the railroad's product not want to be part of designing the product; in this case, designing the best schedule? He asked the marketing chief if he wanted to provide him with any guidelines.

"Don't make it any worse," he was told.

When Harrison arrived, the operating ratio (OR) at Illinois Central was abysmal, in the high 90s. The railroad spent virtually everything it generated. Prospect, the private equity group that now controlled IC and brought Harrison on board, targeted an operating ratio of 84 percent—meaning the railroad would spend 84 cents to produce each dollar, instead of 98 cents. Prospect and IC's CEO, Edward Moyers, told Harrison that a smart guy like him could perhaps get it to 82 percent.

"Two years, and we're at seventy-four," Harrison said with a wry smile. "And they called me in and said, 'Is that all you got?'"

Being bullheaded had a lot to do with it. Early on, Harrison developed the ability to use a powerful two-letter word: no. He didn't just use it with employees, but with customers, a counterintuitive approach in an industry that had always let the customer dictate railroad schedules.

From the 1950s until well into the 1980s, American railroads had trouble making money. Not only had trucking sucked freight off the rails, but rail freight only moved when customers showed up with their loads. As a result, more often than not, they dictated the price. Given its perilous finances, Illinois Central was at their mercy.

In the summer of 1992, unbeknownst to Harrison, Moyers told the board that he wanted to resign soon but would stay until a search turned up a new CEO. When Harrison found out three days before Christmas that there was an executive manhunt going on, he thought, "What are they doin' a search for? They got the man here in the next office and they're out here doin' a search? Don't y'all see me here?"

Alex Lynch, an investment banking advisor to Prospect and an IC director, said that "Hunter was a little bit rough around the edges." When it came to operating a railroad, no one came close to Harrison, but he was still inexperienced when it came to finance and strategy. While it did have him in mind for CEO, the board felt it prudent to do a proper search to satisfy itself. Lynch, who chaired the search committee, advised Harrison to be patient. "And Hunter's not a patient guy."

Meantime, that October, even though he was planning to leave, Moyers announced four-year growth targets. Annual revenue at IC would rise over the four years by $100 million, he forecast, and the operating ratio would drop a point every year to 66.9 per cent.

"I was listening [to the conference call]," Harrison said. "I'm about to faint."

After the call, his phone rang. It was the railroad's marketing chief.

"Where are you getting that four points in OR?" he asked Harrison.

"I said I don't have a clue," he replied. Harrison then asked his colleague where *he* was going to get the extra revenue. "He said 'I don't have a clue.'" Harrison then confronted Moyers, the man who was departing but leaving an ambitious plan for his underlings to execute.

"Well, that's pretty aggressive," Harrison said.

"Nah, you're a smart boy," Moyers told him. "You'll figure out how to do it."

In early February 1993, Moyers fell ill and required heart surgery. Hunter Harrison was made interim CEO of Illinois Central. Moyers would eventually give Harrison his blessing; the board, however, was still unsure about Harrison, who said he was interviewed nineteen times. It's hard to believe, but Lamphere said that Harrison was shy. "Hunter's looking at his shoes. Hunter's shuffling. Hunter's mumbling." The board was concerned he didn't have the public confidence to be the face of the company. When you're trying to implement change, "You are the message," Lamphere said. "The message is you." IC's directors saw Harrison as untested. They got over it.

On February 17, Mr. High Risk, High Reward—as Harrison had become known at BN—took over as CEO of IC. When he got the job, he told a reporter for the *Commercial Appeal* in Memphis that railroading had been his life. "That's all I've ever done. I've kind of sacked groceries and threw papers and railroaded." He'd also worked construction and at a bakery, but the point was made. Railroads were all he really knew.

Among the dozens of congratulatory letters was one from John M. Crothers, his principal at Kingsbury High School in Memphis, where Harrison had been less than a model student. He received a handwritten note from Dick Grayson, his former boss at Frisco and BN, who wrote, "My only regret is that you are not running the BN." Harrison also got a hand-scribbled, supportive note from Jerry Grinstein, who was still the chairman and CEO of BN.

While much of what Harrison did was based on an intellectual approach that had developed over years of observation, thought, and the honing of processes, much of it was also common sense. At IC, there were plenty of examples. For starters, the railroad's main line from Chicago to New Orleans was double tracked. Early on, Moyers—a shrewd character in his own right who'd identified a number of inefficiencies— thought it was one too many. As Harrison would proselytize for years to come, just because the railroad possessed an asset didn't mean it was free. The second track had to be maintained and was therefore expensive. Moyers wondered if the double track could become a single track. "Look at that," Moyers directed Harrison, "and see if I'm crazy." Harrison came to the same conclusion. Much of the track was ripped up and sold, though certain sections of double track were left in place to create sidings to deal with oncoming trains from north and south. The trains also got longer for efficiency's sake, and locomotive power was more precisely matched to the need.

There was also an obvious saving to be had with crews. Normally, engineers and conductors would travel for eight hours, stop, change crews, and spend the night wherever. The next day, they worked a train going back. Not only did the overnight stay result in lodging and meal costs, but crews were away from their families. As an alternative, crews were swapped. Trains would meet halfway, and crews would swap engines and ride back home—instant savings and happier crews.

Then there was Harrison's war on paper. Illinois Central rented a huge amount of square feet to store files. Harrison wondered what could possibly be so precious to warrant paying for such a large repository for old paper. So, he went to see for himself. Rathe described him sneaking into the filing area in the middle of the night to root through the cabinets. As he suspected, what he found wasn't needed. The word went around IC that the boss was on the warpath. The next time Harrison went to Memphis, he saw a dumpster parked next to the yard office, and it was full of old paper and files. Staff there were already on it. Alongside all of these initiatives, Harrison was beginning to articulate the notion of Precision Scheduled Railroading. He was putting words to the concept so it could be spread throughout the organization.

When Harrison took the reins, IC's annual revenue was $547.4 million (1992). He quickly let the market—which he always viewed as the scorekeeper—know what his key goals were so analysts and investors could keep a tally. Harrison promised to increase revenue while at the same time reduce the operating ratio by four points—a point a year. In 1995, he announced *Plan 2000*, a five-year blueprint to achieve annual revenue of $800 million by 2000, up from $595 million in 1994. By 1996, revenue was $617.2 million, and he wrote in *Railway Age* that IC's operating ratio would drop from 65 percent to below 60 percent by the end of 1999. The average across the big railroads in the US was 83 percent. He was forecasting the railroading equivalent of the lunar landing.

Illinois Central had finished 1992 with an OR of 70.9 percent, down from the high nineties when Prospect took over in 1989 and Harrison arrived. If he was right about his prediction for 1999, a further 1100 basis point reduction would mean the profit margin for the railroad would go from virtually nothing when he had arrived to 40 percent.[4] Compounded annual earnings growth almost doubled from

---

4   A basis point is 1/100th of a percentage point.

1991 to 1996, when profits hit $126.6 million. The operating ratio had dropped steadily each year to 64.4 percent for 1996. It would go lower still.

"They said it couldn't be done. [IC] was regional. It's all coal. And it goes downhill." People in the industry and on the street were calling the number an aberration. "It's a small Class 1 and shit," he recalled people saying. "They [IC] don't really count." When IC's board allowed Harrison to get a corporate jet, "the tail number on his first aircraft—a Hawker—was OR59," recalled Lynch, a number that was thought to be an impossible-to-achieve operating ratio.

Harrison's operating ratios were not, however, aberrations. Illinois Central was usually ten points better on OR than the next best—and twelve or thirteen points better than the average. For Harrison, a lot of it came back to his time in the tower as trainmaster.

"Don't forget what got ya there. If that's one of your powers, that's your strength; don't lose it."

As Harrison said, his basic view didn't change during the decades he ran railroads—service customers, control costs, utilize assets, don't get anybody hurt, and recognize and develop people—and over time, he gained more confidence. When he was still at BN and working with Sue Rathe on data collection, notions about Precision Scheduled Railroading began forming. Freight trains ran on volume. Customarily, when the car was full, it would depart. Neither the railroad nor the customer knew when that would be. He said, we're going to flip this very basic premise and run on schedule. By doing so, the railroad would utilize its assets at maximum efficiency and get rid of ones that it didn't need, saving huge amounts of money.

Not long after Harrison became CEO, a tough customer called from Geismar in Louisiana's chemical basin, demanding a meeting. IC's marketing and sales chief was a big, husky football type named Gerry who Harrison said was prone to break into a sweat. Off the two went to Louisiana, where they met the customer's senior VPs. In the past, the railroaders had always met with the local plant manager. Whatever the situation was now, it had obviously escalated.

"Let me tell you something," one of the executives told them. "We do a lot of business with IC." At the time, this particular customer was $80 or $100 million a year, 17 or 18 percent of revenue. Out came the stick.

"You're going to cut the rates," the customer demanded. "17 percent." He then threatened to take his business elsewhere.

Harrison said, "We worked very hard down here to improve the infrastructure . . . the service."

"Fuck your service. It's a fucking commodity. What I'm looking for is low price. You don't get it."

Harrison's colleague was a puddle of sweat. "I just reached over and got my briefcase, closed it up, and I said, 'Let's go, Gerry. The meetin's over.'"

"The fuck it's not," the customer's executive said. "What do you mean it's over?"

Harrison told the man that he wouldn't cut the price. "So, you're not a customer anymore, so I don't have time to fool with you." He said he and Gerry hit the hallway, slammed the door, and drove away. Two years later, Harrison was sitting in his office in Chicago. His assistant Monica told him there was a call for him.

"I bet ya don't remember me, do ya?" the voice said.

"I'm sorry, I don't," Harrison said.

"I'm the asshole from Geismar from the meeting two years ago."

"Yeah, I know you now. You asshole."

The former customer told Harrison he had tank cars sitting in Houston that he'd been trying to move for three months.

"I sure would like to buy some of your service," the man said.

"I appreciate that, you takin' the time," Harrison said.

At a conference years later, Harrison recalled Burlington Northern had put stickers up all over its operation that said "The customer is always right." Harrison joked to a roomful of railroaders that he went around ripping the stickers off the wall. He'd come to the conclusion that if you said yes to everything the customer wanted, you wouldn't make any money. That approach would help him make enormous profits in later years, but it would also eventually result in criticism that would hound him.

Harrison believed improving IC "was about fundamental railroading." Unlike his later assignments at bigger companies, he said Illinois Central didn't need to cut many people. Cuts had occurred before he arrived. But what produced results was the approach he would preach for the next two and a half decades—what train velocity does for efficiency, what longer trains mean for efficiency, and on and on. He saw better processes for everything, base hit after base hit. As for labor, a few years after he was in place as CEO, the union was offered an hourly rate, which gave the railroad scheduling flexibility in return for job security for the workers, an approach he'd helped design. But it took several attempts at ratification. Finally, town halls were held in Memphis, Jackson, and Baton Rouge.

"Throwin' tents up and so forth. Looked like a revival."

In Memphis, the highest-ranking union leader—the local chairman—arrived in what Harrison described as the "prettiest Cadillac" he'd ever seen, "candy apple red." He was, according to Harrison, the highest paid brakeman-conductor on the railroad. Harrison said he wasn't a bad guy, but nonetheless found his questions irritating. He reminded the man that the union had requested the railroad stop contracting out jobs, which he said it had done.

"I've worked with you and I don't think you've worked with us," Harrison recalled telling him. "If you don't ratify this agreement, I'm going to contract out every job on the railroad I can." The agreement was ratified.

While he took on unionized workers, he was also mentoring and coaching. Among the chosen was an Alabama native named Keith Creel who had started working for Burlington Northern in Birmingham in 1992, three years after Harrison had left for Illinois Central. Harrison cast a long shadow over BN, even though he was long gone. After a stint in Lincoln, Nebraska, Creel moved up to trainmaster in Tulsa, Oklahoma, working at a yard that was the sister facility to where Harrison started in Memphis. Harrison was mythical, Creel said, on that section of the railroad. Some of the tales surrounding him—including ones told by Harrison himself—have aged like fine wines. Among the stories that stuck with Creel was one about a switchman who'd gone to sleep on the job. In the middle of the night, Harrison drove by the man's truck and saw feet sticking out the window. As the story goes, Harrison jerked the man out of the truck by his feet. Harrison said this had been "embellished a bit," but the wayward employee soon changed his somnolent ways and became, according to Creel, one of the best operating people at BN. Whether the story is one hundred percent accurate isn't the point. The stories—many akin to parables—were a way to teach a lesson. Creel, therefore, had heard about Harrison and learned from him before he met him.

In February 1996, Creel went to work for Illinois Central as a trainmaster. He met Harrison on his first day there. The executive vice president of operations, John McPherson (now on the board of CSX), showed Creel the railroad's operations center in Homewood, Illinois.[5] He then took Creel, still in his late twenties, into Chicago to meet Harrison at the CEO's office in the NBC Tower. Up to that point in his career, the highest-ranking person Creel had ever met was the general manager, akin to "meeting the President of the United States" and this CEO was an entirely different species. Harrison's office was massive, with a panoramic view of Lake Michigan. Creel described walking through a living room and hearing Harrison's booming baritone. He couldn't see him because partitions separated the outer rooms from where the boss sat. After getting up to shake Creel's hand, within ten minutes Harrison loosened his tie, "kicked back," and began puffing on a Marlboro Red. This was at a time when smoking had become verboten in office buildings, but Harrison made his own rules. Creel said they talked for two or three hours, and Harrison's understanding of the business floored him. "I could just smell it and sense it." By the same token, Harrison could sense the potential in Creel, a future CEO.

It's hard to imagine many CEOs spending that much time with such a low-level employee. But Creel's day didn't end there. Off he went with McPherson to get on IC's office car. Creel had never been on one. There was also a bedroom car. The two railcars were hitched to the back of Amtrak 59, otherwise known as *The City of New Orleans*, a famous train that runs every night out of Chicago to New Orleans. During the evening and the next day Creel was treated to a view of the whole main line. Harrison was puttin' on the Ritz for the young man. "I've hit the jackpot here," Creel was thinking. Along the way, he met Edmond Harris, who would become a top executive at Canadian National, Canadian Pacific, and CSX. They drove the three hours back to Jackson, Mississippi, and then Harris told Creel he'd pick him up for breakfast in the morning.

---

5   Harrison was alerted to Creel by John Kay, a colleague from Frisco days, who told him and McPherson, "I've got a pup that I had over on the BN. You might want to talk to him." Kay also noticed David Ferryman, who went on to a senior VP position.

They went to the Waffle House. "That should have given me a signal." After breakfast, Harris pointed to the train in the terminal and told him that was Creel's ride back to Memphis. "Go to work." Harrison had dangled the carrot; now it was the stick.

Creel worked in Memphis for about a year and a half. It was demanding—twelve-hour days, minimum five days a week—and Creel found he wasn't seeing his family. His old employer, BN, came back to him with an offer of a promotion and he gave his two weeks' notice to IC. The next morning, the phone rang in the tower. It was Harrison. He called to tell Creel he wasn't going to let him resign—he had a future with the company. Creel was gobsmacked. He and his wife, Ginger, had already decided to stay in Memphis with BN. Creel was worried about having given his word to Burlington Northern. Harrison told him to tell BN he'd changed his mind—explaining that changing one's mind wasn't lying. The CEO told Creel that he had a lot of talent; he'd put him there for a reason and would develop him.

"There's a place for you," Harrison told the young man. "If you walk away from this company, you're walking away from a golden opportunity."

Creel said he had to talk to his wife. Harrison said, "Well, go talk to her now."

"But Mr. Harrison," Creel said, "I'm at work in the tower."

"The railroad will run without you," Harrison told him. "Go find your wife, talk to her, and call me back."

Creel went to talk to Ginger, who was at a pool party. The two of them loved Memphis and didn't want to move again. While Creel was talking to Ginger, his cell phone rang. It was known as a "brick," descriptive of the size and heft of mobile phones at the time. Creel thought there must have been a problem at the railroad. But it was Harrison looking for a decision, a replay of how Thompson had dealt with Harrison, giving him just hours to decide on a move.

Harrison had offered Creel a job in Mobile, Alabama—the lure of going home. He and Ginger agreed he should stay at Illinois Central. But before the Creels could even move to Alabama, the location of the job changed. They were being sent to Jackson, Mississippi. Like Harrison's own pinball-like trajectory, Creel would move many times, sometimes on very short notice, in one instance packing up and leaving on the same day so he could make his way to Battle Creek, Michigan. Some fourteen trains were horribly backed up between there and Chicago, a distance of only 166 miles. Upon his arrival, Creel was warned by Harrison to "get it cleaned up or you're not going to have a job."

More than once as Creel moved towns and climbed the ladder, Harrison told him not to build a swimming pool where he lived because he wouldn't be there long. It would be tough to clone a Hunter Harrison, but the railroader homed in on people with potential and groomed them. While his old friend Laird Pitz called him a frustrated cop or even J. Edgar Harrison ("He's got everything solved"), Harrison was also a teacher. He loved nothing more than a hard worker who was willing to learn and wanted to succeed. Bill Thompson and his father had seen something in Harrison, and Harrison had seen something in the twenty-something Creel. The CEO would spend an inordinate amount of time with this junior employee—more than half a dozen levels beneath him in the organizational chart—teaching him the business. It paid off for both of them. He'd put Creel in the right jobs at the right times, which was good for both the railroad and Creel. Harrison had trained someone who would become a standout operator in the industry and years later his successor as chief executive officer at a Class 1 railroad. It was a remarkable example of Harrison's eye for talent and willingness to spend years developing it.

The CEO had invested so much in him that Creel didn't want to disappoint him, a refrain from many who worked closely with Harrison. The pressure was pounding. If you didn't do your job, you wouldn't have a job. Creel had served in the first Gulf War, so stress was not new to him. But this was different. This was his future, and he was always on a knife's edge. At one point, his anxiety crested, and "one side of my face just literally froze," Creel said. It wasn't officially diagnosed (he didn't go to the doctor), but Creel and his wife were convinced it was Bell's palsy. Whatever had afflicted him self-corrected in a matter of weeks, but Creel discovered that he had to learn to manage his stress. Getting the operation working better also made him feel better. Harrison, though, knew human nature and was toughest to work for when the railroad ran well. The boss worried that his people would get complacent.

"When things were bad, it's when he was most supportive," Creel said.

BILL THOMPSON NEVER used the term Precision Scheduled Railroading, but the concept was evolving in the way he operated. Harrison took it further, not only developing it and implementing it, but articulating it for others. Thompson's operating lessons imprinted so strongly that forty years later, Harrison would still talk about him in executive meetings at the railroads he subsequently ran. In the mid-1990s, while he was steering IC, Harrison was invited back to Springfield to play in a golf tournament. Thompson was living there but could no longer play golf due to an accident. The older man came out to the course and rode around with Harrison so the two could have a visit. "Hunter," he said, "I have a question for you."

"Yessir?"

"How in the shit did you get the operating ratio down to 62?"[6]

"I applied some of the lessons you taught me."

"Well, I never got it down to 62."

Their former boss at Frisco and BN, Dick Grayson, was living in Arizona. In later years, Harrison traveled there for a meeting of a company that owned railcars. Grayson called his former employee's office—akin to the Pope calling, Harrison said—and asked if they could have dinner. Harrison said sure, even though he didn't know Grayson well, having been so many levels beneath him. At dinner, Grayson talked about how proud he was that someone from their ranks had become the boss of a Class 1 railroad. He then said he wanted to share something with Harrison. He, Grayson said, had thought of himself as the best operating guy around—until Thompson came along. He admitted that such a realization was hard to swallow. But he then added that before Thompson died, Thompson had told him that Hunter Harrison was even better than he, Bill Thompson, had been.

Harrison also wasn't afraid to put himself in harm's way. In September 1997, a levee broke in Obion, Tennessee, and a new lake—more than a mile in diameter—formed in the middle of IC's 900-mile single-track system. At one point, the track was under nine inches of water. With Memphis at the heart of Illinois Central, trains were backing up.

---

6   According to regulatory filings, IC's best annual OR was 62.3 percent in 1998. Harrison said the best quarterly OR at IC was 61.9 percent.

The crews worked out a plan: run a long train to the closest siding, cut the power and run it to other end, then gingerly "shove the train through the lake to locomotives waiting on the other side," as described by IC's Jerry Peck. They got good at it. Then, when the water subsided to just three inches above the rails, Harrison arrived in Obion. A local manager told him that the engineer still didn't think it was safe to ride the train across the lake, even with the lower water level and assurances that the rail beds were solid. It wasn't just the engineer who didn't want to cross; the conductor didn't want to go either.

"I guess I'm going to be driving a train," Harrison said.

"Sir . . . respectfully, I don't think you should be doing that."

"Are you going to take it?" Harrison asked.

"Uh, no sir."

"Then Mr. McPherson [the operating VP from Baton Rouge] and I will take it," Harrison told him.[7] Both the engineer and the conductor climbed aboard, and the four of them took the train across. While it was perhaps a case of major bravado, it also sent a message through the organization about leadership. Years later, Harrison confessed that only a fool wouldn't have been worried. Hedging his bets, he'd stood on the outside of the engine, ready to leap into the water if something went wrong. It was the full Harrison on display—high risk, high reward—only now, he was CEO.

Not only was the company becoming highly profitable, Harrison was starting to make money. In 1992, he received cash compensation of $338,807, owned 134,155 shares, and received $412,000 in stock. The next year, he received $718,442 in salary and bonus, plus $275,000 worth of options. In 1994, his salary and bonus totaled $1,126,154, and he was granted $4,402,262 worth of options. By then, he owned 195,845 shares, and by 1996, he owned more than $17 million in stock and had 600,000 options. In 1997, his cash compensation was $1,081,849, and he was granted $1,357,705 in options. His share ownership then totaled 665,316, and in 1998, he was paid $8,396,574, more than the CEO of McDonald's Corp. The 1990s were the beginning of what amounted to a quarter of a century of massive

---

7　The incident was described in manuals written by Harrison later at CN.

wealth accumulation for Hunter Harrison. But it wasn't just Harrison getting wealthy. The railroad had created twenty-seven millionaires in its ranks.

"I'm talking about guys who were making fifty a year and became millionaires, just on stock," he said. Jeannie Harrison, who'd been reluctant about her husband joining IC, laughingly said that after such results, "I stopped butting in."

By 1994–95, Illinois Central was virtually on automatic. It was as efficient and profitable as it was going to be. Meantime, the 1990s was the decade of rail mergers. Burlington Northern Railroad combined with Santa Fe Pacific Corporation to form BNSF. Union Pacific would later combine with Southern Pacific to form the largest railroad in the United States, also called Union Pacific. Compared to Illinois Central, they were gigantic. Still, in 1994, within weeks of the announcement of BNSF's creation, Illinois Central's board was looking for its own deal. The only railroad that was an appropriate size was Kansas City Southern. In fact, its track miles were almost identical in total length to IC's. The merged railroads would serve fourteen states in the South and Midwest.

An IC-KCS combination would create a much larger north-south system with connections to Chicago, Kansas City, Omaha, New Orleans, Houston, and Dallas (later, KCS would expand into Mexico). The chairman of KCS from 1987 to 2000 was Landon Rowland, who had also been CEO of the railroad. A Harvard law graduate, he'd been a lawyer in Kansas City for eighteen years prior to joining Kansas City Southern Industries in 1980, the holding company for KCS. He ran it for more than a decade. In Harrison's view, Rowland was not a railroader at heart. But Kansas City Southern, he said, had expressed interest in being acquired by Illinois Central.

"They put the company in play, if you will," Harrison said.

The railroad invited Harrison to Kansas City to speak to its key employees. Harrison said he was not a particularly big advocate of the deal, at the time privately thinking, "I wouldn't give you shit for your company." He thought KCS had "baggage" and was unable to see the synergies in combining. But industry players were merging, and IC didn't want to be last man standing. Besides, IC's board—Harrison's boss—wanted to do the deal. And although Harrison didn't like KCS, he would, throughout his career, welcome opportunities to get bigger, find more efficiencies, and entertain deals that would amplify his role. Harrison went to Kansas City and told KCS employees, "Don't worry, everyone's going to be treated fairly. We're marching forward."

The letter of intent to do the deal was dated July 19, 1994. It would be a $1.6 billion stock swap, while Illinois Central would also assume KCS's debt. Analysts were already onto the Hunter Harrison narrative. One's view was that KCS was an "under-managed franchise." Certainly, nothing Harrison ever ran could be construed as "under managed." More to the point, another told writer Lawrence Kaufman that "IC is going to send a SWAT team over to the KCS and try to drive the efficiencies there." It was clear who the chief of the SWAT team would be.

The plan was to put Illinois Central into a trust, pending approval of the deal. Harrison would run KCS from Kansas City, to get it ready for the merger. Once it was consummated by regulators, the combined enterprise would be run by Harrison. By running a much bigger organization, he would be moving up another notch in the railroad world.

In those days, railroad executives traveled to New York City to announce their companies' quarterly earnings. There, Harrison stood up to begin Illinois Central's meeting, where he would also announce the merger of KCS and IC. As he was about to speak, he said, IC's general counsel waved to him to stop. Landon Rowland had sent a wire, ten minutes before the meeting began, to say the deal was off. The earnings call was delayed by an hour and a half, during which time a press release was drafted. While the board of KCS had told IC they were ready to go ahead with the deal, one IC director, Alex Lynch, said the parties were within eight hours of signing a binding agreement "and they pulled out." Harrison said Rowland, who died in 2015, never believed it would happen, and when he finally realized it was about to occur, he undermined the deal. Harrison's view is that the KCS chairman was fearful Harrison would come to Kansas City and embarrass him in his own community. It would not be the last time this issue would arise.

On October 25, 1994, the *Chicago Tribune,* reporting on the deal's demise, said "both companies said the decision was mutually agreed to after they failed to come to a definitive agreement 'on a number of issues.'" The paper reported that both sides, when asked for specifics, said "No comment," a highly unusual response from Hunter Harrison. The *Tribune* cited analyst commentary that the deal fell apart because IC's stock price had fallen since the intent to merge was announced and that perhaps KCS decided to look for a higher bidder. Harrison felt Rowland had been intentionally working behind the scenes to drive down IC's shares to scupper the deal. Whatever the reason, the deal was off. In spite of him never being crazy about doing a deal with KCS in the first place, Harrison and Illinois Central were suddenly left with nowhere to go.

"We're going to get consumed by all these mega mergers," he thought.

An attempt to do a deal in Canada also fell through. Harrison said Rob Ritchie, who was running Canadian Pacific, called Harrison and asked, "How about running the Soo Line [the US subsidiary of CP] for us?"

"What do you mean run it?" Harrison asked. "Why don't you run it yourself?"

"'Cause you're a better operator," he said Ritchie told him. "We'll give you a management fee."

Harrison said forget that, we'll buy it from you. Ritchie said it's conceivable CP wanted Harrison to manage it, but he said CP would never have sold the Soo Line. A sizeable part of it had been owned by CP since 1890, and it gained full control in 1990. Ritchie confirmed that both IC and KCS were on the block in the mid-90s. Canadian Pacific had looked at KCS, too, but that didn't go anywhere, so it looked at buying IC, combining it with CP's Soo Line, and having Harrison run it as CP's US division. For whatever reasons, the talks disintegrated. IC and Harrison suddenly found themselves short of viable options, yet they wanted to maximize the railroad's value.

"Bottom line was we had nobody to call but Montreal, which was Paul [Tellier]." Two years before, in 1995, Canadian National had been sold by the Canadian government. Its top two executives, Paul Tellier and Michael Sabia, were former government officials. There was a desire at CN to expand southward; IC saw a strategic fit.

The two companies were already doing business. Illinois Central had built a terminal facility in the Chicago area that it had leased to

CN. As early as 1997, there was press and analyst speculation of a possible takeover of IC by a Canadian railway. Harrison had already hinted strongly that because of the consolidation occurring all around Illinois Central, IC would be surrounded and vulnerable, even though it was the most efficient. In February 1997, the chairman of Illinois Central, Gil Lamphere, who was also the CEO of Prospect, called Tellier.

Lamphere and Alex Lynch,[8] the investment banker who advised Prospect and was an IC board member, recognized that Harrison might be able to make shareholders a staggering amount of money at a bigger railroad—not via typical merger synergies, but simply by putting the railroader on the property so he could apply his methods. Lamphere and Lynch had been thinking about this for some time. In Lynch's calendar for October 24, 1996, there was an entry that said "$100/IC-MTL." Lamphere had wagered Lynch $100 that they could convince CN to buy IC. "I'll bet you a hundred bucks it doesn't happen," Lynch said, adding that he'd "be delighted to lose." Both would be at the forefront of negotiations. Although Tellier said "they [IC] were asking for too much," the ground was fertile on both sides. The talks, however, would be on and off for a year before there was a deal.

Harrison had been a star at IC. But Illinois Central was a small Class 1. Moving to CN would put him in the major leagues, the start of twenty years of railroad superstardom.

---

8   Lamphere and Lynch were also brothers-in-law.

4 MERGE OR DIE: IC MEETS CN

HUNTER HARRISON ONCE said, "They ain't buildin' any more railroads." Critical infrastructure was constructed decades, if not more than a century ago, as cities built up around rail lines. The only way for existing railroads to get bigger and more efficient was to swallow others. Merger mania gripped North American railroads in the mid-1990s, and the giants of the West were Union Pacific (UP) and Burlington Northern Santa Fe (BNSF). In the East, the big players also became more dominant. In 1997, CSX and Norfolk Southern each took pieces of the Consolidated Rail Corporation (Conrail). Conrail had been created by the US government out of bankrupt lines belonging to, among others, Penn Central, which went under in 1970 and was then the largest bankruptcy in American history. The other Class 1's on the continent were Canadian National, Canadian Pacific, Kansas City Southern, and Illinois Central.

CN's highly respected CEO was Paul Tellier. He'd been the top official in the Canadian government—the Clerk of the Privy Council and Secretary to the Cabinet, essentially running the country's vast number of bureaucrats. Next to the prime minister, Tellier's position was arguably the most powerful in the federal government. A friendly, gracious, down-to-earth manner was just one dimension of a personality also known as fierce and tireless—a hard-driving, goal-oriented chief executive. His work ethic was such that on weekends, Harrison said Tellier took home two briefcases of documents to go through before returning to the office on Monday morning.

In the early 1990s, Tellier was tapped by Prime Minister Brian Mulroney to head up the government-owned railroad, Canadian National. CN had been cobbled together from bankrupt lines beginning in 1919. Railroads were an economic and social necessity, so the government took them over and created Canadian National. By the mid-1950s, CN had morphed into a beast with more than 115,000 employees and multiple divisions. By the 1980s, it was moving toward a private enterprise model and had sold certain operations. But when Tellier arrived, it was still ripe for pruning, followed by privatization. The Conservative government had already sold Air Canada in the late 1980s, and Mulroney's government was determined to sell off more taxpayer-owned assets. But it wasn't until November 1995, when Jean Chretien was prime minister, that CN, run by Tellier and his CFO Michael Sabia, sold shares to the public.

Tellier had proved his CEO mettle by cutting eleven thousand CN workers in just three years, beating the target of five years and illustrating that the freshly minted public company he ran could be lean and profitable. Sabia was quoted in *The Pig That Flew*, a book chronicling the privatization, "It is impossible to overestimate the importance of that decision. Later everything flowed out of that." As long-time rail journalist Larry Kaufman said in *Trains* magazine, "Tellier's inexperience [as a railroader] was a huge asset. He didn't know what he couldn't do."

Tellier's ambition went beyond simply outdoing CP. He told people, "We want to be the best in North America." Tellier had his staff zone-in on key objectives, and he tracked progress. Not only were excess employees let go, but also thousands of miles of redundant lines were shed. In 2003, *National Post Business Magazine* provided a stark description of Tellier, whose "questioning gaze could freeze the arteries of his managers," saying that he had "methodically renovated the railroad." Sabia, who had worked for him in government, separately described Tellier as a "god-like figure."

Tellier had guided CN from the warm belly of government into the cold reality of the marketplace. When its shares were sold in 1995, it was the biggest initial public offering in Canadian history, raising CAD $2.16 billion. In addition, CN's efficiency was improving because of Tellier's hardboiled, get-it-done approach, cost cutting, and labor reductions. But with the arrival of the North American Free Trade Agreement (NAFTA), CN was only an east-west road. It needed a southern component, a route into the American market. Adding Illinois Central would drastically alter its network into a Y-shape, giving it a pathway south from Chicago to the Gulf of Mexico at New Orleans. On paper, a marriage of Illinois Central and Canadian National looked like a perfect match.

"Just looking at the map makes it extremely compelling," said Jean-Pierre Ouellet, who was CN's chief legal officer and corporate secretary at the time. The graphic image of the route map was also a perfect way to package the story as a logical NAFTA deal. To this day, Michael Sabia has the map framed at Caisse de dépôt et placement du Québec, the huge pension fund he now runs.

Still, despite the logic, there was reticence at CN. In addition to strong management, there was an eminent board of directors. Both the board and Tellier were acutely aware that the record of Canadian companies making acquisitions in the US was poor. CN's identity shift from Crown corporation—owned by the federal government—to publicly traded company had gone well, and the stock offering had gone even better. Why risk screwing things up by paying too much for an American railroad?

Although discussions began in earnest in Chicago in March 1997 (between Harrison, Tellier, Sabia, Lamphere, and Lynch), by May, the talks were off. Sabia said CN closed the file. Tellier was "uncomfortable" and didn't want to overpay for assets that might need updating. There were also unanswered questions. Who were these Americans who ran IC, and why did they want to sell it to Canadians? Illinois Central, in spite of its low OR, was in some respects dismissed as minor-league. The joke was that all you had to do was point it downhill from Chicago to New Orleans and "let it go." Were IC's owners just trying to cash out? Also, while IC's numbers looked great, were they too good to be true? Illinois Central was much smaller than CN, which had an OR of 78.6. Could the IC recipe really be replicated on a larger scale?

While the talks died out, Sabia, who actually became a strong—if not the strongest—proponent of a deal, stayed in touch with Alex Lynch at IC, an indication that all was not lost. In July 1997, CN's interest was rekindled. At the right price, it still wanted a US railroad, and the Canadians reached out to IC. In late summer or fall, Tellier dispatched Sabia—his chief bullshit detector—to Chicago. Sabia was regarded as a brilliant strategist. In possession of a first-class intellect, he worked harder than even workaholics like Tellier and Harrison (Sabia disputed this, saying Harrison was more driven than he is). So committed to his work, Sabia was said to find vacations difficult. While toiling in the federal finance department, Sabia apparently kept working through agonizing, debilitating back pain. He was seen by a colleague dragging himself across the floor to a fax machine, determined not to leave his post at a critical time. Sabia did not remember that episode, but he conceded it was not out of character. Like Harrison, Sabia spoke his mind. Blunt was going to meet blunt.

"We need to come see you in Chicago," Sabia told Harrison. "We" was Sabia and CN's top lawyer, Ouellet. "We need to talk to you, but we'd like to play golf with you too," Sabia said.

"You want to play golf or you want to talk business?" Harrison said.

Sabia said they played and remembered playing a particularly bad round. Harrison then had IC's executive chef prepare a sumptuous meal to be served at his home.

"We had the finest steaks and the best wines. We got the best cigars. Longest, nicest cognac," Harrison recalled. "In my house, on my turf."

"We got a problem," Sabia told the group from IC. "The board's not there yet."

"Whaddya mean the board's not there yet?" Harrison said. "Where are they?"

"They're not in on this transaction," adding that he and the other executives hadn't done a very good job working the board. "Can you give us three or four months?"

"I can't give you shit," Harrison claimed to have said, adding that he then told Sabia if another party called the next day and wanted to buy IC, it could.

Sabia, according to Harrison, "effectively said, 'You're right, this is embarrassing.'"

When Sabia said "the board's not there yet," what he really meant was "largely, Paul wasn't there yet." And if the CEO wasn't there, the board wasn't there. By citing the board, Sabia was being careful not to personalize the negotiations, and he intentionally kept Tellier's name out of the mix. Arriving at a price was one thing; the tougher assignment was ensuring a comfortable relationship between Tellier and Harrison, who Sabia likened to "two cocks in a ring," testing each other out. Both were used to being in charge—"and we were buying *them*," Sabia said. It took time for that relationship to gel.

That was the hardest part of doing the deal, Sabia maintained, because CN didn't just want IC, it wanted Harrison. That desire had been reinforced by Joe Gatto, who was then an investment banker at Goldman Sachs, the firm advising CN.

"Make sure you lock up Hunter as part of this deal. He's going to make all you guys rich," Ouellet recalled Gatto telling CN. For Lynch and Lamphere, the treasure chest would be getting stock in CN, provided Harrison went. Not only could he run a railroad like no one else, but he would make their stock certificates golden. Harrison, Sabia said, was the "secret sauce that nobody else had." CN wanted to buy a regional railroad in the US to exploit liberalized trade, but it was also engaged in "expensive headhunting." Sabia wisecracked that until he met Harrison, he thought the term "railroading genius" was an oxymoron.

Harrison's boast, though, that he could readily sell Illinois Central to someone else was viewed as bluster. "Who the hell was going to come and buy the Illinois Central?" Sabia said. Besides, IC had initially called CN. As for Harrison quoting Sabia as saying the situation was "embarrassing," Sabia smiled and said that's "a little bit Hunterized." Ouellet actually believed it was as much a case of "Michael wasn't there yet." Before he advised Tellier and they made the final pitch to the board, Sabia wanted to be absolutely certain that buying IC was airtight. In November 1997, Tellier phoned IC's chairman, Gil Lamphere, to tell him that, once again, CN was not prepared to pursue a transaction. Harrison said Sabia then went to do some intense research and was ready to meet again in Chicago later that year. Harrison said the meeting mostly consisted of Sabia pumping him with questions.

"I spilled my guts about precision railroading," Harrison recalled.

Until then, Harrison said the numbers team at CN was skeptical. In his autobiography, former CN chairman David McLean suggested that he thought that Tellier and his team were initially too anxious for a deal. But Tellier himself had been worried about the price. He said when the CN team became convinced of the deal, he was actually the holdout. "I was preoccupied with the price and I wanted us to pay the right price," Tellier said, insisting on more talks. Sabia confirmed this. "He [Tellier] was very, very, very disciplined about this," Sabia said. "He never fell in love with the deal." According to Harrison, that session in late 1997 cemented Sabia's view.

Sabia left the meeting in Chicago late that evening and called Tellier, who he knew was regimental about going to bed by 10 pm. He woke him up to tell him Harrison was the real deal—"This guy is no *boolshit*," as Harrison summarized it. Sabia had no memory of this, but Tellier remembered that Sabia gushed that Harrison was "a preacher," so passionate about railroads.

"I know after that meeting it was full steam ahead and that's when we started talking price," Ouellet said. Negotiations intensified in early January 1998. Sabia indicated there could be a deal, and CN got cranked up for a final bargaining session at the Ritz in Chicago. Lamphere recalled IC wanted $42 a share, while CN was "stickin' to thirty-eight." On the CN side, it was Tellier and Sabia.[1] For IC, it was Harrison, Lamphere, and Lynch. The two parties were separated by a small coffee table. The IC side was about to go through its presentation deck when Harrison said Sabia slammed his hand on IC's deck (Sabia doesn't remember doing so).

"The only thing I can tell you," Harrison recalled Sabia saying, "is that this deal is not going to start with a four [as in $40 a share]." Harrison then told Sabia he disagreed with everything he'd said and that his position was that there would not be a deal *unless* it started with a four. Sabia was speaking for Tellier—"Michael and I were always on the same page," Tellier said. Ouellet remembered that the under-$40 ultimatum had been cooked up at a CN executive committee meeting. "Everybody basically whipped themselves up to a fever," Ouellet said.

Emotions ran high, Harrison recalled, saying Tellier and Sabia were playing good cop, bad cop. "It was kind of made up." Tellier laughed at Harrison's description, admitting that it was indeed a bit of a routine.

---

1   Some recalled Jeff Ward from A.T. Kearney being there, but Ward didn't.

Eventually they agreed on price—just below $40 a share—and everyone shook hands. But the negotiations weren't over. Harrison asked Tellier, "When do you want me to leave?" Tellier then put his foot down. All along, CN wanted Harrison as well. "Hunter," he said. "We paid too much for your company. You are part of the assets." No Harrison, no deal. It's hard to believe someone as shrewd as Harrison didn't know he was being hunted or that it hadn't been negotiated prior to that, but Lamphere recalled Harrison had no intention of going to CN. "He was almost dragged," he said. "Hunter wasn't goin' because Hunter didn't want to work for anybody." He was now used to being the boss.

"It was a moment of tension where it was a deal breaker," Lynch said.

Lamphere turned to Harrison and asked him if he'd stay. The railroader's second daughter Cayce was just fourteen (she was born nineteen years after Libby) and a junior in high school. The family had already moved plenty of times for his career, and relocating to Montreal wasn't on his wish list. He also assumed Tellier wouldn't want him. But whenever an opportunity presented itself in railroads, Harrison considered it. He loved working and was only fifty-three years old. Even though he now had money, Harrison wasn't ready to retire to the golf course—he never would be—or to the show jumping circuit that would later preoccupy the family because of Cayce's involvement.

During the devastating 1998 ice storm that crippled large parts of eastern Canada, Harrison and Tellier dined alone at Montreal's Mount Royal Club. Electrical power was lost at the private club, so the two were illuminated only by candle light. Harrison finally agreed, but he insisted on having the authority to run the railroad and being able to see his family in Chicago, which meant he needed a corporate plane. CN told him he could live wherever he wanted and use the plane, as long as he fixed the railroad and made CN money.

He said, "You got a deal." Harrison, an American, went to CN, a Canadian institution, as COO and Tellier's number two. In 2004, *Canadian Business* quoted him as saying, "I told Tellier I only know one way to railroad. If he was willing to go along, I'd stay and work my ass off."

The deal was announced on February 10, 1998. CN offered IC shareholders USD $39 per share in cash and stock valued at approximately USD $2.4 billion—75 percent cash and 25 percent in CN stock. Adding IC's $560 million in debt, the total enterprise value of the deal was approximately USD $3 billion, multiples of what Prospect had originally paid for IC. Harrison, meantime, admitted that he almost made a mistake in the negotiations. Because initially he thought he would leave the company after the deal, he hadn't been interested in taking CN stock as part of the purchase package.

"I was looking for more cash. Cash is king," he recalled. But Lamphere convinced Harrison otherwise. He appealed to Harrison's ego, asking him what he could do with CN's operating ratio. Harrison told him he would get it down.

"Well shit," Lamphere said. "To what?" When Harrison told him how much he could reduce the OR, Lamphere said if he could do that, it was important to get CN stock. And he was right, Harrison said. If the OR could be significantly lowered, CN shares would go to the moon. Several years later, Harrison reflected on what he had received as an enticement upon joining Illinois Central—stock. "It was just a sheet of paper," he said. The chairman, Lamphere, told him Illinois Central had just handed him a $20 stock, even though it was not yet trading. "I'll take ten today," Harrison joked.

"No, you're not taking ten," Lamphere said. "You're going to create value in that piece of paper. We're giving you an opportunity." By the time he joined Canadian National in 1998, Harrison said that piece of paper, which some people thought was worth nothing in 1989, was worth multiples of what had been estimated.

Meantime, Tellier and Harrison were well aware of their respective strengths. "I knew what I didn't know and he knew what he didn't know," Tellier reflected. The now-famous phrase uttered by Tellier became the simple but sophisticated new CN playbook: "I lead the company, you lead the railroad," he told Harrison. Tellier was better with boards, government, regulators, and long-term strategy. He relayed a story about how Harrison told Canada's minister of transport—while in the minister's office—that he "didn't know what he was talking about," indicative of Harrison being, in Tellier's words, "awful" at government relations. He also remembered Harrison advising him not to return a call from the leader of the US Senate. "He said, 'Don't return the call. He's going to ask for something.'" Still, Tellier called their partnership "a perfect combination." Tellier could sand down Harrison's rough edges and deal with areas where Harrison had weaknesses, while the railroader could produce better results for the company Tellier headed. "He was," Tellier said, "the best railroader probably in the world."

While Harrison and Tellier settled into a working relationship, over time it would become apparent that the IC purchase might be the best $3 billion ever spent by a Canadian company—or any country's company, for that matter. Not only did the acquisition of IC add an asset with 2,600 route miles and approximately $700 million in revenue, but also the line through the heart of the continent from Chicago to the Gulf of Mexico gave CN a three-coast network just a few years after NAFTA opened up continental trade. Illinois Central also went west 850 miles into Iowa and Omaha, Nebraska—farm country. IC was the most efficient railroad in North America, with an operating ratio of 62.3 percent versus CN's 78.6 percent (CN's had come down 16 points since the privatization in 1995). Tellier and Sabia were also buying an operation that didn't have to be slashed. Looking back, it's quaint to think that the two sides were fussing over a dollar here or a dollar there, with CN determined not to look like the chump who paid too much. The purchase would move CN from a company with a market capitalization of just over CAD $2 billion at the time of its IPO in 1995 to a juggernaut with a USD $20 billion market value by 2005 and USD $60 billion (CAD $78.5 billion) by June 2018. The railroad also got Hunter Harrison in the deal. "Pretty cheap," he said, smiling.

Harrison's arrival meant the end of Michael Sabia's prospects as a future CEO of CN. Harrison said that before he came on the scene, Sabia was clearly viewed as the number two there. Sabia recalled thinking that it was enough that Tellier and Harrison were going to run the place. His own presence, he concluded, would complicate matters. Harrison claimed he tried to get Sabia to stay. "I'm your supporter. I'm your sponsor. You need to stay." Tellier firmly believed that if Harrison had not come to CN, there was "no doubt" Sabia would have been the obvious choice to succeed him as CEO. In fact, Harrison said that at one point he told Tellier that if the company was going to lose Sabia, he would step aside. Tellier said this happened, but in spite of his enormous admiration for Sabia, he told Harrison "it was out of the question" because he was the "expert" railroader.

Sabia left CN on October 1, 1999, and it may have been the best thing for his career. By 2002, he was CEO of BCE Inc., Canada's largest telecom company, and in 2008 began perhaps his most successful run, as CEO of Caisse de dépôt, the second-biggest pension fund in Canada and a powerful force in the global investment community. At the end of 2017, it managed $298.5 billion.

There was a trace of regret in Harrison's reflections about Sabia, whom he held in high regard.

"Sabia had a whole [lot] to do with the success of that organization [CN]," he said. Tellier agreed, calling Sabia "the best colleague I ever had." For a time, Harrison said they were close. They were often the only two in the office late in the evening, so they talked about personal matters. But they fell out of touch, which Harrison blamed on himself. "When I close the door, I close the door."

As part of the deal, Harrison, Lamphere, and Lynch would get board seats. But once inside the CN fold, Harrison was told he had to wait a year before getting his. There was concern that he and Tellier might not get along, so it was better to see how the relationship evolved. Harrison agreed to wait. But he claimed that after a year, CN's chairman David McLean called him into his office, telling him the board had decided not to make him a director at that time. Ten minutes later, Harrison said he got a call from Tellier, whom he knew had unmatched intelligence sources within the company. "Nobody shit without him knowin' it," Harrison said in textured fashion.

"Did you have a meeting with the chairman?" Tellier asked.

"Yes," Harrison said.

"Can I ask the subject?"

"We've decided not to put me on the board."

"So, what are you going to do?"

Harrison said he told Tellier that after two years, "I'm walkin' away from this sorry sonofabitch," meaning CN. The next morning Harrison said he was appointed to the board. McLean said there was no such attempt to delay Harrison's appointment—Harrison was appointed to the board after the first year, he said, as planned.

Tellier said he didn't recall whether McLean, on behalf of the board, asked to delay. He had a different slant. Tellier wanted to do as many things as possible to integrate IC people into the CN team. "I said to the board it would be useful for him [Harrison] to be in the board room." The directors, however, "told me fairly soon after we started working together—the board said, 'Paul, you are so different the two of you, it won't work.' I said, 'The guy is so good, there is so much money on the table for shareholders, I will make sure that it does work out.'"

"Paul and I got along beautifully. Huge respect. Huuuge. It was just a beautiful experience," Harrison said, adding he loved Tellier's wife and the two were just as nice as could be. "He [Tellier] was like, Eureka. NAFTA, this really fits," Harrison said. Tellier, whose star was already high, rose even higher because he'd parked his ego at the door for the greater good of CN. He let Harrison run the railroad and got the best out of him.

"You just have to give Tellier a ton of credit for having found a way to make this work with Hunter," Sabia said in July 2017. "Because you know, Hunter is not an easy personality."

5 MEMPHIS MEETS MONTREAL

IT WAS BETTER to cross your legs than leave the room to urinate. In the spring of 1998, CN gathered the company's top 200 operating people at Montreal's Hotel Bonaventure to introduce them to Hunter Harrison. And Michael Sabia was right—the son of the lay preacher knew how to preach. Harrison had a hammerlock on the room, mesmerizing CN's people for eight hours straight with no notes. They'd never heard anything like him. Harrison used whatever he needed to get his point across—storytelling, personal anecdote, humor, anger. He was both folksy and foxy. According to Jim Gray, who served on CN's board for more than a decade, it became obvious that Harrison was very unusual. "I've never seen a guy grab hold of a company," Gray said, "and change the culture and the results in such a short period of time." Was it all warm and fuzzy? Gray asked rhetorically. "Not on your life."

Harrison was a "change-agent," and the status quo, while comfortable for most people, was uncomfortable to him. Railroads, Gray said, were slow to adapt. The industry had not evolved for a generation. Given that the sector was ripe to be whipped into shape, he said it was inevitable that someone like Hunter Harrison would come along eventually. "I'd never seen anybody who was more appropriate for the time and the changes required than Hunter."

Ed Lumley, who served on the board for nineteen years and was involved in taking CN public, said Harrison's arrival "filled a real gap that we had." Lumley added that although Harrison was not the easiest person in the world to deal with, "He was my kind of guy. He was straight. Said it like it was. Got things done."

Looking back, the merging of talents at CN then was astonishing. Tellier, the consummate Ottawa insider who'd run the federal public service and engineered CN's IPO and initial turnaround, had locked arms with the best operator in the business. What's more, there was Sabia and Claude Mongeau, a detail-oriented future CFO and chief executive of CN. The four of them were a dream team. All would eventually become CEO, in nine different instances at six public companies and one giant pension fund.[1] It's hard to think of another recent confluence of talent at one company, with the possible exception of the Jack Welch days at General Electric. Not only did the group not suffer fools gladly, Lumley reflected, but "they didn't suffer fools, period."

While Tellier and Sabia had cleaned up CN prior to and after the IPO, according to Harrison their turnaround had gone almost as far as it could, given that they were non-railroaders. While Harrison recognized that their contributions and support of him were crucial, his job was to take CN to the next level—to get it operating as efficiently as Illinois Central. To do so, Harrison needed to convert CN's people. Preaching alone wouldn't be enough. To really make them see the light, he had to find "a winner," something startling to show CN's managers how the railroad could be more efficient, an achievement that would ripple through the organization and send a message—even a shudder—that there was a different way to run the company. That something would be a reduction in the number of locomotives.

Within fourteen to sixteen months, the company would reduce its locomotives by about 600—some 35 percent. By 2003, another 186 had been sold, stored, or leased out. With each locomotive then worth $2 million (now approximately $3 million) the cost savings were significant. Two million multiplied by almost eight hundred was about $1.6 billion—real money. With that came reduced fuel charges, parts, and mechanics.

The question was how to get by with fewer locomotives. As Harrison would say, you don't build the church for Easter Sunday—you build it

---

1 Harrison was CEO of Illinois Central, CN, CP, and CSX. Tellier was CEO of CN and Bombardier. Sabia has been CEO of BCE and Caisse de dépôt, while Mongeau was CEO of CN.

for the capacity of the other 364 days of the year. Instead of running three dayshifts, one afternoon shift, and no nightshift—which equaled four eight-hour shifts that added up to thirty-two engine-hours—he suggested spreading the work around the clock. To fill the church, so to speak, for those three dayshifts, the railroad needed three locomotives for each, a total of nine. Adding in a spare or two, that could mean eleven locomotives. Adjusting the schedule to two dayshifts—sixteen engine-hours—plus one afternoon shift and one nightshift to make up the other sixteen, the highest locomotive requirement for the day would now be six engines for the two jobs on the dayshift. Add in a spare and it was down to seven locomotives instead of eleven for the daytime job. If CN had fifty locations where this could be applied, that alone was 200 locomotives—or $400 million saved.

Aside from locomotives, Harrison said there were various ways to take such expensive assets out of the system and the drop in the OR would be material. In his view, you could solve the world's problems, including poverty, with such productivity gains. Next stop was freight cars—you could do the same, he argued. At the end of Reverend Harrison's sermon, there were some born-again railroaders at CN. Still, he was careful. "I was cautious to just go in there with an axe," Harrison said, "like Paul hadn't done shit and I had to fix it." Besides, he only planned to stay for two or three years, never figuring he would be heir apparent.

Harrison had fine-tuned and proven Precision Scheduled Railroading at Illinois Central, but running IC wasn't anywhere close to running CN.[2] Illinois Central was a regional railroad with three thousand employees. CN, with IC folded into it, was a continental "road" with more than twenty thousand employees. It was the big time. To achieve what Harrison envisioned, every CN employee had to become a precision railroader.

Previously, CN quoted delivery times in days—plus or minus a day or two for flex. Edmonton to Chicago was seven to nine days. Sometimes it was five or six, other times ten or eleven. That drove Harrison nuts. He wanted to quote in *hours*, not days. If a train was scheduled to leave at

---

2   Initially at CN, A.T. Kearney consultant Jeff Ward said Harrison's system was called the scheduled railroad.

8 am, Harrison wanted it to leave at 8 am, whether there were sixty or one hundred cars. If you measured in hours, everything got more precise. Taking it even further, if you measured car inspections in seconds, they got faster too. Things began to change at CN in the latter part of 1999 when precision railroading kicked in. Faster trains and better service resulted in better market share—and yield followed.

Years before Uber shattered the taxicab business, Harrison was trying to modernize an industry that had been Uber'd for decades by another segment of the transportation sector. Until the 1950s, the rails were the dominant means of shipping freight. But during that decade, US president Dwight Eisenhower built highways. The interstates led to the growth of new businesses, like Holiday Inn (founded by another Memphian, Kemmons Wilson), but they spawned new competition for railroads. All of a sudden, trucks were a viable alternative to freight trains. From the 1950s until the 1980s, railroads lost business to trucks. As a result, railroads had to improve.[3]

While at CN, Harrison penned (with the help of CN human resources executive Peter Edwards) two highly readable manuals on precision railroading, quoting everyone from Arthur Schopenhauer to Norman Schwarzkopf. In *How We Work and Why: Running a Precision Railroad, Volume 1*, he makes it plain: "Railroads are very capital intensive. Every $1.00 of rail revenue requires about $2.50 in net property, plant and equipment. In contrast, every $1.00 of truck revenue requires only about 40 cents in company-owned assets. The roads are paid by your taxes." As a result, Harrison argued that "capital decisions must be made very carefully because we live with the consequences a long, long time." If you were buying locomotives, you'd better know your business because you might have them for forty years.

So much of what Harrison taught came down to assets. Few things bothered him more than underutilized ones. If an asset isn't used, he wrote, "it's a liability" because of the costs associated with owning it. "Railroads only make money when cars are moving. Track is a railroad's most expensive physical asset. Track has a 40-year life. So why

---

3   As drones and autonomous trucks evolve, some believe railroaders may be faced with yet another Uber moment.

would we lay down tracks just to have cars sit idle?" He got specific—one mile of track in 2005, which was used to store about one hundred cars, cost USD $1 million. If you *moved* cars instead of stored cars, you saved a million bucks. The more efficient the operation, the fewer assets it needed.

Railroads, he wrote, "were awash in long-lived assets"—track, locomotives, and cars. He went deeper. What if dwell times in yards were cut to eight or twelve hours instead of twenty-four? What if customers unloaded faster so their cars were there for half the time? What if average velocity went from twenty-five to thirty miles an hour? "Now we're getting more cycles from the same equipment." As he would say, a thousand little things equal a lot of money.

Tony Marquis comes from a family of railroaders in northern Ontario and spent twenty-five years at CN. Not only did Marquis and his six siblings work for the railroad, but so did his father and two grandfathers. When Harrison was CN's COO, Marquis flew to Montreal to request five million dollars to expand a terminal in Brampton, near Toronto. Marquis thought he knew his file and his facts. But Harrison quickly zeroed in on why the terminal was so full. Marquis and his team weren't turning the containers fast enough—get 'em in and get 'em out. If you improved velocity, you created capacity in the terminal. Marquis learned a classic Harrison lesson—don't spend a dollar of capital when all it takes is improving processes. "I felt like I was the smartest guy going in," Marquis said. "He kicked the shit out of me, but he didn't de-motivate me." Harrison was again pushing accountability to the regions. He also hadn't made it personal, so Marquis left feeling inspired. He became one in a long list of rail executives smitten by Harrison, people who would work with him (Mark Wallace, Keith Creel, Laird Pitz, and Peter Edwards, to name a few) and prosper in other periods during his lengthy, multi-company career.

The word also spread beyond CN. The first of Harrison's books was translated into Chinese and given to the Chinese National Railway. He spoke to other North American railroads at their invitation about precision railroading, and he shared his ideas and books. But just because they got the Beatles' songbook didn't mean they could make music like the Beatles. Many—including Harrison—have asked why every other railroad doesn't do or accomplish what he did. One person who worked with him years later said no one else had the same "unbending will" to see it through. Harrison believed that even if you're successful, you have to work harder every year.

"Success is a lousy teacher," he wrote. "It seduces smart people into thinking they can't lose." He preferred types like those who came up with the household lubricant WD-40, named numerically because the inventors failed thirty-nine times before coming up with the magic formula. When it came down to it, he simply hated inefficiency. If something was wasteful or inefficient, it created a ruckus in his head, and he didn't stop until the noise was fixed.

Reading people, getting to know what motivated them—good or bad—was one of his strengths. Mostly, he believed money and a sense of purpose were the principal motivators, but he professed that some people needed to be hollered at while others needed to be stroked. He didn't like the word "empowerment" and believed that when employees were permitted a long leash, it was a way for managers to ditch the responsibility to manage. He was also not big on the old saw that patience is a virtue. "I hate it when people say that."

He invoked "the team" and studied great sports coaches of the modern era. While many CEOs love reading biographies of political leaders, Harrison's shelves were full of books about winning coaches. While he drew lessons from all of them, he favored the no-nonsense, tough-guy styles of the past—Vince Lombardi of the Green Bay Packers and Bear Bryant of the University of Alabama. Both were feared and respected.

"Great teams don't allow people who don't want to really play to stay," he wrote in his first manual. "It has to be the same with us. So, we have to convert these people or cut them. To be fair, we have to be very, very clear of the negative consequences of their unwillingness to give good efforts. If after all this, they refuse to pull with us, they can't work for us. We must protect the livelihood of those who do care. I can't let these few damage it for us all. I will not let this happen on my watch."

One of the first things he tackled at CN were "early quits," employees leaving work before their shifts ended. In some cases, he said, certain people were packing it in for the day after only four hours and claiming eight hours' pay. It was, in Harrison's view, "out of control" and "its leaders never wanted to address the situation." When Harrison confronted a supervisor about the problem, he was told, "It's worse than this at other terminals."

"Stop it now," he told the supervisor, his voice louder than normal.

"Some of those places won't like this too much," Harrison was warned. "They'll shut the place down."

"Then start with them."

"What?"

"I said start with them. If we're going to have a fight over this, we might as well start at the toughest place." That was Vancouver. His approach was to fly there and confront "the meanest sonofabitch" at the terminal and read the riot act. His stance worked. People snapped to attention. Harrison's view was that you didn't have to win too many fights to establish a reputation. Once you did, it would rapidly waft through the company. Change-agents like Harrison weren't looking for votes to be re-elected. Although he could be extremely charming and a crowd pleaser, he claimed he was never interested in winning a popularity contest, although he clearly enjoyed it when adulation came his way and reacted badly to criticism. He was only half joking when he said he was even tempered. He came to work madder than hell and left work madder than hell.

"Were there deep affections for Hunter? Not necessarily," Jim Gray observed. "Was there respect? Certainly."

It wasn't just the workers—and managers—who had to figure out a new way to survive at the company. Customers had to adapt to Hunter World. When deliveries changed to seven days a week and customers had to receive goods when they weren't accustomed to receiving them, there was friction. Gray said pushback came from the agricultural community and container customers. For his part, Harrison said the only time he heard about griping from customers was in media reports, but clearly board members knew otherwise. Other CN executives heard it from customers as well. One customer was quoted as saying, "CN's message to customers is: here's our service, take it or leave it."

Still, over time, it wasn't just that costs were coming down at CN; revenue was rising. The railroad obviously still had customers—and in return for faster service, they were expected to pay a higher price.

Requests for price cuts were denied. This would not be Harrison's last scrape with customers.

A cultural shift was occurring at CN, and it was agonizing for those who had difficulty embracing change. Harrison quoted the former chief of staff of the US Army, General Eric Shinseki: "If you don't like change, you're going to like irrelevance even less." He pointed no further than the fate of the cassette tape and the compact disc. As for those who say businesses just mature and get commoditized, Harrison wrote in one of his manuals, "This is simply the excuse of losers . . . Time after time, people and organizations entered stable, mature markets and turned them on their ears. Häagen-Dazs did it with ice cream, Starbucks did it with coffee, and CN keeps doing it again and again with railroads."

Harrison was fond of the word "mud," arguing it built up in organizations—just like under railroad tracks—and created rot. The so-called Hunter Camps were retreats where he would sermonize to employees about washing away that mud, the obstacles to communication in an organization.[4] As he told *Progressive Railroading,* the company was trying to convert people. "These camps are a way for us to get to the masses quicker." Harrison was taking the church of railroading to wayward parishioners.

The company started the camps in 2003 to indoctrinate or "Hunter-ize" 2,000 of CN's 3,500 non-union employees from all levels of management within five years. They were also the basis for writing the manuals. Co-author Peter Edwards went to almost every one of the retreats, taking notes each time or whenever he spoke with Harrison, jotting down what he said on bar napkins or hotel pads. Once, when Edwards was stuck in traffic with no writing paper, he pulled the insoles out of his shoes so he could scribble down what Harrison was telling him on the phone. It was another indication of a Harrison staffer running through walls to do his best for him. Edwards allowed, however, that, unbeknownst to Harrison, he was once hospitalized for a heart

---

4   Harrison did not invent the name "Hunter Camp." According to Mark Wallace, the retreats were initially leadership camps with Harrison. Soon, he said, CN people began calling them Hunter Camps. They evolved from discussions between Harrison and the SVP of People at CN, Les Dakens.

issue, presumably because he drove himself so hard, not unlike Keith Creel experiencing what he believed to be Bell's palsy due to stress. Harrison drove himself hard and expected the same from his people.

Campers were put up in luxurious digs like The Breakers in Palm Beach. The message was that CN was first class and expected first-class results. Attendees were encouraged to ask questions, which got Harrison fired up and also illustrated an employee's level of engagement.

"I'm impatient. I'm demanding," he told *Progressive Railroading*. "I'm asking people to stretch."

Hunter Camp sounded fun, and for many it likely was. But it was serious business. The course was formalized in a zip-up folio; Harrison's voice could be heard in every word. The folio also included ten DVDs. At these sessions, he quoted industrialist and oilman J. Paul Getty, who in the 1950s and 60s was the world's richest person: "In rapidly changing times, experience can be your worst enemy."

Harrison, the "change-agent" personified, was giving everyone at camp a big, fat clue: Get ready to change your ways. He confronted those in the room, telling them he could see the skeptics in the crowd. "I can read a room, okay? I have a pretty good sixth sense for reading a room. And I'm reading this one now," he said. "There are a couple of you that are sitting there, internally, saying '*Boolshit.*' (pause) And I know who you are, okay?" The room broke into nervous laughter. Those assembled could submit to the brainwashing, he told them, or life would become much more difficult. The manager of a Montreal yard had told Harrison that American operating methods wouldn't work in Canada. He was soon gone.

Watching the DVDs from a camp held in August 2005, you could be forgiven for thinking you were at a Sunday church service in the Deep South. A few months shy of turning sixty-one, bringing together more than forty years of experience and analysis, Harrison was arguably at his peak. Barrel-chested, with a thundering voice, pointing his finger for emphasis and conducting the equivalent of a railroad revival meeting, he was convincing. Calling Harrison a "self-educated dynamo," the late Purdy Crawford, the one-time dean of Canadian boardrooms who joined CN as a director leading up to the company's privatization, wrote in the foreword to *SwitchPoints*, a book about CN's transformation,

"Most business leaders talk about the importance of people, but Hunter actually lives and breathes that belief."

Harrison wanted the campers to internalize his key principles—provide service, control costs, utilize assets properly, concentrate on people, and not get anybody hurt. He didn't necessarily want the smartest people in the world, he wanted the hardest working people in the world. "Y'all take the technology and give me the good worker and I'll beat you to death," he told them. "Don't let 'em just be a worker bee," he implored, "'cause that's what you'll get." And if there was a great person working in another industry, he wanted that person at CN. "Find me a good athlete and we'll develop 'em," he said. "We'll make 'em into what they need to be."

He wanted those in the room to be passionate, arguing that people—employees—were dying to do something that mattered, to be inspired. *"Just care,"* he pleaded. In fact, Harrison drew inspiration by speaking to them. He told the room he viewed Hunter Camps as the most important thing he could do at the railroad—changing the culture. He lectured that most people underestimate themselves, while he wanted them to give their all.

Furthermore, he said, the team needed to develop a plan, analyze it, and then execute it—over and over, like a great football team that painstakingly reviewed its game films and changed its strategy.

He urged those in the room to do what they promised for customers, but that they should also be willing to "say no," writing it with a flourish in magic marker on a big piece of white paper that sat on an easel. He emphasized his firm belief that while customers were vital, the railroad had a right to make money and wouldn't do so if it agreed to every customer request.

While he taught employees the principles of railroading during that camp in August 2005, CN was reeling from the collision of two trains in Mississippi the previous month that killed four employees. A fire followed the crash, destroying evidence. A visibly agitated Harrison told the room that it was unlikely the cause of the crash would ever be determined. Twelve years later, Harrison still remembered the name of a man killed in that accident, Buddy Irby. He told the silent room that the railroad's rules were "written in blood." To underline the point, he recounted a grisly incident he'd witnessed early in his career.

Future CEO.

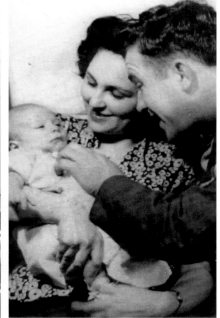

TOP: The family home in Memphis. Photo by author.

LEFT: The only boy in the family.

RIGHT: Baby Hunter with Dorothy and "Tank" Harrison, 1944.

TOP: "Tank" Harrison, pitching prospect.
BOTTOM: "Tank" Harrison during the Second World War.

FACING TOP: At TV studio for *Top 10 Dance Party*. Hunter Harrison is in the top row, second from right. Jeannie Day is in the second row, far right.

FACING LEFT: Hunter and Jeannie at prom, 1962.

FACING RIGHT: All-around athlete.

ABOVE: High school graduation, 1962.

TOP: The second wedding, July 10, 1970. (L to R) Jeannie, Libby, the pastor, Hunter Harrison, "Tank" Harrison.

LEFT: Starting out at Frisco, December 1963.

RIGHT: Late 1960s, Frisco.

TOP: Manager, early days.
LEFT: The tower in the Tennessee yard, Memphis. Credit: Erin Kay.
RIGHT: W.F. "Pisser" Bill Thompson. Credit: Burlington Northern Santa Fe.

With Jeannie and Libby, 1970.

A colleague had been run over by a caboose because the employee had ignored a rule and run across a track. Harrison had fetched his trench coat and covered the man, not only for warmth, but so the injured worker couldn't see what had happened to his leg, which he would lose.

While focusing on safety was first of all morally right, it was also good business. If you wanted trouble, he would say, have a derailment. Trouble was often avoided by a deep understanding of railroading—and a deep understanding also meant measurement, something Harrison was big on. Railcars presented a good example. CN classified them by Originating and Destination points, or O&Ds. When he wrote the first book at Canadian National, the railroad had more than 200,000 O&D combinations.

"Although this is a daunting number, about 5% of these O&D pairs account for more than 80% of CN's traffic volume. Optimize that 80% and the remaining 20% pretty much takes care of itself." When you read that quote, you can visualize Harrison the young trainmaster in the tower in Memphis, moving boxcars. Now, he was trying to teach thousands of employees to be smart trainmasters on a grand scale.

In 2002, with Harrison having been COO for more than three years, CN's OR was 69.4 percent, already far and away better than the pack. CP's was 77; Norfolk Southern's, Union Pacific's, and BNSF's were in the mid- to high 80s; while CSX's was the caboose at 92. Back when he was at Illinois Central, he said outsiders viewed its league-leading operating ratio as an aberration, achievable only because IC was so much smaller than the rest.

"Then we got to Montreal. Big time. No more little-bitty-doesn't-matter aberration." Along with Tellier, he proved you could get a low operating ratio at a major-sized railroad. By the time his second manual was published, CN's operating ratio had moved from the worst in the industry (more than 97 percent in 1992 when Tellier took over; 89.3 in 1995, the year of the IPO; and 78.6 the year before Harrison arrived, in 1998) to 61.8 percent for the year in 2006, the best in the business. If you'd invested $75,000 when CN went public in 1995, it was worth a million dollars by 2008. The railroad had moved light years from the early 1990s, when Michael Sabia had said to Tellier that "just getting to *one dollar* of positive cash flow would be good." In those days, the expectations were low to say the least, particularly for CN, but also for those in the industry who had never dreamed of such a low OR. "At the time," Sabia recalled, "people thought that it was just contrary to the laws of physics that a railroad could run at an operating ratio meaningfully south of 80." Not only was CN in the 60s, but it would eventually break through with quarters in the 50s, unfathomable to the other Class 1's.

More than half of the employee base at CN had joined the stock purchase plan, and improvements in the operating ratio and the stock price benefited many. It wasn't just employees and the broad shareholder base that benefited. The man who was for years the world's richest human, Bill Gates, profited mightily as well. His investment vehicle, Cascade Investment LLC, was and continued to be the largest shareholder of Canadian National.

While Harrison monitored hugely successful investments, he never hesitated to get in the trenches. In 2008, while scrutinizing CN's network via one of his screens at home, he saw a problem. Something was amiss between Jackson, Mississippi, and Memphis. As described in *Trains*, Harrison called the dispatcher in Homewood, Illinois, to investigate.

"I'll do the dispatching tonight," he told the employee. "Just stay on the phone and I'll dictate the needs and priorities. Here's what we want to do." Ultimately, he pulled an all-nighter—*as dispatcher*—to solve the gridlock that was affecting the whole railroad. While he did, the employee was treated to a master class. Such boots-on-the-ground moments are now Harrison lore. "Great leaders," Laird Pitz said, "they kind of have this thing where they can feel the pulse of the business." Harrison traveled constantly, so employees everywhere saw him in action.

Although he argued strenuously with him and said he had to tolerate his lectures, Buzz Hargrove, the former head of the Canadian Auto Workers union (CAW), which represented CN workers, liked Harrison. This was in spite of recognizing the CEO had "an ego as big as a house" and also enduring a strike when union members didn't ratify an agreement, which infuriated Harrison.[5] "Nobody can bullshit him," said Hargrove in 2017. "Not the management, not the union, not the

---

5   There were two strikes at CN during Harrison's years there, in 2004 and 2007.

workers." Harrison knew their jobs. That gave him credibility in the field, but it also created angst among employees. Militaristic management was not unusual at railroads south of the border, but it was new in Canada.

There was also a bigger picture. While Tellier purchased IC to build his NAFTA railroad, there were other attempts to expand CN's network in the United States, among them a dalliance with Kansas City Southern. Harrison wasn't crazy about the idea. Tellier said he knew Harrison wasn't supportive, adding that Harrison didn't get along with the then-CEO of KCS. Harrison also knew KCS from his IC days and, against his better judgment, had come close to buying it before that arrangement fell apart. To Harrison, there was no strategic value in buying what was the number seven railroad and smallest Class 1 in North America. "My strategic objective," Tellier said, "would have been to acquire Kansas City and to connect with one of the Mexican railroads." Mexico, however, just added risk, Harrison believed. Nonetheless, Tellier was the boss who'd taken time to get to know the US railroads and their CEOs.

Among them was Rob Krebs, the chief executive officer of BNSF, who would be retiring soon. CEO retirements can be catalysts for mergers and takeovers because only one of the two CEOs involved can run the new company, and an executive departure solved that problem. That fact, combined with Tellier's sense that word had gotten out about CN looking to buy KCS and that Harrison was rather disinterested in the deal, led to discussions about combining CN with BNSF. Jeff Ward of A.T. Kearney, who consulted for CN for several years, said Tellier got a call from Krebs. Ward went with CN's CEO to meet Krebs at a Montreal airport. Ward said CN was then assessing both KCS and BNSF "in parallel." While Harrison didn't want anything to do with Kansas City Southern, he liked the prospect of a BNSF deal. He'd worked there and knew its potential, and it was a major asset in comparison to KCS. Tellier, he said, called him one evening and asked which railroad he thought CN should do a deal with—KCS or BNSF?

"I said, are you kidding? Shit, do BN."

CN's focus quickly turned from KCS to Burlington Northern, Harrison's old employer that he felt had spurned him. While Tellier said he did most of the negotiations with Krebs, Harrison furnished CN with a high level of business intelligence about BNSF.

The parties met in Chicago. Like any good storyteller, Harrison was prone to the occasional exaggeration for effect. He said the dingy motel where they met was the kind of place where you put a quarter in the bed and it shook. This undisclosed location near Midway Airport had what he described as a filthy conference room, detached from the motel. He shook his head at the fact that this was where the heads of two of North America's biggest railroads had met to discuss their merger.

The transaction between CN and the second-biggest American railroad, BNSF, was announced on December 20, 1999—just six months after CN closed the IC deal. If consummated, CNBN would have created a company that could ship from Halifax to Vancouver to Los Angeles to New Orleans. It would have been the biggest freight railroad in North America, with a market value of USD $19 billion (CAD $28 billion). That was enough of a threat that in January 2000, other Class 1 railroads went on the offensive, taking out ads in major American newspapers objecting and requesting the regulator intervene. On March 17 of that year, the US Surface Transportation Board slapped a fifteen-month moratorium on new rail mergers. On July 20, CN and BNSF announced their joint termination of the deal, citing a possible two-and-a-half-year wait for a decision from the US regulator. The railroads said the lengthy timeframe was not in the interests of their shareholders. There has not been a major railroad merger in North America since then. But in 2009, Warren Buffett's investment vehicle, Berkshire Hathaway, bought Burlington Northern Santa Fe, taking it private. "The day I read in the papers that Buffett had bought BN, I felt pretty good," Tellier laughed.

At the time of the proposed deal, CN was strong financially and stacked with talent—and Tellier had a powerful, sound strategy to continue expanding into a truly North American railroad. "After the Burlington thing, they [management] scrambled," CN board director Ed Lumley said. "I think that caused them some frustration. *I don't think. I know.*" Even stationery with the imprint "CNBN" on it had been printed. Two years after the deal had been called off, Harrison said he found it on the shelves in the mailroom at CN.[6]

---

6   CN would add to its North American network by buying Wisconsin Central in 2001, BC Rail in 2004, and the Elgin, Joliet and Eastern Railway in 2009.

After the CNBN deal fizzled, two American directors at CN who'd been instrumental in Harrison's rise at IC and subsequent move to CN—Alex Lynch and Gil Lamphere—wondered about another way for Canadian National to take a piece of another US railroad without being blocked by regulators. And if they could orchestrate it, they believed that utilizing Hunter Harrison to replicate his methods elsewhere would mean a massive benefit for CN shareholders. Elsewhere meant America. Unbeknownst to Harrison, Lynch and Lamphere had fixated on CSX, one of two American railroads that dominate the eastern half of the United States, from the Mississippi to the Atlantic (the other is Norfolk Southern). CSX covers the eastern US, from Florida to New York state, up to Montreal and west to Chicago, Nashville, and Louisiana. Based on the political rumor mill, Lynch said they had a hunch that its CEO, John Snow, was interested in leaving railroading for politics and that a deal could provide an "elegant way" for him to move on. Even someone who knew nothing about railroads could imagine the fit between CN and the American railroad. CSX would take CN from Montreal to Florida and all the important stops in between, while CSX would get access to the ports of Western and Eastern Canada.

In late summer and fall of 2000, after the US Surface Transportation Board announced its moratorium and the CNBN deal was called off, Lynch said he and Lamphere met an advisor to Snow in Richmond, Virginia. They suggested to the intermediary they had a structure that could work for both companies. That trip, Lynch said, was followed by a second that included lunch with Snow. At that lunch, he said they told Snow they'd devised a means whereby CN would buy just under 20 percent of CSX, not enough to be considered a control position. One of the railroads would then be put in trust, pending approval, but the transaction would not be a merger or takeover. They had a lender for the deal but still needed a major equity investor. The wrinkle was the way they made the approach: "We're not here representing really anybody other than CN, although CN doesn't know we're here." Lynch maintained that he and Lamphere were well aware of their fiduciary obligations to CN and were acting in the railroad's best interests. The equity investor they had in mind was Kohlberg Kravis Roberts (KKR), the New York private equity firm. Lynch said he and Lamphere had an initial meeting at KKR that fall. He said they also spoke by phone with Warren Buffett. Lynch said that once there was a nibble from KKR, they then informed CN management, which, according to Lynch, liked the idea. Harrison said he was not part of the earliest discussions. Lynch said he and Lamphere had been careful not to let him know (or anyone else) before informing CN. If a transaction were to occur, Harrison said he found out later that the plan was to make him CEO of CSX. Tellier said he had only a "vague recollection" of the situation, but he added, "I cannot challenge his [Harrison's] views on that."

Should the deal proceed, the idea was that CN shareholders would benefit from Harrison putting his railroading know-how to work at CSX. In turn, CSX would become more profitable and CN shareholders and KKR would reap a portion of those profits because of their ownership stake. Perhaps a full merger would be possible later. Once Harrison had been told at a business dinner, he was advised to retain counsel because if the deal were consummated, he would have to separate himself from CN and become an employee of CSX. He said he went back to his suite at the Queen Elizabeth Hotel adjacent to CN headquarters and began looking for suitable legal advice.

Soon, members of CN's team traveled to New York to visit KKR, legendary in the world of high finance and deal-making. The railroad's advisors made clear that Henry Kravis, one of the partners, would listen for about twenty to twenty-five minutes and then lose interest—so get to the point.

The scene at KKR, according to Harrison (who said he attended, as did Lynch), was something to behold. The room with a long table had the obligatory spectacular view of Central Park. Projected on a video screen was the R in KKR, George Roberts, with a magnificent room as a backdrop. Dressed in a crewneck sweater, he was seated on a piano bench in front of a baby grand.

"Shit, this has been made up," Harrison thought.

Someone on the CN side began running through the slide deck, telling people to start on page fifteen.

"What about the first fourteen?" Kravis asked.

"Well, they're not important," he was told. Kravis then asked why those pages were there.

"I want to hear about scheduled railroading," Harrison recalled Kravis saying. The railroader started talking.

"Don't you need a deck?" Kravis asked.

"Nope, I don't need the deck," Harrison said. He said he talked for about two hours, with Kravis listening intently.

The problem, however, was back in Montreal. Harrison said certain CN directors "got inflamed" about the discussions, which had only been going on for a matter of weeks. "That's when the shit hit the fan," Lynch said, describing "a bit of a trial before the board." According to Lamphere, "They [the board] were pissed that [things] were being done without their knowledge." KKR planned a trip to Montreal for a follow-up meeting, they said, but the talks died and the meeting never happened. CN's then-chairman, David McLean, said, "I don't think it went very far at all. I think it was a very preliminary board discussion." Lynch said he and Lamphere believed they were doing the right thing, developing an idea quietly. "No question," Lamphere said. "We knew fiduciary responsibility very well," saying he and Lynch did what they did only because it would be in CN's interest. "We did what an investment bank would do," he said, "just have some preliminary discussions." But the board had another view. "They saw it as somebody going out on a limb and possibly putting CN at risk," Lamphere said. Separately, Lynch said CN's board was "worried that they would lose Hunter to CSX." As an investment banker, Lynch said "most of the blowback was directed at me." At the end of 2000, he said he was diagnosed with non-Hodgkin lymphoma. Given that, combined with what he described as strained relations with the board, Lynch "felt that the high road for me would be to resign." His resignation as a director was effective January 22, 2001. Lamphere remained on the board until August 29, 2005. To Harrison's knowledge, discussions about CSX-KKR never came back. However, Tellier said that there were further discussions about CSX and CN—without KKR—in late 2002. He said he and CSX's CEO John Snow discussed a CN-CSX combination. Within days, though, both of their lives changed dramatically, and those talks evaporated as well. On December 9, 2002, Snow was named President George W. Bush's choice for US treasury secretary.

ALSO IN DECEMBER 2002, Paul Tellier informed the CN board he was leaving the company on short notice. He couldn't tell them where he was going. The directors were shocked. Top executives were called into

Tellier's office late in the day, said Mark Wallace, who was then manager of investor relations and would soon become Harrison's long-time lieutenant. "We had assumed he was going to tell us Hunter was leaving to join CSX!" The next morning an announcement would be made that Tellier would be the new CEO of another transportation company—plane, train, and snowmobile maker Bombardier. Based in Montreal, "the Bomber" had been the pride of Quebec. It was the world's leader in manufacturing regional jets. Bombardier was also a global leader in rail manufacturing, building subway cars, trams, and high-speed trains. Its legacy business was the snowmobile, plus other recreational products such as the Sea-Doo. But with the cataclysm of 9/11 and the impact on its aerospace business, Bombardier had faltered, as had many aviation-related businesses, and it wanted new leadership.

Although Tellier's departure was unexpected, fortunately for CN, there was a CEO-in-waiting. Harrison was already running the railroad as COO. He would take over as CEO on January 1, 2003. Harrison called his protégé, Keith Creel, who was now working for CN and living in Winnipeg. Creel said he was sitting in his car in the parking lot of supermarket Sobeys when Harrison told him he would be the new CEO of Canadian National.

"You're shittin' me," Creel said. He couldn't believe an American was going to run CN. As it turned out, it would not be the only major Canadian company Harrison would lead.

6 CN HIGHS, CN LOWS

ON **SEPTEMBER 20,** 2005, an analyst's report hit the street. It was written by Morgan Stanley's James Valentine, at the time the pre-eminent transportation analyst. The Wall Street firm singled out Harrison, calling him, "arguably the most dynamic and shareholder-focused CEO within the railroad industry." Valentine went on to say that CN's Precision Scheduled Railroading philosophy was a "way of life for front-line employees" and that it wasn't "simply a schematic created by a management consulting firm." CN employees, he wrote, knew there were consequences if they didn't perform to plan. "We don't see the same sense of urgency on all the other properties." Again, it was a dig at the other Class 1's.

"A CNI [CN's New York Stock Exchange ticker symbol] manager's pay, promotion, and job security can be significantly influenced by how well that manager complies with the plan," Valentine said, and that "results in better decisions down to the front line." With CN's 61.2 percent OR in the most recent 2005 quarter (the only North American railway sporting one that began with a six), Valentine pointed out that CN's OR was 1200 basis points (12 percentage points) better than its nearest peer. It was a staggering difference. Then the capper.

"We consider Hunter Harrison one of a kind, an industry maverick blazing the trail to a 60 per cent (or lower) operating ratio (i.e., 40% margin)," Valentine said. If anything would make Harrison the envy of the other major railroads, it was that phrase, "one of a kind." Valentine was essentially saying Harrison was so good that the others could only be embarrassed. In fairness to Tellier, Valentine had also published a report on June 4, 2001 (while Tellier was CEO and Harrison was COO) declaring that "CN is to freight railroading what Michael Jordan is to basketball and Tiger Woods is to golf."

Four years into his tenure as chief executive, Harrison continued to set records. The OR continued to fall—for the year ending 2006, it was 60.7 percent, and shareholders were rewarded accordingly. Adjusting for stock splits, CN was worth less than USD $4.44 per share in mid-1998. By the beginning of 2007, it was worth USD $21.48. Harrison was rewarded as well. While he was highly paid at IC, his compensation ballooned at CN. In 2004, his pay packet was USD $12,520,646. In 2005, it was $13,379,624, and in 2006, it rose to $16,345,845. Beyond that, by the beginning of 2007, he'd amassed USD $99,289,071 in equity holdings in the company, either via options or stock units. His contract as CEO ran until the end of 2008 and was extended a year until the end of 2009. At that point, he would be sixty-five. His last year at CN, however, would be awkward.

There are various accounts of what happened. At the beginning of 2009, Harrison said he was preparing to serve out his last year as CEO when he received a visit at his Florida home from the then-chairman, David McLean, and Robert Pace, the current chairman who was also then on the board. He said the two sat across from him on a sofa. During the discussion, Harrison said he was asked to extend his tenure for at least a year. CN, like other companies, was coping with the global financial crisis, and the CEO recalled being told that his planned departure date at the end of 2009 was no longer ideal. "We need you to stay," Harrison said he was told. "Bad time in the market." Harrison remembered asking if he could reflect on what he believed was said. He and Jeannie had made post-retirement plans, but he felt the company had been good to him. He said he'd speak with her and get back to them quickly. Three or four days later, Harrison said Jeannie told him that although she wished he'd retire, if staying on at CN was what he needed to do, she understood—she knew he was not looking forward to retirement. He then said he relayed to the chairman that he'd be happy to do it. Within a few weeks, Harrison said he went to Montreal for an evening board meeting that was almost entirely in camera—he was excluded for several hours until 10:30 or 11 pm.

"What are they talking about?" he wondered. They'd asked him to stay and he'd agreed, adding that he wasn't asking for any new compensation and felt he had been loyal and fulfilled his duty.

"Made them a lot of money. We—I'm not saying I. The team made a lot of money."

Finally, he said they summoned him, and Harrison maintained he spoke to the board that night. He described saying to the assembled directors that he'd been asked to stay on, and then a couple of them said "stop." We didn't know you were being approached, they said. Eventually, Harrison said one of the directors—the former chairman and CEO of Toronto-Dominion Bank, Charlie Baillie—spoke. He said he couldn't always read Baillie and didn't always agree with him, but he gave him credit for speaking up. Baillie, he said, told him at the meeting that he was one of the ones opposed to an extension—and not because it had anything to do with the job Harrison had done.

"He said we've got to learn to do without you sometime and if we keep extending, we're saying to the market we've got a weak team here," Harrison recalled. "So it's time for us to stand on our own two feet and so we don't need you." Baillie said at that point, he didn't think there was any director who felt there should be an extension. In Harrison's mind, though, he thought there was a faction that believed it was okay to keep him while the company was making money, but as soon as possible it was important to appoint a Canadian as CEO. He was asked for his reaction to the situation.

"I feel like I've been kicked in the nuts and I'm disappointed," Harrison recalled saying. "I'll see you down the road."

McLean had a different recollection. He said Harrison's description of the Florida visit "was not the way it went." McLean said he went alone to Florida that January. "I don't think it was with another board member. I was by myself," he said. "Because my habit was to meet with each of our directors once a year."[1] Later in Montreal, McLean said Harrison did not appear before the board that evening when it held a dinner

---

1   CN did not make Pace available for an interview.

meeting prior to the regular meeting the next day. That was also how Baillie remembered it as well.[2] But McLean said that he and Pace went to Harrison's office that night to tell him his tenure would indeed finish at the end of December 2009. McLean added that Harrison was then offered the opportunity to speak to the board the next morning. He recalled Harrison's emotions being "first very mad, then very sad."

"There's no question he was hurt," Jim Gray said. "On the other hand, Claude [Mongeau, the CFO] was ready" to succeed Harrison. (On April 21, 2009, CN announced that Mongeau would be Harrison's successor.) Once something was inevitable, Gray said, it was better to get it behind you and move on. But he allowed that "running a railroad with Hunter is a very personal thing." It had been lucrative for him over the years, Gray said, "and that [was] very important to Hunter," adding that CN was exceedingly generous when it came to his compensation. He did not recall Harrison saying something so graphic to the board (neither did Lumley or Baillie), but Gray added, "that doesn't for one minute mean he didn't say it." McLean said, "[Harrison] might have said that."

One director had difficulty recalling the details, but thought it more likely "you'd have two people doing it [telling Harrison he was no longer needed] rather than humiliating him in front of the whole board." If that had been the case and McLean and Pace went to Harrison's office that night, did he say it to them rather than to the full board?

McLean indicated Harrison's renewal issue became complicated in December 2008. He recalled a board function where a few directors were musing about Harrison staying on as CEO past 2009. Did Harrison hear them? "Oh fuck, he was with them," McLean said. "And I took these guys aside after and I said you guys can't do that, you have no authority, you're undermining the board. Christ, stop it." By then the damage was done, he said. "Hunter got the bee in his bonnet that you know, maybe the board wanted him to stick around a bit longer and so when I went to see him in January, the first thing he said is I've talked to my wife and yeah, we're prepared to stay. And I said, Jesus, Hunter.

---

2 A former director's calendar indicates there was a Human Resources Committee meeting at 6:00 pm, Wednesday, January 21, 2009, and a board meeting at 8:00 am, Thursday, January 22.

No. You know that's not the decision of the board. That was the musing of a couple of directors," McLean said. At the evening, in-camera
board meeting—which McLean said went on for four hours—there was
a lengthy discussion "about whether the board wanted to change the
decision we'd taken and the decision was no, not to change it."

Lumley said, "I was probably the main one who went to McLean [say-
ing] why don't we extend again?" But Lumley also said that the board
"did not want to lose Claude. And the results showed, thank goodness.
Claude was a tremendous replacement for Hunter."[3] Lumley reflected
that many directors were already focused on the successor and were
under the impression Harrison was leaving. Another director who was
in the room interpreted the situation as though it was Harrison's view
that had changed, not the board's. He said that Harrison had "thought
it would be a good idea to retire and then as it got closer, he didn't."

It was certainly McLean's view that it was time for a new CEO. While
he viewed Harrison as an effective change-agent, McLean said that once
Precision Scheduled Railroading had been implemented, running the
railroad day to day was not Harrison's "strong suit." He had done his job,
McLean felt, and it was time for him to leave. Mark Wallace, who worked
closely with Harrison for years, believed this missed the point—that the
CEO's model was about continuous improvement. Harrison added that
if he had any strength, "it would be leadership-coaching stuff more than
even the scheduled precision railroad." While McLean gave Harrison
credit for running the railroad, he said there were also negatives. "The
positive is you pick up a lot more cash flow," McLean said. "But in the
negatives, we had some pretty unhappy people working in the railroad
who were tired of getting those phone calls telling them to kick this
guy's ass off the property and stuff like that."

"It all seemed to blow up," Ed Lumley said, thinking back on the
episode. "It's just one of those unfortunate things that a very happy marriage dissolved to the satisfaction of no one." In defense of the amount
he was paid by CN, Harrison said that he had never negotiated "one inch

3   At the end of 2010, Mongeau's first year as CEO, CN's OR was 63.6 percent. Revenue was
$8.297 billion and net income was $2.104 billon. At the end of 2015, his last full year as
CEO, CN's OR was 58.2 percent, revenue $12.611 billion, and net income $3.538 billion.

of anything in the contract" there. When people said that he made too much, it was "because no fuckin' body thought the fuckin' company was going to get turned around and make that fuckin' much money. It wasn't something I negotiated in options or issues or anything else."

McLean wrote in his book that he "always liked Hunter Harrison." He said Harrison "marched to his own drummer," found him to be a "smart, charming, and very engaging individual," and said "he was a very good CEO in a lot of ways" and "a fabulous guy." But as Tellier recalled it, there was no love lost between the chairman and Harrison. Still, McLean wrote that it was actually him who had encouraged Harrison to pay more attention to the board while he was COO. McLean said Harrison never expected to be CEO of CN—that once Tellier was gone, Hunter Harrison would be gone—and that he, McLean, nudged him to forge board relationships so when Tellier did leave, the board would be more prepared for the prospect of Harrison as CEO.

In some respects, during the Tellier years, Harrison was shielded by the protective armor of his boss, the expert diplomat who knew politics and could offset some of the American's rough edges with government, the board, or investors. "Could've been," Harrison said. "I wouldn't argue with that. I was not your typical Canadian operating chief or CEO," Harrison said. "CEOs in Canada are not operators, they're politicians. They don't really get their hands dirty with the business. I'm not a big back-slappin', banquet-goin', CEO club" kind of guy, he added. "Nobody said anything to me about running for office in Canada."

Certainly, Tellier was more involved with the board than Harrison ever was—even though CN, by Harrison's own estimation, had a very good board. He admired a number of the directors—the late Purdy Crawford,[4] Ed Lumley, Jim Gray, and Raymond Cyr—all Canadians. "When you've got people like Purdy Crawford saying you're the best CEO that he's ever dealt with, non-financial," Harrison said combatively, "that goes a long way in my fuckin' book." But it was still a board. In fact, Keith Creel noticed that when Harrison got irritated at board meetings, he would turn his diamond wedding band around and tap it on the boardroom table, leaving dents. Harrison understood why boards

---

4 Crawford died in August 2014.

existed—to monitor—but for him, everything came down to adding value. Did a board add shareholder value? In the final analysis, he would say no, at least at a railroad. It's possible there were directors who felt that vibe from him and simply had enough of Hunter Harrison. He certainly viewed boards as an "encumbrance," said one director privately.

"You name me a top-notch CEO who really believes he or she really needs a board," Lumley said. "Some CEOs are better strokers of the board than others." CN had a strong board and a strong CEO, he said, so there were bound to be clashes around the table. "I think that's healthy. What I think is not healthy is not talking."

Part of what bothered Harrison about his Canadian experience was the heightened focus on corporate governance, particularly when it related to compensation. After the Enron and WorldCom accounting scandals of the early 2000s and the passage of the Sarbanes-Oxley Act in the United States in 2002, boards and top executives had to be more accountable for financial disclosures and audits. This included Canadian companies, in particular those listed on American stock exchanges, like CN. But clipping the wings of CEOs on compensation and aircraft use was not productive, in Harrison's view.

At CN, as part of his compensation package, he said he was entitled to 500 hours annually of personal use of a corporate plane. The first four or five years, he said, it wasn't an issue. A problem arose in 2008, Harrison said, when the price of fuel surged alongside the price of oil, which topped $140 a barrel in July of that year. Harrison's number of hours put the cost of his aircraft use at a level that he said caught the attention of Institutional Shareholder Services (ISS). ISS monitors governance issues, including executive compensation–related matters on behalf of shareholders, and advises on how to vote at company meetings. Harrison believed the board, and specifically members of the compensation committee, felt pressure.

"It was the board that got the criticism," Lumley recalled. "Some people on the board were more sensitive to governance issues than others."

Harrison believed the board had hit its limit. A month or two before the meeting in which he said he was asked to extend his contract, Harrison said McLean asked him to pay back some of the money related to aircraft use. He said he refused. For his part, McLean said no one ever asked Harrison to pay back money related to aircraft. "Not a factor," he said, adding its use was "not a big item" because it was part of his compensation and Harrison only used a plane under conditions to which the company had agreed. CN policy at the time required the CEO to use the company aircraft for both personal and business use "for efficiency and security reasons." As well, use of the aircraft was a condition of Harrison's employment. McLean said he believed Harrison was treated fairly.

Whether the aircraft was an issue or not (one former director called it "an irritant"), could it have been one more case of Harrison's dismissive attitude toward optics? If there were issues around his generous compensation and aircraft use, it would be characteristic of Harrison to not deploy political astuteness to mitigate the situation. Others, he said, were sensitive about driving around in company limos in front of workers. He wasn't. With aircraft, in one instance, some CN directors boarded one private plane and noticed Harrison boarding another by himself. He often ignored what others thought and there's no question he got lots done that way. But it made him vulnerable.

He also aggravated the board by committing CN as a major sponsor of Spruce Meadows, the prestigious show jumping event in Calgary founded by his friend the late Ron Southern, the founder and chairman of ATCO Group. The promise was in the millions of dollars, one director said (Harrison said it cost four to five million annually). "Why didn't they say something?" Harrison protested when queried about it. He said that he didn't even know who Southern was when the sponsorship opportunity was first brought to him (Tellier said it started under him), although they later became friends. Although the director said Harrison told the board he would extricate the company, he was soon gone and CN "was stuck with it," unaware there was "a forward commitment" (it was a "rolling" five-year commitment). Looking back, Harrison defended it, saying "we got recognition all over the world for it." He said prior to the sponsorship, "CN was viewed as an arrogant eastern Canadian company that didn't do anything for the West."

WAS THE CN board—rightly or wrongly—worried about safety issues when Harrison was CEO? The question received an emphatic no from several longtime directors. Paul Tellier said Harrison was "always a very strong promoter of a safety culture" and would "lose his temper" if the right safety measures were not taken. Buzz Hargrove said it was true that Harrison was tough about safety in the yard. "He would hammer the hell out of people who didn't wear their hard hats and their safety shoes in the yard." But at the other end of the spectrum, Hargrove said Harrison would load down locomotives with as many cars as they could pull, running longer, faster trains to reduce delivery times. "That was great for him and the shareholders, but it's not good for communities where the accidents occur." Indeed, in his first year at CN, velocity increased by 16 percent. It also kept improving and trains got longer. Harrison took Hargrove's point about train length and speed as fair, but said society made tradeoffs all the time. He used driving as an example. At one point, the interstate speed limit in the United States was reduced to fifty-five miles per hour in the wake of the 1970s energy crisis. It saved gasoline, but drivers were frustrated. They wanted to go faster. The reduction in the limit didn't last.

Reviewing the record at CN during his time there, in 1998, the year Harrison arrived, the railroad had very strong safety data. The following year was difficult, but then things improved markedly. There were certainly some high-profile accidents while Harrison was CEO, particularly in 2005. The Lake Wabanum derailment in Alberta on August 3, 2005, resulted in a spill of 184,920 US gallons of bunker C fuel, as well as 23,247 US gallons of another form of oil (pole-treating oil), all of which led to a high level of public anger directed at CN. The cause was a defective rail. The company spent some $35 million on environmental remediation and compensation and in 2009 pleaded guilty to three charges related to the Fisheries Act, the Migratory Birds Convention Act, and an Alberta environmental protection act. Two days after Lake Wabanum, a CN accident resulted in 10,566 US gallons of toxic caustic soda being spilled into a river north of Squamish, British Columbia. An estimated half a million fish perished. Investigators cited human error, supervision, and the length and assembly of the train. There was also the head-on collision in Mississippi in July 2005 that cost four lives. Investigators said the probable cause was "failure by the crew of the northbound train to comply with wayside signals requiring them to stop" and that "the crew's attention to the signals was most likely reduced by fatigue," although without supporting evidence, other factors could not be ruled out.

"The loss of life we sustained in 2005 will remain with me for a long, long time," Harrison said. There were also CN-related deaths in 2003 and 2006, but in fairness to Harrison, there were work-related fatalities while his predecessor and successor ran the company.

While deaths can certainly overshadow statistics, the data clearly show that CN's safety record improved over Harrison's tenure. At the end of 1999, the injury frequency rate per 200,000 person hours was 7.3 and the accident rate per million train miles was 2.2. In the last three years of Harrison's time as CEO, the injury frequency rate per 200,000 person hours fell from 1.87 to 1.78—a vast improvement from his first full year at the railroad—as did the accident rate per million train miles, which dropped from 2.73 to 2.27 (it had fallen to 1.6 in 2004 but was up to 2.7 by the end of 2007 before starting to fall again). Both indicators improved in the year after he left and also by the end of 2011, arguably a carryover of the changes he had made.

In the final analysis, the biggest issue for the board was not aircraft use or safety—it was customer complaints. One director said it was as though Harrison saw customers as "a bit of an inconvenience." Harrison bristled at this, challenging critics to present a specific example. He cited a line from the biopic of Steve Jobs, based on Walter Isaacson's book, in which the Jobs character said, "I guarantee whoever said 'the customer is always right' was a customer."

The fact remains that scheduling the railroad rather than letting customers dictate its schedule was one of the major factors that led to CN's exceptional results, which the directors shared in and enjoyed. Charlie Baillie, for one, gave Harrison credit for recognizing the ability to price, a result of offering reliable, faster trains. Such premium pricing made CN shareholders a lot of money and was the byproduct of Harrison's product—a scheduled railroad. The board may have become uncomfortable with Harrison, but the financial and operating achievements were hard to ignore. In the end, though, he'd worn out his welcome with many on the board.

"It should have been a lovefest" at the end, said one director, but it wasn't.

CN did, however, throw a big retirement party for Harrison at Navy Pier in Chicago in December 2009. An enormous sculpture of a horse graced the room, emblematic of the Harrisons' deepening involvement in the equestrian scene. Jeannie Harrison recalled David McLean acting as emcee of the event. She said the chairman gave her a gold bracelet with bears engraved on it. The theme song that evening was Tina Turner's "Simply the Best." Yeah, Harrison thought, but you don't need me. What *boolshit*, he said to himself.

When a blow or even a personal slight came his way, he was touchy and defensive about it for years. He was a star performer—how could they do this to someone like him? The money was important, but the feeling of being betrayed was undeniable. Reflecting on his departure from CN seven years after the fact, he allowed that his feelings may have been immature. The people at CN were great, except for a handful who, for whatever their reasons, had grown tired of him. Companies, he said, don't do very well with executive exits, adding that perhaps executives shouldn't be so sensitive. But there was no disputing it—a gulf had built up between Harrison and CN. It would expand into an all-out fight two years later.

7 PROXY WAR

ONCE DONE AT CN, Harrison never imagined he'd run another railroad. He was angry and felt sorry for himself. Certainly, "CP would be the last one" he ever thought he'd lead, given its long-running rivalry with CN. However, in an interview I did with him just prior to his leaving CN in 2009, he said people expected him to "fail at retirement." His sister Mary said, "He wasn't ready to retire then." He had worked 24/7 for more than forty-five years in an industry he loved. He was also accustomed to being the boss and the sense of identity and stature that went with being a CEO.

Fortunately, he had a hobby—horses. His daughter Cayce became involved in show jumping at the age of ten when they lived in Chicago. Jeannie began traveling to events with her as the family became involved in the sport. While she went with Cayce during the week, Hunter would drive her to the barn on weekends. "He was really supportive of anything I wanted to do in the sport," Cayce said. Eventually, she would marry another rider, Quentin Judge.

Harrison ultimately ended up with three luxurious horse farms. One is in Connecticut and was originally one of the state's oldest dairy farms. The subject of a cover story in *Equestrian Quarterly,* it's set on eighty-seven acres of rolling New England farmland. There are twenty stalls in the main barn, and a total of forty on the property. There is a 3.5-acre Grand Prix field, a foaling barn, apartments, and a party barn (a.k.a. games room) near the tennis court and swimming pool. There are three homes—two of which have in the past been occupied by his daughters and their families, and the main home, 15,000 square feet, made of timber and local stone. It has indoor and outdoor kitchens, a cinema room, a golf simulator, a putting green (at one point Harrison was a two or three handicap golfer), a trophy room, and a wine cellar. For more than five years, the expansive estate was looked after and managed by Libby when Hunter and Jeannie weren't there. The other two farms are in Florida in a ritzy enclave where the Gates, Bloombergs, Spielbergs, and Springsteens nest (their daughters are also equestrians). The main one is set on one of the last large parcels within walking distance of the Winter Equestrian Festival. It too has three dwellings that include homes and apartments, a spectacular barn with another packed-to-the-rafters trophy room, as well as a "quiet room" on top for Harrison, with a panoramic view of the property and no electronics (he liked quiet "think-time" each day). The third farm, which is nearby, was an investment in partnership with a Pittsburgh real estate magnate. Double H Farm bought the partner out in late 2017 and then listed it for sale at $36 million. The Harrison residence is a few minutes away in an exclusive community.

Cayce and Quentin run the family's horse business, although Harrison hovered. Post-CN, "he was involved more in the barn . . . which I simultaneously dreaded and appreciated," Cayce said in May 2017. "Because he's tough and he's argumentative and the two of us can really butt heads." Quentin said Cayce and her dad were very much alike. In spite of Harrison becoming an instant expert on horses, Cayce came to value being challenged by him. She's not alone. McLain Ward, winner of two Olympic golds and top ranked in the world in 2017, was in professional partnership with Harrison during two phases of his career and considered him a mentor. Whether it was big railroads or big sports, "there are a lot of similarities," Ward said. "You're held accountable." Harrison, Ward said, reminded him of his late father—forceful and demanding, like a football coach from the 1950s or 60s. People who want to do well in life were drawn to him: "You aim for the stars." Together, they owned world championship horses—and like any professional sport, they tried to draft a strong team. Similar to how he recognized railroading stars, Ward said Harrison had an eye for talent in show jumping. As a result, the family's Double H Farm is "one of the most, if not the most, respected private teams in the sport," Ward said. "There isn't an event that they haven't won."

Although he loved the sport's scene, created a prestigious brand with Double H, invested in a major equestrian center in Florida, and successfully bred and sold many animals, by 2010 and 2011 Harrison was bored and frustrated. Libby said he was "just kind of lost." He'd be in the kitchen telling people how to cook and clean. Jeannie also noticed her husband pacing in the stalls around the farm. "When he's not happy, no one is happy," his granddaughter Mackenzie said. Her sister Morgan added that, "He drove everyone crazy." Like a tiger in a cage, Harrison wanted out. He needed to work. On top of that, the joke was that Jeannie was simply sick of having him around the house.

"He'd be like, 'Jeannie, where are you going?'" Cayce said. "He's never asked her that in fifty years of marriage, probably because every single day he was doing his own thing and worried about his own schedule."

His farm-bound purgatory wouldn't last long. In August 2011, Harrison got a call from Pershing Square, an influential, headline-making American hedge fund run by activist investor Bill Ackman. After identifying what they believe to be an undervalued company, activist investors buy large positions of that firm's stock, agitate for seats on the board, and press for change in order to increase the value of the shares. Pershing managed $11 billion in assets and had a roster of investors that included, among others, endowments, pension funds, charitable foundations, and individuals. It made concentrated, research-intensive investments wherever it saw value. The caller was Paul Hilal, Bill Ackman's colleague, former college roommate, and close friend. Hilal had first taken note of the railroad sector in 2008 when two other investment funds bought a major position in CSX. (Harrison was approached then by a former colleague who was associated with those investors—Gil Lamphere—to see if he was interested in running the American railroad, but Harrison was still running CN and he declined.) Hilal didn't think about the sector again until 2011, when over dinner his brother Philip heard about poor performance at a Canadian railroad and called his brother, suggesting there might be an opportunity. It didn't take a rocket scientist to identify the candidate.

CP and CN were galaxies apart when it came to performance. CP's operating ratio that year was 81.3 percent, while CN's was 63.5. Paul Hilal, then in his mid-forties, also noticed during his research that whenever anyone mentioned railroads, one name kept coming up—Hunter Harrison. According to Pershing's calculations, while CEO at IC, Harrison had made shareholders 450 percent and another 350 percent at CN.

In early August, Hilal said things were relatively sleepy in New York's financial community. He started sniffing around Canadian Pacific, was immediately intrigued, and said he canceled his own vacation. Over the next nine weeks he estimated he logged one thousand hours researching the company, the sector, the regulatory environment, and Harrison—an average of fifteen hours a day, seven days a week. Hilal had been working at Pershing since 2006 and was always hungry for opportunity. CP looked like a possibility—if Pershing could persuade the railroad's board to replace its CEO with the retired railroader.

Anxious to speak with Harrison, Hilal got a number for the farm in Connecticut. He got through to the barn and identified himself as a New York financial type. The person who answered connected him to Harrison's office in the house. The retired CEO picked up the phone. Hilal was careful not to let Harrison know the real purpose of his call—to secure him as Pershing's candidate to run CP. Hilal positioned it as a "teach me" call about the industry. Harrison thought it would be a ten-minute conversation. But Harrison was a talker and so is Hilal. It was three and a half hours. Although he was fascinated with what Harrison was saying, Hilal was extremely uncomfortable during the call. He had to go to the bathroom, but he was afraid to end the conversation because he worried that he might never get Harrison on the phone again.

"Gold is coming out of the phone and I had to go to the bathroom," Hilal said.

At the end of the call, Hilal asked him if he would consider consulting for Pershing. Harrison said yes but added that he didn't come cheap. "You're going to pay me X a day and I'll work my ass off for you," Harrison told him, and charged $10,000 a day. Harrison didn't need the money, but he wanted it to determine whether Pershing was taking his time seriously. Hilal described what Harrison said to him on the phone as a "masterclass," an unbelievable exposition on Precision Scheduled Railroading. "I was blown away." After some basic valuation work, Hilal thought Pershing could triple its money if it landed Harrison.

After their initial conversation, Harrison spoke at length on the phone with Hilal several times as a consultant, as well as in marathon meetings at Pershing that included Hilal's twenty-five-year old associate, Brian Welch. Welch was a new hire who, alongside Hilal, did "deep dive" research on railroads and, in particular, CP. Hilal and Welch grilled Harrison on the rail sector.

"There was no [mention of] CP. I had no idea," Harrison said. With Harrison on board as a "consultant," Pershing used him to check the work of other consultants. Pershing would get Harrison to listen in on calls with paid advisors and then ask what he thought. The firm, Hilal said, told the consultants they had someone else listening, but did not reveal who it was. The consultants had no idea it was Hunter Harrison.

"You're payin' for that?" he said to Pershing.

It was ironic Harrison was being paid as a consultant, given the dim view he had of such types, which he characteristically dismissed as "washouts." Little did Harrison know that on September 23, 2011, Pershing bought 330,814 shares of CP at USD $46.41 (CAD $47.72). It continued buying for the rest of the month and throughout October as the price rose.

"We started piling in and at times we were buying 20 or 30 percent of the daily volume, driving the shares up in the process." Hilal said. Still masking his intentions with Harrison, he asked hypothetical questions about what would happen if this railroad or that railroad implemented Precision Scheduled Railroading. Hilal had a backup plan. If he couldn't land Harrison, "I was going to go for Keith [Creel]," who became COO at CN in January 2010, less than a month after Harrison's departure as CEO. Hilal kept Creel's cell phone number on a Post-it note stuck to his computer monitor for months, resisting the urge to call for fear of being in violation of a non-solicit clause in Harrison's agreement with CN. Eventually, though, he tested whether Harrison would be receptive to running another railroad. Hilal told me that Harrison said he would, and that CSX made the most sense, but that no board would hire him. Hypothetically, Hilal raised the notion of CP.

"Well, why would I go back to run a smaller railroad?" Harrison asked. Hilal made the case that the opportunity was sizeable compared to other railroads. CP was in the worst shape; therefore, the opportunity was greater. He also cited the fact that Harrison knew CP as a competitor, knew Canada, the regulatory environment, the weather, the customers and unions. Contractually with CN, Harrison had a two-year non-compete clause restricting him from taking such a job until 2012. But Hilal made a seductive argument—he, Hunter Harrison, was uniquely qualified to create astronomical shareholder value at CP.

"Then at some point, he's just kind of quiet and you could tell he's thinking about it," Hilal said. "I mean, it's a complete layup for him."[1]

On October 13, 2011, Harrison was sitting in one of the conference rooms at the fund's offices.[2] In one corner, there was a peculiar-looking contraption, a 1951 rocket-powered ejection seat from a Canberra Nuclear Strike Bomber. It had been put there as a graphic reminder to staff at Pershing to bail out if an investment went bad. Pershing is known for making big bets on investments that Ackman and his team have rigorously targeted and researched. The firm has made a fortune on certain investments and lost a fortune on others, but Ackman has been considered an investor to reckon with—and one who causes friction, not unlike Harrison.

The forty-second floor offices Harrison visited are heavy on glass and modern design, with a view of the entirety of Central Park. He heard somebody coming down the hall and then saw a tall man walking in an animated, energetic manner toward the conference room where he was sitting. Ackman bounded into the room and introduced himself.

"Why don't you and I go to lunch?" Ackman said to Harrison. Hilal said he had arranged the lunch, booked the time in Ackman's calendar, and made the reservation for just two people so Ackman could independently form his own judgment of Harrison. He also believed a one-on-one would allow each man to size the other up and develop

---

1   Harrison said he didn't hear that CP was Pershing's actual target until he went to lunch with Ackman, while Welch said Harrison was told about CP being the bullseye while at Pershing's offices. "[Welch is] probably the most accurate," Harrison said dryly. (Ackman said Harrison was told just before lunch.)

2   October 13 is a "best guess" by Pershing, based on emails.

trust. The duo then walked to The Modern, the upscale restaurant at the Museum of Modern Art. Ackman has long legs and is a fast walker. Harrison, who'd had a vascular procedure in his legs that summer, was huffing and puffing by the time they arrived. Ackman, an advocate of healthy living, soon became Harrison's informal nutritionist and exercise coach.

"When I would sit with him at dinner, I would pull away the wine bottle. I wouldn't let him eat dessert," Ackman said. "He must have thought I was a fucking pain in the ass."

They went to a table in the right corner by the window, the least conspicuous part of the restaurant. Ackman is a familiar face in certain circles in New York. He said that if someone recognized Harrison, he worried they'd put two and two together. The lunch lasted a couple of hours.

"We want to get CP and we want to know your thoughts and I want you to run it," Ackman said, cutting to the chase.

"Bill, you can't afford me," Harrison said, half-kidding. Ackman told him what he had in mind for compensation.

"Looks good to me," Harrison said. "Ackman and I made that deal in a day." The chemistry was good. So was the potential for each of them to make a lot of money. Ackman said, "in the first five minutes, you could tell he was the right guy."

"I mean this guy's a general. He's like Patton," Ackman said. "And running a railroad is like running an army, right?" Harrison had made the same reference about Bill Thompson, his mentor.

While Harrison had a consulting agreement with Pershing as of September 23, 2011, they went back to the office where Hilal and Harrison finalized the outline of a compensation arrangement in the event Harrison became CEO of CP (ultimately, the railroad's board would have to hire him, not Pershing). Their agreement, according to Harrison, consisted of eight or nine lines on a legal pad. His salary would be modest for Harrison, $550,000 a year. That would be on top of his $1,500,000 annual pension from CN. What he really wanted was a significant stack of stock options—650,000[3]—on the company, plus access to a jet so he could commute to Calgary from his homes in

3   The option grant meant he could buy CP stock at $73.39 per share, well below where it would ultimately trade.

Connecticut and Florida. Later, Pershing would also indemnify Harrison in the event CN tried to take away his pension and other post-employment compensation owing, in the neighborhood of $40 million. That agreement was dated January 28, 2012 (Pershing ultimately raised Harrison's protection to $100 million). While these amounts are stratospheric for most people, Ackman thought Harrison's demands were reasonable given how much he thought the railroader could make for Pershing and other shareholders. Besides, according to Ackman, when it came to running railroads, "there's Hunter and there was everyone else." To Pershing, the huge premium to get Harrison was worth it.

ON THE SURFACE, if you were to sketch two characters who would be polar opposites, you might draw Bill Ackman and Hunter Harrison. Ackman is a New Yorker who went to Harvard Business School, while Harrison went to work as a grime-covered laborer at a railroad. Ackman is a polished, northeastern intellectual, while Harrison was a rough-around-the-edges, self-educated Southerner. Ackman grew up in an affluent suburb; Harrison came from working class stock. Nonetheless, they had much in common. Ackman reads financial statements on vacation and Harrison didn't like to take holidays, or at least ones that lasted more than a few days. A book about Ackman, *Confidence Game* by Christine S. Richard, describes him as "brash, blunt, almost neurotically persistent." The same could be said of Harrison. Both were fierce, competitive, single minded, and brainy. Both were fervent believers in their own ideas and skills. Both would yell at people when they deemed it necessary, a manifestation of their zealotry. As Ackman told Jacquie McNish in the *Globe and Mail* in 2012, "I'm exactly who I appear to be. I am unfiltered, for better or worse." No one would ever accuse Hunter Harrison of being otherwise. They liked and respected each other, and Harrison said they could do business on a handshake (Harrison said he could do same the same with Hilal).

On October 28, Pershing disclosed its investment in CP. After the news broke, Jim Gray, who was on CN's board during both Paul Tellier's and Hunter Harrison's tenures as CEO, was at the TV studio in Toronto to tape a segment for my program, *Headline*. Prior to going on set, he mentioned that he'd bet Harrison was somehow involved in the

Pershing situation. All the signals were there. CP had a bad operating ratio, it was a long-haul railroad, and Harrison was familiar with the Canadian market.

"It made such eminent sense," he reflected. "Who the hell better to turn CP around?" Besides, he knew Harrison was ambitious and wanted to work. "He's going to die with his spurs on," Gray said presciently in a 2017 interview. "He has no choice. He's addicted."

Meantime, the executive committee of CP was on a train about to travel from Toronto to Montreal for a board meeting. The railroad's chief legal officer, Paul Guthrie, who'd been with the company for more than twenty years, got a message that a Mr. Ackman wanted to speak with the chairman. It was then that the upper reaches of CP found out Pershing had purchased the railroad's stock. Before the group traveled on to Montreal, lawyers and bankers were called to advise the company. They boarded the train. The whole way to Montreal, the top echelon of the company conferred with advisors.

Ackman and CP's chairman, John Cleghorn, spoke twice by phone on October 29, 2011. On November 2, Ackman, Hilal, and Welch flew to Montreal on a private jet, a G550. At the airport in a so-called FBO—a fixed-base operator where private planes pull up—they met with Cleghorn and the railroad's CEO, Fred Green. Ackman knew Cleghorn was interested in military history, so he brought him a book as a gift. Cleghorn gave each of the Pershing representatives a poppy—the red pin Canadians wear in the run-up to November 11, Remembrance Day, a solemn day designated to honor Canada's war dead.

John Cleghorn—the former chairman and CEO of Royal Bank of Canada (RBC), the biggest company in the country—embodied blue-chip Canada. Ackman suggested to Cleghorn in advance of the meeting that it would be awkward for Green to be present, given that Pershing was looking to replace him. He said Cleghorn insisted CP's CEO be present.

Green, who had a marketing background with the railroad and had been its chief operating officer, took over as CEO of CP in 2006. During his time as chief executive, CP vastly underperformed its century-old competitor, CN. CP had toiled in the private sector since its completion in 1885. CN, meanwhile, had been a Crown corporation (owned by the government) for more than seventy years. It was also a classic east versus west enmity, the kind that has roiled Canada since time immemo-rial. While CP had indeed been a private company since the late 1800s, the construction of the railroad had been financed and backed by the federal government, with the country's first prime minister, Sir John A. Macdonald, its biggest cheerleader. CP had also been the recipient of 25 million acres of government land to facilitate the building of the track across Ontario, the prairies, and the Rocky Mountains to the Pacific. While its construction was an incredible achievement with participa-tion of private investors, it would be inaccurate to say Canadian Pacific Railway bootstrapped it; it would not have been built without the federal government's assistance.

Although CP had originally listed on the NYSE in 1883, over time the company added other businesses such as steamships, telecommu-nications, and an airline. From 1971 until 2001, the railroad operated as a division of Canadian Pacific Limited, a conglomerate that included CP Hotels (now Fairmont), CP Ships, Pan Canadian Petroleum (a pre-decessor of Encana and Cenovus), and Fording Coal, now owned by mining company Teck Resources. On October 3, 2001, the five Cana-dian Pacific siblings were spun out of the mother company, independent of each other. Once the railroad was again an individual, pure-play stock, its operating results came into sharper focus. Compared to CN's, they were wanting.

Even Harrison would be awed by the incredible feat of building a railroad in the 1880s from eastern Canada to the Pacific in *five* years, half the time mandated for the job. During that period, not only did it have to be constructed throughout fierce Canadian winters, but passes had to be found through the imposing Rocky and Selkirk Mountain ranges in western Canada. While Apollo 11's moon landing or Lindber-gh's solo flight across the Atlantic are among the twentieth century's major achievements, the pounding of the last spike of the CPR in 1885 was arguably on the same scale, given the era.

It's a coincidence that the person who's best known for spearhead-ing the building of the CPR—aside from Sir John A. Macdonald—was a bullheaded American, William Cornelius Van Horne, who also hailed from the Chicago railway scene. He had been the former general superintendent of Chicago, Milwaukee and St. Paul Railroad. As with

Harrison, Van Horne's reputation preceded him. He was ruthless and blunt, and he wouldn't tolerate laziness or poor productivity. He was another hard ass American who triggered visceral feelings north of the border.

"He wants to know why this was not done and why this was done. If the answers are not satisfactory there is a dark and bloody tragedy enacted right there," wrote Pierre Berton in *The Last Spike*. But like Harrison, Van Horne also celebrated ability, with his own as a shining example.

"It was said he could make eight hundred freight cars do the work of a thousand by his ingenious methods of loading." Van Horne "used locomotives to their fullest capacity over the protests of engineers who wanted to treat them like horses and let them rest quietly in the shops. He had a reputation for doctoring sick railroads until they were made to pay," Berton wrote. "He seemed to know a terrifying amount about railroading. He knew about yards and repair shops. He understood the mysteries of accounting. He could work out a complicated system of scheduling in his head while others sweated laboriously with pins and charts."

Like Harrison, Van Horne was a man obsessed. Also like Harrison, he was a man of large appetites—good cigars, fine wines. It was as though more than a century later, the railroad industry had spit out another Van Horne–like creature, someone who would impact CP in another way.

Meantime, Harrison said he'd only met Fred Green briefly on two occasions. While their tenures as CEOs of CP and CN had overlapped, he said he'd never had a substantive conversation with him. Harrison wasn't aware of how Green felt personally (Green's predecessor Rob Ritchie maintained that Green "liked Hunter," while Guthrie said he'd never heard either of them say anything negative about the other) but was aware of the tension between the two railroads. While at CN, Harrison had noticed Tellier's and Sabia's reactions whenever the other company was mentioned.

"You could say 'CP,' and their ears would just twitch with red blood at the lobe." He said it was the same at the other end. "They hated CN as much as CN hated CP." Michael Sabia said that when he and Tellier were at CN, some CP executives were utterly scathing in their condescension toward the two former government bureaucrats who were now running the railroad. In the 1990s, an attempt at a deal between the two companies to swap assets and combine in the east had failed.[4]

In the small, second-floor airport conference room in Montreal on November 2, 2011, were John Cleghorn and Fred Green from CP and Bill Ackman, Paul Hilal, and Brian Welch from Pershing Square. While Harrison and Ackman shared certain personality traits, it appeared as though Ackman and Cleghorn shared none. As one person close to Cleghorn put it, "Ackman and Cleghorn were like oil and water." Hilal described Cleghorn, a big man who had played defensive lineman for the McGill University football team, pulling him in close with a tight and forceful handshake, looking down at him. Cleghorn was polite, but "he grabbed me unusually firmly and pulled me unusually close." Still, Hilal and Ackman were impressed with Cleghorn's credentials and had every reason to respect him. They settled in to talk. After saying deferential things about both Cleghorn and Green, Ackman dropped the "H" bomb. Pershing, he said, wanted to install Hunter Harrison as CEO.

"And Fred, like, blanched," Ackman recalled. "All the blood drained out of his face." Cleghorn appeared ready for a fight. Both Ackman and Hilal described Cleghorn putting his arm around Green and saying that the CEO had unanimous board support. When things stalled, Ackman requested a one-on-one with Cleghorn, a move Hilal said Pershing had planned. Hilal, Welch, and Green split off into another room. Hilal said he told Green that Pershing's request to have him step down was not personal, adding that it was obviously an enormous sacrifice to ask of someone "making mid seven figures." Although Hilal did not promise anything, the implication was that Green would be looked after if he stepped aside in favor of Harrison.

"He was completely stone faced," Hilal said.

Meantime, in the other room, Ackman said Cleghorn "flat out turned me down." In CP's proxy filing, it said Cleghorn "advised that Mr. Harrison was well-known to the Board from his time at CN and expressed

---

4   Author Harry Bruce wrote that CP's cancelation of the talks pushed CN "onto a fast track to privatization."

reservations about Mr. Harrison's suitability to lead Canadian Pacific." The Pershing contingent then left. It looked like they would have to launch a proxy contest to get what they wanted. Pershing was smart, but it didn't mean things always went according to plan. In March 2017, for example, it threw in the towel on an investment in pharmaceutical company Valeant, losing billions. Canadian Pacific was also a huge bet. At its peak, Pershing would own 14.2 percent of CP, an investment of USD $1.4 billion, making it the largest shareholder of the railroad— at the time, its "largest single initial commitment" to any investment.

"The pressure on me was enormous, enormous, enormous, enormous," Hilal said. Not only were Pershing's staffers his friends, but the firm was run by his dearest friend, Ackman. Hilal, after all, had been the one who'd pushed for investing in CP. Failure was not an option. He assured Ackman and Welch that he'd planned out the proxy fight and Pershing would start calling major Canadian pension funds immediately to gauge support. Then something happened.

"We then leave and it's a short hundred feet to the airplane," Ackman said. He and his colleagues boarded the jet and the door was closed. The pilot started the engines but then called back to Ackman (Hilal said it was the chef on the aircraft who signaled to them).

"'Bill, there's some guy waving us down on the runway, on the tarmac.' And I look out the window and it's Cleghorn."

The pilot powered down the engines and Ackman walked down the stairs. Hilal said there were two inches of snow on the ground and neither man was wearing a coat. Their conversation, Hilal said, was brief, just a minute or two.

"Bill, I've had a chance to talk to Fred and we're delighted to have you [as] a shareholder of Canadian Pacific," Ackman said, quoting Cleghorn. "Welcome to Canadian Pacific." The summary of events in CP's proxy circular confirmed this in general terms and said Cleghorn had offered to discuss Pershing's proposal with the board. Ackman said he got the strong impression Green had seen the logic of Pershing's presentation. Others familiar with Green's thinking confirmed he was indeed prepared to leave CP. Rob Ritchie, Green's predecessor at CP, said Green told him that "he wanted to protect the board" and would leave the company at the right price. "He wasn't *ready* to go,"

Ritchie said, "but he was willing to be part of that transition that was being proposed."[5]

Ackman got back on the plane. Hilal recalled his friend had a "Cheshire cat grin on his face."

"We're like, all high-fiving on the plane," Ackman said. "We're like, oh my God, it's going to be so easy. Fred realizes he's up against Superman." Hilal recalled dancing on the aircraft on the way back to New York.

CP's board then convened meetings on three successive days to discuss the proposal with advisors. That included "the legal implications of Mr. Harrison's contractual obligations to CN." During in-camera sessions, the board also "discussed its knowledge of and experience with Mr. Harrison, including his relations with customers, employees, and government regulators."[6] His baggage from CN was following him. There was, however, continued communication with Ackman. On November 21, CP's directors agreed that Ackman should be interviewed for a board position. However, "the board did not believe it appropriate to meet with Mr. Hilal, given that he had no particular railroad industry expertise and offered no additional complementary experience." This irritated Ackman. It was also ironic because while Ackman was leading the charge, it was Hilal who was immersed in railroad research. At the same meeting, CP's board continued to consider the "suitability" of Harrison to lead the company.

On December 11, things took a turn for the worse. Ackman flew to Calgary to meet the governance committee of the board. Hilal traveled with him, and Ackman asked again that the board meet with his colleague. It wouldn't. Ackman also "reiterated his demand that Mr. Harrison be installed as president and CEO of Canadian Pacific." The temperature clearly rose and would soon be off the charts. According to CP's management proxy circular, on December 14, Cleghorn advised Ackman that directors "had approved in principle his joining the Board, 'subject only to entering into the customary confidentiality and standstill arrangements.'" On December 23, Pershing's legal counsel contacted CP's to advise that it would not sign the confidentiality

---

5   Cleghorn and Green each declined an invitation to be interviewed for this book.

6   On November 25, 2011, the *Globe and Mail* published its annual corporate governance rankings. CP ranked highly, tying for fourth place out of 253.

and standstill agreement "and had no interest in negotiating it." Ackman refused to be bound. Pershing viewed the request as "excessive." Relations between CP's board and Pershing deteriorated quickly. Ackman said, "the board or somebody had a change of heart and said, look we can't. This is embarrassing, we can't do this." On December 30, the story broke. The *Globe and Mail* reported that Ackman wanted to replace Fred Green with Hunter Harrison. A series of increasingly pointed emails and letters released to the public foreshadowed what would occur over the next five and a half months.

On January 3, 2012, Canadian Pacific Railway Ltd. made public a letter from Cleghorn, on behalf of the board, to Ackman stating: "We are troubled by the inaccuracies and mischaracterizations that have appeared in the media. Contrary to media reports . . . no member of CP's Board of Directors has 'expressed enthusiasm for Mr. Harrison and requested a meeting with him.' Indeed, no invitation has been extended by us to Mr. Harrison, either directly or via Pershing Square . . . Leaks to the media are counterproductive, and we hope that they are not attributable to you personally. With that said, we are willing to continue our dialogue in order to advance the best interests of the Company."

Ackman replied later that day.

Dear Mr. Cleghorn:

. . . neither I nor any representative of Pershing Square has made any inaccurate statements to the press . . .

Contrary to your statement in the letter that no one at Canadian Pacific expressed an interest in meeting with Mr. Harrison, on the Saturday after our Wednesday, November 2 meeting, you called me at home and asked that I arrange a meeting with him. Neither you nor Canadian Pacific expressed concern about Hunter's contract with Canadian National at the time. Rather, on that Saturday call and in subsequent communications, it was I who explained to you (and subsequently in communications among our respective counsel) that Hunter was subject to a non-compete agreement which would prohibit him from meeting or speaking with representatives of Canadian Pacific until January 1, 2012.

Contrary to your statement in the letter that we "acknowledge" that we have no plan to improve Canadian Pacific's operating performance, we do have a plan... Our plan is to transform Canadian Pacific from the worst performing railroad in North America into one of the best by effectuating a cultural and operational transformation of Canadian Pacific which begins with a new leader...

... In order for Hunter to be successful, he must have the full support and backing of the board of directors. For this reason we have asked for two board seats so that we can work with the board and Hunter to effectuate the changes that are required.

Ackman went on to say he was appreciative of the offer of a board seat but unwilling to be bound by a standstill agreement. A standstill meant Pershing would have to go along with whatever CP's board decided. In essence, it would be a gag. Among other things, it would prevent attempts at a hostile takeover and limit a shareholder from buying more stock. Ackman said he was not willing to sign. As Cleghorn had done, he concluded with a conciliatory tone describing their dialogue as "constructive." But he pushed for a meeting that would include Harrison and Hilal "as soon as practicable."

A day later, on January 4 at 7:22 am, Ackman unsheathed his ballistic missile, a three-page email to Cleghorn with the subject line "War and Peace" (the subsequent exchange was released by Ackman to the *Globe and Mail*). The email threatened a dramatic escalation,

a proxy contest for the upcoming annual meeting where we will seek to replace a greater number of the existing directors... we will take the largest public hall you have available in Toronto and will make a presentation to shareholders and the public (which will be simulcast on the Internet) about management and board failure over the last 10 years at CP...

... This proxy contest will not go well for the board and Fred. The track record is very poor, shareholders are disgruntled, and we are offering an alternative with a legendary reputation. An analyst at Morgan Stanley, your advisor in this matter, is now writing of a "super-bull" case if Hunter is hired... We will win the election likely by a landslide vote...

... the probability of war occurring has gone up meaningfully. War is not my preference... War is also not inevitable. I think the failures so far have been largely ones of communication...

. . . I took it quite negatively that the committee was unwilling to meet with my proposed director, trusted partner and good friend Paul Hilal in light of the fact that he left his newly born baby girl and beautiful wife to travel a fair distance on a Sunday night.

. . . You explained that Paul was not a CEO, that I was "the man" at Pershing Square, and as such the board would not consider him.

. . . Two months have passed. We are still left out in the cold. I have been accused by you in a public letter of making false and misleading statements. We are not in a great place.

. . . My impression of you when we first met was quite favorable. You seem like a solid, good man . . .

. . . Let's avoid having a border skirmish turn into a nuclear winter. Life is too short. Please call me when you can.

Sincerely,

Bill

At 5:47 pm the same day, Cleghorn responded with a brief email. In it, he reiterated the desire "to reach an agreement which advances the best interests of the company," adding he would discuss Ackman's email with CP's board.

Eleven minutes later, Ackman wrote back.

John,

I greatly appreciate your email. I shared the email with my colleagues after I sent it and they said that it may be perceived as overly blunt by you.

When we met, I promised to be extremely straightforward and you promised the same. I hope I did not offend with my directness and I apologize if I did so.

Please also note that I am not talking to the press and that a business story that appeared this afternoon on BNN sourced from a "source close to the action" was not me or anyone else affiliated with Pershing Square. I don't have any intention of speaking to the press unless and until we are unable to resolve this matter. I look forward to hearing from you.

Sincerely,

Bill

The rest of January saw no resolution. CP fired back on January 9 with an open letter from Cleghorn. It said Pershing had "not presented any detailed, credible plan" and did not "fully take into account structural differences between CP and peers." Ackman's and Hilal's OR promise of 65 percent for CP was "unrealistic" and had "never before been achieved by any railway management team." Changing management at CP—i.e., parachuting in Hunter Harrison—"would be detrimental to the company and its shareholders." Alternatively, CP was confident it could get its OR to the low 70s over the next three years.

Early the next month, "nuclear winter" began. On Super Bowl Sunday, February 5, 2012, Ackman and Harrison were shepherded to the offices of Davies LLP, a prominent law firm in Toronto, to meet with media. I recorded a half-hour television interview with Ackman for BNN. Then I recorded a half hour with Harrison, who wore a tie that featured the maple leaf. He told me he was "itchin'" to get back to railroading. He said Jeannie hadn't seen him so excited about anything in a long time.[7]

Ackman and Harrison were launching a proxy contest and would present their case the next day to investors, analysts, and the media at the Hilton Toronto. Pershing was looking to oust CP directors, install its own slate, and then appoint Harrison as CEO. It was bold. Canada's business establishment is tight. Aside from Cleghorn, there were several major names on the board—a virtual who's who—including, among others, the late Rick George, the two-decade CEO of oil sands giant Suncor; and the late Roger Philips, the former head of steel company Ipsco. Ackman and Harrison were aiming at big game. There were 101 days until CP's annual meeting in Calgary, and the battle would dominate business headlines in Canada for months.

It wasn't just Ackman on the assault. Harrison helped. In a speech at the University of Memphis, where he donated a million dollars, he said, "I might be back as a railroader here in a couple months. My former employer [CN] is not happy about it. But they'll get over it." He was referring to a lawsuit CN filed on January 23, 2012, alleging it

---

7   During the entire battle between Pershing and CP, more than once, interviews were requested with either Cleghorn or Green, but the invitations were declined.

had a reasonable basis to believe "that Harrison was in breach of his non-disclosure and non-compete undertakings sometime in 2011." The suit went on to allege that if Harrison were to accept a position at CP, "he would be in unquestionable breach of his non-compete undertakings; and his disclosure of CN confidential information in breach of his non-disclosure undertakings would be inevitable." As a result, CN suspended retirement-related payments to Harrison "subject to further factual discovery." The amount was significant—pension payments of $1,500,000 per year, valued at $20,614,000, and a restricted stock unit payment of approximately $17,900,000. That day, unsolicited, CN sent me an email at Business News Network with the lawsuit attached. "Exhibit A" of the court filing was Harrison's contract as CN's CEO. I phoned him at his barn in Florida. He said it was the first he'd heard about the lawsuit. I told him that it included his old contract.

"Fascinatin' readin'," he said, vintage Harrison. He was, however, miffed. His contract had expired and he believed he'd sat out his two year non-compete. "If you're playing for a fuckin' hockey team and your contract expires after five years and the fuckin' people across the street offer a hell of a lot better deal, are you disloyal if you go take it?"

The suit did not come out of the blue. The situation between Harrison and CN had started getting tense in late 2011. According to the complaint, on October 31, 2011, Harrison had a phone conversation with an unidentified official at CN in which he disclosed to his former employer that he'd signed a confidentiality agreement with Pershing. CN subsequently sent him an email reminding him of his obligations under the employment agreement he'd signed with the railroad. On January 5, 2012 (after his non-compete had expired), in another call with CN, he said that during 2011 he'd worked as a railway sector consultant in Europe, Russia, and Australia on various short-term projects and that in late October 2011, Pershing asked him if he'd be willing to return to work as the next CEO of CP. Harrison had responded that he was. When Harrison asked CN if there was any way it would allow him to become CP's CEO, he was firmly told no. According to the court document, Harrison also got firm. The document claimed he said to CN that if the railroad didn't make his January payment, he might be required to take legal action.

CN's suit was clear in its allegation. "Harrison is not the only executive who could run CP; but he is the only executive who possesses the unique body of CN Confidential Information, access to which by CP would be devastating." Former board members Jim Gray and Charlie Baillie said that on behalf of shareholders, CN had no choice but to file the suit. "Frankly, it pissed the board off," former chairman David McLean said. Directors felt CN had been very generous to Harrison, but "they lost their sense of humor" when Harrison "jumped camp." Harrison felt, however, that he had honored his contract by sitting out the two-year non-compete—he wasn't running a Class 1 railroad during that time. Additionally, one of his consulting opportunities during that period had come to him via a recommendation from a CN board member. Winston Churchill and Ronald Reagan had switched political parties (Churchill twice) and subsequently led their respective countries, but Hunter Harrison couldn't work for another railroad, especially Canadian Pacific. In March, Harrison's lawyers responded in a court filing, calling the suit "a baseless, petty effort to avoid paying Harrison the money it owes him" and that he "complied fully with the two-year non-compete provision of his Employment Agreement." Any material, non-public information he may have had, the filing said, was now stale.

Although he had left CN in 2000, the company's former head of legal, Jean-Pierre Ouellet, stayed in touch with Claude Mongeau, Harrison's successor. When the lawsuit was filed, Ouellet called Mongeau. "Claude doesn't easily get upset," Ouellet said. "I've never seen him as upset as he was at that time." The message conveyed was that Harrison was screwing over CN and Mongeau wasn't going to let him get away with it. "He was determined to see it through."[8] While the CN lawsuit was a dramatic development, it was later resolved without the allegations being tested in court.[9]

The battle for the hearts and minds of shareholders began on Monday, February 6, 2012, at the Hilton in downtown Toronto. The town hall was organized for Pershing by Kingsdale Advisors, led by Wes

---

8   Mongeau declined an invitation to be interviewed for this book.

9   Pershing indemnified Harrison so he wouldn't lose anything that would have been owed to him by CN.

Hall. Hall said a proxy fight in Canada had never been launched via a town hall and his firm was unsure how many people would show. In case attendance was sparse, he said Kingsdale had one hundred people on standby to fill the room. Hall didn't have to worry. He said more than four hundred filled the conference room, and Hilal said another thousand watched live on the web. In addition to investors and media, Harrison loyalists were there. His two former chiefs of staff at CN— Mark Wallace and Nadeem Velani—slipped into the conference room. Bill Ackman strode onto the stage and began laying out the case. Sixteen percent of his fund was concentrated on CP.

"We're in to win," Ackman said. He said Harrison was "stepping out of retirement for the trifecta," suggesting CP would be his third turn-around. However, he said that "the ultimate decisions about who will run the company will be made by the full board. We think the board will make the right decision."

That statement would foreshadow a confrontation in Calgary a little more than three months later. Pershing was not only looking to make Harrison CEO, but it also wanted new directors on the board. Ackman introduced Pershing's three independent board candidates, while he and Hilal would round out the five-person slate (two more nominees would be added).

Ackman said that when Pershing started buying CP shares, Canadian Pacific had an enterprise value of $13 billion, while CN's was $39 billion. The disconnect, he said, was that CP had about 70 percent of the assets that CN had but was worth only a third as much. By bringing in Harrison, Pershing would narrow that gap. He then introduced Hilal, who was operating on four hours' sleep. Hilal broke down CP's metrics, chapter and verse. It was not pretty. In addition to the titanic amount of work Hilal had done, large parts of the research and analysis had been done by Brian Welch, who was getting married five days later in Guatemala. The date of the town hall had been moved earlier to accommodate Welch's wedding, which the Pershing team attended.

"Importantly, this is not an attack on Fred Green personally," Hilal said. "This is an analysis of the performance of Fred Green and this company under his rule over the past five and a half years." He went on to say that during that period, North American rail investors earned 50 percent on their money, including dividends. Investors in CP, he said, lost 18 percent. While the ORs at American railroads were improving, CP's had worsened. In 1999, Pershing reported that CP's OR was 78 percent. In 2011, it had deteriorated to 81 percent. There were severe weather-related disruptions that year, but the railroad, Hilal said, simply wasn't efficient. It moved 70 percent of the freight of CN but used 80 percent of the cars. CP cars were "sitting around too much," compared to CN's. When they sat around, they didn't make money. CP's cars made fewer trips than CN's and its trains went slower. It was a devastating deconstruction.

Hilal then went after CP on pricing. He argued that CP's service was so sub-standard that it had to cut prices to keep customers. "CP," he said, was "in a vicious cycle." The company's response, he said, was scattered. Hilal told the audience ten distinct plans had been outlined by the company in recent years, but the results were dismal.

He sat down and Ackman got up again. Playing the diplomat, Ackman said CP's directors were extremely high-quality, smart, capable people, but for whatever reason, the railroad's results were the worst in North America "by a long shot." He then turned to Harrison, saying Pershing found it "shocking" that once the railroader's non-compete ended, "we offered him up to be available to meet with the board," but the board declined. He then began his evisceration. Exhibit A: the company had five chief operating officers in five years and three chief financial officers. "There's something wrong with the CEO if you have that much turnover." With such turnover, it was the board's job to look very hard at the person in the number one spot.[10] Regarding Green's compensation, Ackman also expressed surprise that the CEO had achieved seventeen of the eighteen targets set out for him by the board. How could a CEO achieve almost all of the targets, yet the company produced a negative shareholder return? Executive compensation as percentage of net income, he argued, was also going up at CP.

Piling on, the board, Ackman said, had very little skin in the game, owning just 0.2 percent of the company, and generally through shares that were awarded rather than purchased. If a director had $100

---

10 Later, during Harrison's time as CP CEO, there would also be several CFOs and three chairs.

million of his or her own money invested in CP, he argued, the company would not be run by the current CEO. What the company needed was the proven hand that belonged to Hunter Harrison. He could fix the culture and make the operational changes, and he knew Canadian railroads. At IC, Harrison had improved the OR 1700 basis points and the stock had increased five and a half–fold. At CN, the OR had improved 1100 basis points after he arrived[11] and shareholders had made four and a half times their money. Ackman reckoned that CP could be a double from where it traded that day. Without his plan, the business was at risk, he said. He then brought Harrison on stage for a Q&A.

"I feel like Paul Newman in *The Color of Money*, his final statement when he broke the balls open—'I'm back.'" (Newman won the Oscar for Best Actor in the 1986 Martin Scorsese film about a pool hustler.) But why *did* Harrison come back? He told the crowd that he loved the business and it was all he'd ever done. Furthermore, a few days before, he had personally invested $5 million in CP stock. As for the so-called structural challenges inherent at CP—specifically, the higher grades of the Rockies—he dismissed the argument. "It snows everywhere. It snows on CN and it snows on CP." All railroads used structural challenges as excuses. US railroads, he told the room, had complained they couldn't catch CN because the Canadian railroad had the advantage of Canadian healthcare.

"There's no perfect franchise that I know of," he said. "You start believing your excuses." For him, it was all about execution. "Clearly, the execution's not been there." It was time to do things differently. CP issued a statement in response to the town hall, saying "Harrison has no detailed plan to improve CP's operating performance," adding that "Pershing Square still has no plan or clear timetable to improve CP's operations." It also called Pershing's math "hypothetical."

That evening, Pershing had reserved a private dining room with seating for twenty-five people at Sassafraz, in Toronto's glitzy Yorkville district. Major CP investors would get a close-up view of Bill Ackman

---

11 CN's operating ratio had actually improved by 1400 basis points by the end of 2007 to 63.6 percent, but the impact of the financial crisis in 2008–09 pushed it back up to 67.3 percent by the time Harrison departed.

and Hunter Harrison, plus a chance to have a dialogue, specifically to showcase a softer side of Ackman and address lingering concerns that Harrison was rough with customers. The diners that night, according to Hilal, represented more than half the ownership of CP. He said he choreographed the seating to match whom he wanted to speak and in what order. His plan was to start with the most vocal shareholder who, he said, let loose. Once that person aired his grievances about CP, others felt emboldened, Hilal said. One by one, in descending order, they made their dissatisfied feelings known to Pershing. When they were done, Harrison spoke for about fifteen minutes. Even though Wes Hall said shareholders were "very, very guarded" about whom they'd vote for, by the end of the dinner, Hilal said Pershing felt "strongly encouraged" it would have support to unseat the board and replace Green with Harrison.

After the events in Toronto, Hilal, along with Hall, flew with Harrison on the railroader's personal jet to meet investors in New York, Baltimore, Los Angeles, San Diego, San Francisco, Vancouver, and Victoria, all in five days.[12] "Hunter's an animal, right," Hilal said. "He's like all over it." Hall says he got a "mini-MBA" from Harrison on the trip, not only on railroading, but on how to manage a business. He wasn't the only one. Hall said the railroader educated shareholders at each stop.

It was all part of a full frontal by Pershing and Harrison. Both were more than willing to speak with the media and both did so effectively. CP, though, was mostly unwilling. Cleghorn did speak with the *Globe and Mail* (published January 9, 2012), saying "This is a longer-term issue, rather than a few days on the market. Replacing our CEO and jeopardizing our successful multi-year plan is not in the best interest of CP or its shareholders." Four days after the town hall, CN amended its lawsuit against Harrison. His former employer canceled his pension and certain other benefits.

Meanwhile, Canadian Pacific hunkered down. It was worried not only about Harrison's approach, particularly with customers, but also about the potential legal implications of hiring him, given his arrangement with CN. But Pershing was its biggest shareholder and the stock

---

12   After leaving CN, Harrison bought his own jet, a used Hawker.

had also appreciated significantly since Pershing started buying it. It was now well over $70 a share. The railroad's board was getting boxed in by the move in the stock.

On March 7, CP made another letter public. It included testimonials from CP customers, but offered little else. On March 22, CP launched its strongest attack on Harrison. In a letter to shareholders, Cleghorn said CP's board "believes that Mr. Harrison is not the right leader for Canadian Pacific." Five days later, Fred Green lit into Harrison at CP's investor day, saying that he didn't seem to understand the physics of curves and grades, two factors faced by Canadian Pacific. He also brought up the familiar refrain about customers—that Harrison's previous time in Canada "was not pleasant" and that "virtually every statement made by Mr. Harrison about this franchise has been just plain, flat wrong."

Cleghorn capped the session with a statement that tempted the gods. "My fellow directors have had, like everybody in this room, I suppose, from time to time, the odd bad day in business. But insofar as I know, no real association with failure, and we don't intend to start here." On April 20, CP reported first quarter results. Its operating ratio was 80.1 percent—Pershing and Harrison were promising to get it to 65 percent in 2015, the fourth year of a turnaround. But on April 26, CP said hiring Harrison "would delay and damage CP's value-generating plan." The railroad's defense sounded weak in comparison to the attack.

On May 3, just two weeks before the annual meeting, proxy advisory firm ISS said shareholders should vote for the Pershing slate, a devastating blow to CP's board.

"I can tell you that if I'm running a fight where there is 70 percent of the stock held by institutions," said Wes Hall, "and ISS is not supportive of my side, I have a problem, a big problem."

The CP board went down swinging. In its response, the railroad went harder at ISS than it had at Pershing. In a multi-page release, CP called the report inaccurate, misleading, and flawed. Two days later, CP said the verdicts of two other shareholder advisory groups had "reached the wrong conclusion in recommending that shareholders vote in favor of all seven of the Pershing Square nominees."

But it was a lost cause. The night before the annual meeting, in the bar of a Calgary hotel, a last-minute surrender was arranged by outside lawyers for both sides. Just prior to the meeting, CP announced that Cleghorn, Green, and four other directors were resigning. Ackman's read was that until the last minute, Cleghorn was convinced he would win the vote. The American activist said that Canadian investors were too polite—they weren't telling Cleghorn to his face that they were going to vote for Pershing's slate. A former CP director, however, countered this, saying it was very clear from major institutional shareholders that they couldn't take a chance on the stock. "We're voting for change," they said. "You gotta go cut a deal with Ackman." He didn't buy Ackman's view that Cleghorn hadn't realized it.

Ackman had encountered northern resistance when trying to recruit Canadian directors and pension funds—resistance to coming out against the country's establishment. You're right about CP, they told him. We love your idea, but we can't do it. Call us after the vote. The first Canadian director Pershing secured was Rebecca MacDonald, the furthest thing from a member of the establishment. A woman, an immigrant, and a successful business person, she was suggested to Pershing by Vancouver billionaire Jimmy Pattison. But MacDonald said she was sent a message by another billionaire friend, who passed along a warning of the implications of joining Pershing's slate of candidates for the board. After a dinner with Ackman at her estate in the Dominican Republic, she signed on anyway. Paul Haggis, the former CEO of the Ontario Municipal Retirement System—a large pension fund—was also recruited. He said he had been on the board of the bank of the iconic retailer, Canadian Tire. His announcement, he said, that he was joining the Pershing slate had raised concerns at the bank's parent company, and he stepped down from the bank's board. One friend who was also an institutional investor reacted to Haggis's joining the Pershing slate by joking, "Well, as long as you don't want to go to the Toronto Club, you're fine," a reference to the establishment haunt of the corporate elite.

In all, the Pershing slate was seven people, including Ackman and Hilal. Pershing's victory was a landslide—shareholders voted overwhelmingly in favor of its nominees.[13] The fact that three proxy advisory firms recommended voting for the activist firm's slate was "the kiss of

---

13 During the proxy fight, a major Canadian pension fund CEO said in a road show meeting that "they [CP] need a kick in the teeth," a strong signal CP's board would lose the vote.

death" for the incumbent board, according to Haggis. At the brief annual meeting, Ackman said Cleghorn told him, "Don't screw it up." One of Pershing's advisors said Cleghorn then "gracefully" left the meeting.

Harrison was in Calgary but did not attend. Given that it was ultimately the board's decision to appoint the CEO, he didn't want his presence to affect—or appear to affect—the outcome. But immediately after the annual shareholders' meeting, there was a board meeting. Ackman described it as "the most tense board meeting I've ever had," even "very hostile." It was important that a healing process begin. But there would be one last battle. Pending the result of a CEO search, the surviving board members wanted to install CP's CFO Kathryn McQuade as interim chief executive and Tony Ingram as chair (Ingram was a former COO at the American railroad CSX and appointee of the previous CP board). In Ackman's estimation, this indicated that the old board wanted to retain control and block Harrison's appointment. It did not go over well. Ackman's yelling could be heard outside the room in the hallway. Did you not see what happened in there today? he asked the board.

"There was no grace about him [Ackman] at all. He berated people," said a person familiar with what happened. "He hit like a bully in a school yard."

The activist investor said he tries "to be very gracious," but he told the holdover directors that if they didn't respect the vote, Pershing would force another vote and replace them all. Ackman said that Pershing wanted Steve Tobias (now deceased) as interim CEO. Tobias was the former COO of US railroad Norfolk Southern and a widely respected railroader who had also joined the Pershing slate, the pro-Harrison contingent. The board ultimately relented; Tobias was appointed interim chief executive and Paul Haggis became chairman. Hilal described Haggis as someone with superior social skills and emotional intelligence who could help salve wounds on the board.

Within weeks, other legacy board members resigned. Meantime, Harrison flew home to the US, landing in the wee hours of the morning. He would have to wait another six weeks to be appointed CEO. Harrison was under the clear impression he would run CP, but one shareholder, British Columbia Investment Management (BCIM), wanted a proper search process. To get BCIM's support, Hilal had promised an executive search for the CEO position. This, however, came as something of a surprise to Harrison. On April 23, 2012, Mark Wallace and his wife, Josée, were at home in Toronto watching Ackman being interviewed on my program when the Pershing CEO said that once the proxy war was won, there would be a search for a CEO. Their jaws dropped. Suddenly Harrison had gone from fair-haired boy to part of a search list.

"Hunter said, 'What the hell is this?' I remember," Hilal said.

Hilal described the search as "perfunctory" yet appropriate. But the result was never in doubt. Ackman said "it was ridiculous" but "we did it to appease the corporate governance folks." An executive recruiting firm was paid $40,000 to do a search that was, for all intents and purposes, for show. It would have been a very short list of candidates. Who was going to beat out Hunter Harrison? In fact, Paul Haggis, the new chairman, said that he wrote the memo outlining the criteria that the search firm would have to consider when scouring for a CEO candidate. In essence, Haggis said he detailed all of Harrison's qualifications for the job. There was only one person who could possibly check all the boxes—Harrison. "And he was available," Haggis laughed.

But if he was hands down the best person for the job, why had Cleghorn and the CP board fought so hard to keep him from replacing Fred Green? It remains a vexing question, and there is no shortage of opinions as to the answer.

WHEN HARRISON LEFT Quebec after his tenure at CN, many were happy to see him go in spite of the exponential increase in the value of the company during his stewardship. While the results he achieved were highly respected, he did not go out of his way to endear himself to the establishment, French or English. When the Montreal Expos became the first Major League Baseball team to be located outside of the United States—in a Francophone province, no less—the team's first star, Louisiana-native Rusty Staub, made an effort to learn some French and became a folk hero in Quebec. Harrison made next to zero effort. At one gathering, he opened with "Bonjour, y'all," which was pure Harrison and good for laughs, but not much more. According to his daughter Cayce, he used the language training course Rosetta Stone once and then packed in any efforts to learn.

In 2007, Harrison said former prime minister Paul Martin contacted him to ask CN for help with Martin's efforts to assist Indigenous communities. While he said Martin did not specifically ask for a donation, Harrison became aggravated, explaining to Martin that at that time, certain members of an Indigenous group were blocking CN's main line east of Toronto (the protest was to educate Canadians about a range of issues affecting Indigenous peoples, including poverty and land claims, as well as dropout and suicide rates).

"Mr. Martin, do you know what those people have done, or are doing to us as we speak?"

While it may not have been ideal timing for the call, the old school-yard brawler with the "rabbit ears and red ass" was never far from surfacing. Harrison could have said that, given the protests, it was awkward for the company to make a gift. He could have offered to send Martin a personal donation, but he did not view optics as part of his job. Martin said he called a lot of companies and would have called CN but did not remember the call Harrison described.

Given certain perceptions of Harrison, when it came time for John Cleghorn to decide whether to meet the railroader or to accept Bill Ackman's proposal to bring Harrison aboard, it's conceivable Cleghorn and others on CP's board had formed an unfavorable view of him. Cleghorn is also a history buff and a generous supporter of efforts to teach Canadian history. The notion of an all-guns-blazing type from south of the border—backed by a US activist hedge fund—barging in to run a historic company like Canadian Pacific could have added to the resolve to block the Ackman-Harrison alliance.

Bill Ackman thought it was Canadian pride. He said the board was embarrassed at the prospect of an American hedge fund and an American CEO coming in to run a company so woven into Canada's national fabric. "It was almost like the board was a board of an important charitable institution," he said. "Like it was an honorary society." This was in spite of the fact that through the fall of 2011 and all of 2012, Americans held more CP stock than Canadians.

As for Ackman's pride analysis, "That wouldn't be the full answer, but you can put a small tick mark beside that, absolutely," said one former director. "It would be naive to not give it some weight." Additionally, a person familiar with CP's board at time said that Ackman "triggered" something in Cleghorn that made him want to fight. While a former director said important constituents had advised against hiring Harrison—that he was "past his best-buy date"—the resistance was less about Harrison than it was about Ackman, who had "the most irksome, prickly, negative style that made it very difficult for people to hang around for more than fifteen minutes."

Cleghorn, according to one account of what happened when Pershing made its demands known, went around the boardroom table and individually asked each director if they were 100 percent behind Fred Green, as though they had to swear "a pledge of allegiance." Another person in the room said that it would have been a stretch to say all the directors were 100 percent behind Green. Some wanted to engage with the activists and look for a solution in the best interests of shareholders. "There were differences of view," one said, resisting the use of the word factions. Certain of the board's advisors had encouraged CP's directors to cut a deal. But it was Ackman's style—particularly his abrasiveness—that really bothered the board. "Those guys [Ackman and Hilal] were never going to negotiate," said one director. In particular, long-time CP director Roger Phillips was said to be in high dudgeon about the American activists and was also influential with Cleghorn. "Just keep telling these guys to go to hell," said the unnamed director. "That would have been Roger's thing."

"From the perspective of some of the legacy directors, this was their sandbox," Hilal said. "This was their playground, and no one was welcome to it unless they invited them. And they didn't want to risk losing control of their sandbox, and they would if Hunter became CEO."

Certainly, when Harrison left CN, his successor was not another American, although that wouldn't be unusual. A Canadian, Claude Mongeau, who had been the highly regarded CFO of the railroad, got the job and performed admirably. But prior to Harrison being hired at CP, Paul Tellier said his former colleague flew to Montreal to have dinner with him. Harrison wanted to know what his old boss thought of him vying for the top job at CN's arch rival. They dined again at the Mount Royal Club, where they'd sealed the Illinois Central transaction during the ice storm.

"Well, it's not my style," Tellier told Harrison. While it was a friendly dinner, Tellier told him, "I wouldn't do it." He said he viewed it as a cultural issue—that it would be frowned upon in Canada but perhaps accepted in the United States. Americans, after all, had seen auto executive Lee Iacocca run Ford, then Chrysler. Tellier also said he sensed Harrison's bitterness about his departure from CN. Charlie Baillie, TD's former CEO, who'd been on CN's board, said, "I was a little disappointed when he retired and he went to run CP." Baillie said that in the Canadian banking sector, with just five or six large banks, it would have been inconceivable for him to have jumped to another bank, "and we only have two railroads in Canada." Baillie added that he "wasn't the only banker with that reaction." Although he wouldn't identify any other banker, it's not unreasonable to surmise Cleghorn might fit the description. Granting that Harrison had "every right to do it," Baillie said he viewed the railroader jumping to CP as "not dishonorable, but disloyal."

Harrison may not have endeared himself to other CEOs across the country either, a closely knit, relatively small and influential group of people. Jim Gray, the former Alberta energy executive who was on CN's board for more than a decade, said, "Hunter was never one to toady up to the bureaucracy in Ottawa or other executives in Canada." Indeed, on the latter point, Gray recalled trying to convince Harrison to attend meetings of the Business Council on National Issues (later the Canadian Council of CEOs and now the Business Council of Canada), a gathering of the company's top chief executives.[14] It didn't work. Harrison had no time for that. Gray said that such an attitude "projects an aloofness" to Canadians. As a result, other Canadian CEOs, many of whom served on the boards of other companies, may have been less inclined to go to bat for Harrison when he wanted to return to Canada. Harrison said then-director and former Suncor CEO Rick George told him that he needed to be more involved in the community, meaning charitably. "You don't give back," he said George told him during his formal interview for the CP job. It wasn't enough for the corporations that Harrison ran to donate money to local causes; Harrison had to step up himself, was the message from George. Once again, as in the late 1980s at Burlington

---

14 Since 2015, I have been contracted to moderate at the Council's conferences.

Northern or in the 2000s at CN, there were clearly those who'd been irked by him.

"Hunter is an in-your-face guy," Ackman said. "And by the way, the board of Canadian National was sick of him," adding that Harrison could be "a bully in the boardroom." Ackman said he's sure that word got around.

But while Harrison was a thorny character to some in the Canadian business, political, and regulatory circles, in many respects the resistance of the CP board may have been more about Ackman. While Ackman said he tries to be gracious, others didn't view him that way. Reacting to Ackman's comments about *him* being a bully in the boardroom, Harrison fired back, saying, "Bill's pissed more boards off than I ever thought about" (and the two were friends). Ackman had also targeted a large Canadian company. The country's business elite didn't have to think far beyond CP—to their own companies. If they let an activist take charge of one, which one would be next? Most certainly, the trend has gained momentum. In subsequent years, activists took positions in very large public companies—General Electric, Nestle, General Motors, and Proctor & Gamble.

This Canadian resistance to activist investors played out in another sphere in this timeframe. During Pershing's attempt to install Harrison at CP, the hedge fund tried to enlist a major Canadian institutional investor—specifically, a major pension fund—to join Pershing as a financial partner in its crusade to change things at CP. Pershing went to several pension funds, but it was a non-starter at all of them. One of the pitches was at a luncheon meeting. When the fund was told by the activists that they had a plan to turn around CP, one person in the room wisecracked, "What are you going to do? You're going to hire Hunter Harrison?"

"Yeah, that's exactly what we're going to do," Pershing said. As Hilal described it, one of the fund's executives was slathering mustard on his bread when Ackman told the group that Pershing had recruited Harrison. At first, Hilal said the executive who'd been making the sandwich thought Ackman was joking. When he realized that he wasn't, the mustard knife stopped—mid-spread. The pension fund, according to Ackman and Hilal, had a short position in CP. That meant it had borrowed CP stock and sold it in the market, betting that it could buy it back at a cheaper price and pocket the difference. Without the information about Harrison, Hilal said there was a good argument for the short position. But now that the pension fund knew about the Harrison factor, which was arguably a catalyst for the stock, the fund was exposed to the possibility of a loss on its position. Arguably, with Harrison in the picture, CP's shares were more likely to go up than down. But a person familiar with the situation said if there was a short position, it would have been small, and explained the surprised reaction in the room another way. The pension fund would "probably" have joined in the investment as a partner, he said, but was miffed at Pershing because the activists were approaching the fund later in the game when CP's stock was already higher. It would have liked to participate from the get-go, the source said.

The hedge fund also spoke with Michael Sabia, who had moved on from CN (and later Bell Canada/BCE) to become CEO of the giant provincial pension fund, Caisse de dépôt et placement du Québec. Pershing wanted to know if the Caisse would invest in CP with Harrison as the new chief. Sabia said Pershing had a "very well done book on what Hunter was going to be able to do at CP." Hilal described Sabia rifling through the pages of the presentation deck at rapid-fire speed, head in his hands, shaking his head.

"These are the numbers that Hunter looked at when he was evaluating the railroad," Hilal quoted Sabia as saying. He said the pension fund boss told them they were going to make a fortune, but "we can't do it." Hilal interpreted Sabia's response as an indication that politically in Quebec, the Caisse couldn't invest in something that could hurt or be perceived to hurt CN, a Montreal-based company. While the Caisse's job is to make money for Quebec pensioners, it has a dual mandate—it's expected to be supportive of businesses based in the province. Sabia "deeply respected Hunter," Hilal said, but "you could see him suffering because he couldn't take advantage of an opportunity he knew would be a home run."

Sabia emphatically said that the Caisse's decision to not participate with Pershing had nothing to do with the so-called dual mandate and "had absolutely nothing to do with Hunter." Principally, Sabia said, he didn't want to get involved with—or go "anywhere near"—an activist investor. Sabia said he wasn't saying "what they [Pershing] do is necessarily bad," but the Caisse, he argued, was a brand, and he was determined to propagate the image of an institution that invested for the long term, patiently. That brand, he maintained, would vaporize in a moment if the Caisse joined forces with Ackman and Hilal. His second reason was personal. CN had been good to him, life was long, and he felt it would be inappropriate to join with those trying to bolster the fortunes of its competitor. The Caisse was also a large shareholder of CN. Sabia said he knew, however, what Harrison would do at CP. "This was a layup," he said in July 2017. "He's probably the only railroading genius on the planet. I didn't have any doubt what was going to happen at CP." He was right. CP shareholders would make a ton of money.

Most certainly the upper reaches of Canadian business have the characteristics of a tight club. Many titans of Canadian commerce went to the same schools as children. As adults, they summer and winter in the same enclaves. They see each other in Muskoka or the Eastern Townships in July and August and then in Naples or Palm Beach, Florida, at Christmas. And that's just the East. The West, where CP is headquartered, is an even smaller community when it comes to the business elite. But it also makes sense that Canadian business is clubby. Canada is just a tenth the size of the United States, not only in population, but also in the size of the economy. Canada's business leaders have to do business with each other constantly, in the concentrated arenas of a few major cities or, for that matter, a few blocks. At a certain level, they have to get along in order for the country to work, and they don't like to feel as though they're the fifty-first state. Hunter Harrison may not have been blind to that reality, but he paid it no heed.

Of course, there is also hypocrisy in Canada's clubby stance. While Canadian business people might fiercely protect the club, they also want to be global players. Witness the country's pension funds acquiring assets all over the world or the Canadian banks and pipeline companies buying operations in the United States—not to mention Canadian railroads buying American ones.

Ultimately, as the proxy contest evolved and just days before the annual meeting, two prominent Canadian pension funds, Canada

Pension Plan Investment Board and Ontario Teachers' Pension Plan, said they would vote for the Pershing slate. It was a crucial public endorsement, Hilal said, "permission to other Canadians that it's not unpatriotic" to vote on the side of the Americans.

On June 29, 2012, CP announced the appointment of Hunter Harrison as president and CEO. The money that Harrison was to be paid by CN had been canceled, but it would ultimately be covered by CP, having been initially guaranteed by Pershing.[15] Meanwhile, CN's legal proceedings against Harrison were still ongoing and his former employer released a statement that was part congratulatory, part warning. It wished him well at CP but said it would "monitor events, and, if it appears that Mr. Harrison is using confidential CN information, CN might seek injunctive relief." Against all odds, Hunter Harrison was back, larger than life.

---

15 Harrison's compensation would be what was agreed to with Pershing Square. Annual salary of $2,050,000 (base salary $550,000 plus what he had been owed by CN for his annual pension), 650,000 options and 25,000 deferred share units vesting over four years, eligibility for annual equity awards based on the company's profitability and other factors as determined each year by the Board of Directors, eligibility for tax equalization payments to compensate for higher tax liabilities in Canada, if any, compared to those applicable in the United States, as well as personal use of company aircraft.

8 TURNAROUND

IT WASN'T A good start. Hunter Harrison walked into CP's head office for the first time at the beginning of July 2012. Other than Harrison and his chief of staff, Mark Wallace (who'd rejoined his old boss after an interlude working in other industries), there were few senior people in the office. One was Peter Edwards, the VP of human resources who had helped devise and run the Hunter Camps at CN and co-written Harrison's two manuals. The other was Paul Guthrie, CP's chief legal officer. Guthrie was wearing a cowboy hat, cowboy boots, and jeans. He recalled Harrison looking at him and saying, "Who the fuck's this guy?" Harrison wanted to know, "What the shit is goin' on?"

"It's Stampede," said one of the secretaries.

"Who gives a shit it's Stampede? This company hasn't made a penny and we're worried about Stampede, having a few shooters at noon?" While the annual Calgary Stampede is huge in the life of the city, being absent that morning wasn't the way to make a positive impression on the new boss.

Guthrie's office was right next to Harrison's. He could hear the new CEO hollering through the wall. Harrison wanted action and he wanted it fast. Guthrie quickly learned his new boss had no tolerance for lawyers like himself telling him they'd have answers to his questions in six weeks. But Harrison would also use his gruff sense of humor to disarm Guthrie, telling him that his "judgment had been clouded" by the fact that he'd had legal training.

Once people were back in the office from Stampede, Harrison imme-diately began assessing them. According to Guthrie, "He made quick decisions. Okay, I've spoken to you for two minutes and I don't think you're needed on the voyage."

Harrison also didn't like head office, which he called the "glass house" in downtown Calgary. It would not be long for this world. For starters, he didn't like floor-to-ceiling windows.

"There was virtually no privacy."

It was also the opposite of what he thought a revamped railroad needed—in-your-face contact with railcars. Harrison would soon announce that he was relocating head office to *a rail yard.* CP's head-quarters would be where the action was—next to the tracks. That would be at Ogden yard, which, when Harrison went to see it, was covered in graffiti. The lease was coming up for renewal at the office downtown, and he told Wallace they were getting out of it. Fortunately, ConocoPhil-lips was looking for space and paid CP a $5 million bonus to move out quickly. Building a new headquarters at Ogden would cost $38 million, but Harrison said the company saved between $20 and $25 million by being out of downtown, so the new space paid for itself in a year and a half. Ogden not only includes the control center for the entire railroad, directing approximately four hundred trains a day and some 50,000 railcars, but also has a gym, running track, and sumptuous executive offices. This was all in keeping with Harrison's view that it was import-ant to work in comfortable spaces and put forward your best.

Like he had done at CN, Harrison also visited the mail room, a place he believed sent profound signals about a company. To him, it looked "like *Sanford and Son,*" a reference to the 1970s sitcom about a junk-yard. But instead of an irascible Fred Sanford and his frustrated son Lamont, the CP mail room was staffed that day by a woman who Harri-son said was "scared to death" of the fire-breathing new CEO prowling around her lair. Scanning the room, Harrison noticed a large FedEx box with several laptops inside, sitting on a scale.

"Where's that goin'?" he asked.

She told him it was being shipped to Alyth, a nearby yard in the southeastern part of the city.

"We use FedEx? To go to Alyth?" Harrison asked, dumbfounded. "To go eight miles away?" Her day was about to get worse.

"Young lady," Harrison said, "Do you know where it goes? It goes to Memphis [then FedEx's main hub]. I can put it in the back of my car and have it there in two minutes."

It might have taken him more than two minutes, but the point was made. Things would be done differently. Like at CN, nose-to-nose encounters with the new chief had a way of resonating throughout the organization. Harrison also said he made a point of breaking something while he paid his visit. In fact, he didn't hide the fact that he did, in such situations, purposely break a piece of equipment or throw something out the window—a phone, for instance—to send a message that quickly spread. Although he denied that his purposeful performances created a culture of fear, those on the receiving end could be forgiven for feeling differently. He was nothing if not an expert at getting his point across, in a way that suggested serious consequences if he was not obeyed.

"He really meant that. I better do it," was the signal, loud and clear. Harrison knew he could be viewed as a "time bomb," and for the most part he didn't care, although he was highly sensitive to criticism that he was mean or had created an environment where employees were scared of him.

Guthrie saw it differently. Yes, Harrison was very direct. "But it was always on the basis of 'this is what we need to do in order to succeed.'" He said Harrison was "incredibly inclined to educate people" and gracious to those who wanted to learn. He'd get out charts and explain where they'd gone wrong the night before with their operating plan. "He explained it," Guthrie said, adding, "I bought into it." Guthrie was unlikely to be cowed. He was an experienced, older lawyer, former marine, and former police officer. Still, whatever your rank, the worst thing you could do was lie, Guthrie said. "He [could] smell a lie. You can do anything but tell a lie." Guthrie managed to survive the transition from the old CP to Harrison's CP. Now back in private practice in Calgary, he maintains Harrison was able to get people to follow, calling him "the best leader of all the people I've had as leaders."

One of those who followed was Nadeem Velani, who'd been Harrison's chief of staff at CN after Mark Wallace. In 2013, Velani went to work at CP. "I missed the action of being in the midst of it all," Velani said, "getting a second chance to work with Hunter."

Velani had moved to Canada from Nairobi when he was two years old. He couldn't get over the fact that an immigrant from East Africa had prospered under the tutelage of the street fighter from Memphis. He rose from trainee at CN to investor relations to chief of staff. He conceded, however, that while working for Harrison at CN, he paid a personal price. Velani didn't take a vacation for four years.

"You could never turn off," he said. "The railroad doesn't turn off." Velani's words could have come out of Harrison's mouth. It had, however, paid off career-wise. Velani ultimately rose to become CP's chief financial officer after the company went through several who didn't last. He believed Harrison got the best out of people, but they had to buy in just as he did. When he awoke at four in the morning, unable to sleep, Velani would check the railroad's daily revenue tally. Harrison trained people to care so much, they worked around the clock.

It wasn't long before Harrison's tried and true efficiency practices started to kick in at CP. "No quits, locomotives, the car fleet, the downsizing . . . the standard story," he said. One of the first questions he asked was how many employees there were.

"I don't think anybody knows," he was told. "It depends on how you want to count it." For starters, the company had a different head count depending on the season, not to mention contractors and consultants. Once again, it was not what you wanted to tell the new CEO, but better to tell the truth than to fudge it. When it was clear he wasn't going to get an answer, he had a suggestion.

"Let's just count paychecks."

That number was 19,200. Again, it was the simple query that yielded the answer Harrison wanted. In the first year, 4,500 reductions were earmarked. Rule number one: no consultants without Harrison's approval—and he added they wouldn't get his approval. By the time he left, the number of people getting paychecks from CP was approximately 11,300 to 11,400. Eighty-five percent of the reductions were via attrition, according to his reckoning. Most people moved on or retired. Some, however, couldn't accept change and were let go.[1]

---

1   By 2017, CP was hiring again. Workers, for example, who'd been laid off in Smiths Falls, Ontario, were being hired back. As for reductions by attrition, Peter Edwards estimated the number to be 90 percent.

FOR YEARS, THE railroader had been studying CP from afar, first as CEO of its arch-competitor, CN, then as a CEO-in-waiting. He knew where the fat lay.

"I had a sense of intuition, gut feel, but not a lot of facts," he said. "Their culture was pretty permissive." There were indications of this while he was running CN. During one of the Hunter Camps, a top CP executive had come as an observer. When the session finished, Harrison said the man raved about it.

"Would y'all ever do something like this [a Hunter Camp]?" he asked the CP executive. Harrison recalled that the man started laughing, adding that there was no one in their organization who could do it.

On his second or third day at head office, Harrison noticed a large group of people—perhaps thirty—gathered in a conference room.

"I said, who is that in there?"

"That's the practice team."

"For what?"

"For the earnings release."

Kaboom.

"Y'all go waste your time doing something productive," he advised them. "I don't practice."

Every second he was at head office, he was evaluating the team, particularly the senior members. As usual, he didn't hide his sharp edge. At the time, CP owned the Delaware and Hudson Railway (D&H). It had been purchased in 1991 as a link from Montreal down through New England and New York to Pennsylvania. Harrison didn't think CP should own it and eventually sold it to Norfolk Southern. But soon after arriving in Calgary, he asked for a one-pager about the D&H. Instead of a one-page synopsis of the key issues, Harrison said he was handed two sheets of graph paper with one line going down and one line going up. There were also two circles on the paper. He took it to mean, "Here's what you get. Nuthin'." The next morning, he called the person who'd drawn it to his office and said, "This ain't going to work."

"What?"

"You. Workin' for us."

"Could I ask why?"

"Sit your ass down there and about three hours later I'll be through with your ass."

"You're right about something," the executive told him. "This isn't going to work."

Harrison, meanwhile, was privately worried "nobody might work" at CP. To him, there were clearly personnel problems. As he told me in a TV interview in December 2012, six months into the job, "Look, I'm the coach. The game is won on the field. They are the players." He needed some new players and had to teach new skills to the ones who were there. Still, among the rank and file, there was embarrassment about being the worst performer of the big railroads. "No one likes to be in last place," said Tony Marquis, who, after leaving CN and then running a Colombian railroad, moved to CP to become a senior VP of operations.

Soon, non-operating people like computer programmers would be trained as conductors. Managers would learn how to drive trains. This would not only give the company flexibility, but office workers would learn what it was like on the front lines of actually operating a railroad. "Nothing was sacred" was the message. Shape up or get out. And it had to be done quickly. Harrison didn't have the benefit of Paul Tellier having run CP for six years before he, Harrison, arrived. He had a four-year contract with CP to make drastic changes. Harrison wanted everyone to do it faster. Soon the whiteboarding exercises began, redesigning train schedules and closing four hump yards. As a result, CP would, day by day, become more efficient. Ackman and Harrison had promised investors that the railroad's operating ratio would, over the course of four years, drop to 65 percent from an embarrassing industry high of more than 81 percent.

Edmond Harris, a former CN executive who was one of two railroaders appointed to the CP board in late 2011 in order to bolster its industry credentials, told the *Financial Post* in March 2012 that "I fell out of the chair when I heard that." He went on to tell reporter Scott Deveau that Harrison had no apparent strategy to get to that number and that while Harrison had a reputation as an operator, he was unfamiliar with Canadian Pacific's property, geography, and structural challenges. Harris had worked for Harrison and added that he came with "a bit of baggage" and had "left Canada maybe not with the best relations with regulators as well as elected politicians and certainly some of the customers."[2]

That same day, Harrison appeared on my interview program and responded: "I would suggest to you, relationships don't make business. So, maybe I'm a little harsh. Maybe I have a little baggage," he said. "Everywhere I've been at, we've gained market share and been able to increase price. And I think that's the important thing, and that's driven on the product you have."

In fact, the OR had been lowered from an even higher level in the quarters prior to Harrison's arrival, as CP's old team desperately tried to prove it was making progress. In Harrison's words, the operating ratio improvement he promised would mean "billions of dollars" for shareholders, of which he was now one.

He was right. After only eighteen months on the job—the fourth quarter of 2013—the operating ratio was 65.9 percent, an all-time record for the company. It would soon surpass that. Two and a half years into his tenure—the end of the fourth quarter of 2014—CP's OR was 59.8 percent, better than CN's 60.7. The stock rose from CAD $47.72 when Ackman first bought in the autumn of 2011 to $241 in the fall of 2014. CNBC's Scott Wapner reported "it is being called the greatest corporate turnaround in corporate history." It was huge, but one could certainly make the argument there had been bigger corporate turnarounds than CP. Apple, for example, was on the verge of bankruptcy in 1997 when Microsoft injected $150 million to help it creep back to life and become the world's most valuable company with a market value of $943 *billion* in May 2018. Nonetheless, Harrison had orchestrated a startling turnaround at CP. It was a massive success for shareholders. The Apple contrast is intriguing, however. While Harrison, the unrivaled operator, did not envision a global computing goliath, in certain respects, he was the Steve Jobs of railroading: uncompromising, unrelenting, fierce, antagonistic, confrontational, and a winner.

Over time, however, comments from the disgruntled would leak, not unlike what happened under Steve Jobs. There was fatigue. No matter

2 Harris declined an invitation to be interviewed. On January 8, 2018, he was named executive VP of operations at CSX.

what you did, more was always expected. Ken Lewenza, who followed Buzz Hargrove as president of the CAW, said that what happened under Harrison could be seen in the number of grievances filed at CN and CP. "No sector had more grievances on the books than Hunter Harrison's era," he said. While he said he respected Harrison's direct, no-BS approach and realized that a more efficient, profitable company was generally good for workers, Lewenza said it was Harrison's way or no way. He was heavy-handed, Lewenza said. "I could put GM, Ford, and Chrysler's grievances combined together and their [the railroads'] grievances would be ten times higher." Change, as Harrison had himself said many times, was hard.

Even among Harrison's staunchest supporters, though, there were questions about him going to extremes. "I mean, he's amazing," Michael Sabia said, citing the upside of what Harrison had been able to accomplish—his record results and inspiration. "But, you know, there is another side to the coin." Sabia went on to say, "He can be, sometimes I think, probably too tough on people." His point was that while it was one thing to maximize returns for shareholders, there was an array of stakeholders that had to be considered. Among others, employees fell into that category.

Some CP workers complained that under the Harrison regime, they were afraid to call in sick. So many people had departed that there simply wasn't the backup. By the same token, as an employee, you knew that if one of your co-workers got sick, you'd be covering for them too. There was also, among some, a hesitancy to be uprooted and moved to other locations across the country. Their families, communities, and social lives were important to them. Harrison had no time for either grievance, countering that the company had supervisors off all the time for sickness.

"I worked a lot of days when I was sick," he responded, unable to resist. "Go somewhere you don't have to work when you're sick." Harrison did, in fact, work while he was sick—through his last year and a half at CP and after. But the people raising the issue earned a fraction of what he earned, plus they may not have shared his obsession for railroading, even though they might have loved their jobs. And few employees are interested in how hard the boss's life is. But that wasn't enough to sway Harrison. As for being transferred, he was not the one to complain to about that, having moved repeatedly. You don't want to move to Moose Jaw? Well, accept the fact that your career at the railroad will not blossom, he warned.

"If you want to be a supervisor and you're not mobile, it's going to be difficult to meet your optimum potential," he said. What he believed in, however, was incentivizing people to go to out-of-the-way places—extra money and a bonus if you stuck it out for a certain amount of time. He was rewarded along the way and believed money motivated people. In addition to a pat on the back, it was a way to get the best out of them.

Harrison also changed supervisory schedules. Instead of having people on three twelve-hour shifts a week, he proposed five eight-hour shifts. He favored straight salary plus bonus. In other cases, hourly wages. If a supervisor needed to work forty-five hours a week to get his or her job done, that person wouldn't get overtime. But if he or she did a good job, there was the opportunity for a bonus. At CN, he had faced resistance after suggesting five eight-hour shifts.

"I don't think the boys are going to like that," said one Winnipeg superintendent.

"We're runnin' this railroad," Harrison said. "Put 'em on five-eights."

He said he took the superintendent position away from that employee and sent him to Edmonton to work nights. Over time, Harrison gave him another chance. That person became CN's chief operating officer, Mike Cory. Cory said the friction with Harrison was actually over another issue, but the message was the same. "I wasn't pushing people hard enough." The CN executive said he took it as a lesson in management. "He was the greatest teacher I ever came across, next to my father."

Harrison said just because a policy was set at the top didn't mean it would be administered as it was meant to be. "Which ones do you keep and which ones do you fire? You can't have it both ways," he says. "If they don't do what they're told, how can you handle it equitably below them?" In spite of the criticisms of Harrison when it came to labor— that he was a merciless cutter—one point was overlooked. When he and Pershing Square got involved in CP, the company's pension plan had a deficit of $884 million. Its investments were doing poorly and it was borrowing to meet its obligations to retirees. Aside from recruiting Harrison, Bill Ackman said his best contribution to the CP turnaround was advising the pension fund to shift its holdings from predominantly low-performing bonds into equities. Peter Edwards maintained pension issues were already being addressed by CP's human resources team prior to Pershing's arrival. But either way, by 2013, under Harrison, Ackman, and the new board, the pension fund moved from deficit to a surplus of $801 million. By 2015, the surplus was $1.1 billion, a clear plus for CP's workers and retirees. Still, former union leader Ken Lewenza said that while achieving a pension surplus was good for CP's workers, Harrison and Ackman dealt with it through the lens of shareholders. "If anybody thinks he [Harrison] did it because he genuinely cared about workers, I don't buy it." That may have been the case, but unions also hadn't seen Harrison go to bat for them behind closed doors. Initially in 2006, he was one of ten Canadian CEOs on then–Prime Minister Stephen Harper's North American Competitiveness Council. At a meeting, Harrison said he mentioned that he didn't notice any organized labor represented on the panel. He said his comment was brushed off and added he never went to another meeting.

For someone who crowned his career in Canada, Harrison had mixed feelings about Canadians. Being viewed as the ugly American stung. But he admitted that he'd come to Canada under the mistaken impression that Canadians were just like Americans, an uncharacteristic misfire for someone who prided himself on taking the measure of people. Harrison hadn't taken the time to understand the culture he was entering. Not that it would have mattered. Railroad efficiency was what mattered. Politics, pleasantries, and diplomacy did not. By the same token, many Canadians may have formed a simplistic, ignorant view of Harrison—a loud, brash, Southerner with a strong accent. Any thoughtful analysis would likely have ended there, with a one-dimensional stereotype of someone from Tennessee. While fond of many well-known Canadians— Paul Tellier, Michael Sabia, Jean Chretien, Frank McKenna, David Dodge, Ed Lumley, Buzz Hargrove, and the late Ron Southern—Harrison railed profanely at the country's "inferiority complex." The fact that Canadians have had to share the border with the most dominant nation in history, ten times its economic might and population, didn't register with Harrison. Equally, a sense that there was a muscular way—a Harrison way—of running a business would be lost on many Canadians who'd been accustomed to gentler methods. This was a man who was born and raised at the zenith of American power and influence. By dint of his own focus, determination, and talent, he prospered within that realm. Without a doubt, he embodied the strut that went with it, nor was he ashamed of it. In fact, he was fiercely proud of it. As a result, in a country that has traditionally celebrated low-profile behavior—knocking people down to size before they get *too big for their britches*—Harrison's time in Canada was, in certain respects, a head-on, cultural collision.

He said he and Paul Tellier joked about the different treatment they got on opposite sides of the border. In Jackson, Mississippi, the locals pulled out the Southern hospitality and fried up catfish for Tellier. Meanwhile in Montreal, to Harrison, it felt like he was public enemy number one.[3] According to former CN executive Bill Fox, there was certainly tension. Harrison's job was to change the railroad, and "it was a spectacularly inefficient place." He'd also arrived in the decade after the nationally divisive free-trade debate in Canada, Fox said, which raised the specter of a watered-down Canada—a fifty-first state where Canadian culture would disappear. "And then," he said, "you have this kind of larger than life, almost folk-figure with a heavy Southern accent coming in. And everybody kind of says, 'See?'"

But since 1999 and the IC acquisition to June 2017, the value of CN had increased some 967 percent, not including dividends (by that time, it had increased 3,605 percent, not including dividends, since the IPO in 1995). The rough-and-tumble American had helped create tens of billions of dollars in shareholder value—stemming from the purchase of *an American railroad by a Canadian company*. You can't have it both ways—buying American companies and then not wanting Americans operating in Canada. Although many shareholders of the two Canadian railroads were American, many were also

---

3   Although no one fried catfish for him, Harrison did garner accolades in Canada. In 2006, he received the B'nai Brith Canada (Quebec Region) Award of Merit. In 2007, he got an honorary doctorate from the University of Alberta and was named CEO of the Year by the *Globe and Mail's Report on Business Magazine*. In 2009, the Canadian Chamber of Commerce named him Canadian International Executive of the Year.

Canadian—including employees who owned stock—and they couldn't deny that he'd made them money, the reason they'd hired him. It brought to mind something said to Jay Leno by his manager and executive producer, Helen Kushnick, whom he fired in the early 1990s for being too tough. In the November 9, 1992, issue of the *New Yorker*, Kushnick was quoted as saying to the talk show star, "I've been serving you steak dinners for the last eighteen years. I just haven't bothered showing you how I slaughtered the cow." Truth be told, shareholders of both CN and CP were interested in the steak, not what happened to the cow.

Certainly, his sister Mary confirmed that after the CN-IC deal, Harrison felt there was culture shock on the Canadian side of CN. A lot of people didn't like a Southern sheriff coming in and telling them what to do. Still, Americans had run other Canadian companies without creating the kind of reactions associated with Harrison. Rick George, who'd been on CP's board and resigned at the board meeting when Harrison was appointed CEO, was also from the United States. But he'd built and run oil sands giant Suncor for more than twenty years without being a lightning rod.[4] As well, Scott Hand had run Inco and Dick Evans had run Alcan. Both were from the United States. Although both controversially sold their companies to foreign buyers (for rich prices), they didn't create anywhere near the static Harrison created.

To call Canadians anti-American is also too simplistic. Some are. But many Canadians like Bill Clinton and Barack Obama, while many dislike George W. Bush and Donald Trump. Frankly, there were many who worked at CN and CP who *welcomed* someone like Harrison, who shared his knowledge, took the time to teach, and wanted to make them and their companies better. The fact was, Harrison had always caused wires to arc everywhere, ever since he was a kid. He was one of those people—a confrontational, defiant, short-tempered, never-back-down-from-a-fight, agent of change. His sister Mary, who spent thirty-eight years in railroading at Frisco and then BN, said that her brother created tremors wherever he went, not just in Montreal and Calgary, but

---

4 A person familiar with George's thinking said that he accepted Harrison as chief executive but was concerned that once on the CP board, Ackman wouldn't be receptive to advice.

in the US too. His nickname at Burlington Northern, she said, was "the Headhunter."

"He would come in and he would cut," she said.

When he was assistant VP of BN's Seattle region, there were complex and difficult union issues. They stemmed from mergers and legacy collective agreements that prevented workers in different unions from doing certain work or people not working for the number of hours they were paid. Harrison changed things. One trainmaster said to Mary that he "personally knew six guys who would back their trucks up to the door and help him if he was moving." He'd eliminated positions and was not popular. He wasn't just the ugly American to Canadians, he was ugly to his fellow Americans too.

"That's exactly right," he conceded. "I am—like it or not—a stern, disciplinarian taskmaster that thinks people ought to do their job." Apparently, though, "Headhunter" was a polite nickname for him. His former colleague Sue Rathe said that in Seattle, he was also called "Seagull." Why was that? she asked Harrison. "'Cause I swoop in and shit all over everything and go away."

Once, when the "Seagull" visited CP's yard in Montreal, he was shocked at how messy it was and ordered that it be tidied. Cleanliness was important. In his view, if a place looked disorganized, it probably was disorganized. The next time he came, it looked like Mr. Clean had visited. One of the employees asked the executive who accompanied him, Guido De Ciccio, what Harrison wanted to see.

"Blue smoke," De Ciccio said.

Blue smoke? What in the hell did that mean? It meant the boss wanted to see activity. Blue smoke came out of a diesel engine as it picked up speed. Harrison grabbed a chair and plunked himself on the roof of the yard's building to eyeball the scene. Soon enough, a locomotive belched blue smoke. The crew waved to the chief sitting on the roof.

HARRISON, MEANWHILE, WASN'T getting any younger. Jeannie knew her husband better than anyone and would call Cheryl Parks, his executive assistant in Calgary, instructing her to remove any cigars and liquor from Harrison's condo. When he couldn't find his Ashton Churchill stogies, he would call Parks.

"Why'd you move them?" he asked.

"Jeannie told us to," Parks replied, having no choice.

"You're not workin' for Jeannie."

Harrison would also stay up late, often talking to employees for hours on end. He'd leave the office at 9 pm and then go out for dinner. By the time he got to bed, it would be one in the morning. Although he'd built an outdoor track and gym for employees at the new Ogden head-quarters, Harrison wasn't using either. Golf was a way he often liked to relax, and he did get a membership at an exclusive Calgary country club. But apparently, he rarely went. After Harrison departed CP, the railroad's CFO, Nadeem Velani, got his former boss's locker at the golf course. In a bizarre twist, the door of the locker had a name plate bearing the name of F.J. Green, CP's ousted CEO and Harrison's predecessor in the job. Velani said it appeared Green's personal effects were still in the locker. (Harrison said he'd never used it.)

But as Harrison began implementing his turnaround, there was great concern at CN that the railroad would lose a slew of senior employees to CP. High on that list was Keith Creel, the chief operating officer at CN, whom Harrison had nurtured from the day Creel arrived at IC in 1996. Losing a number two is serious, and not just for the day-to-day operations of the business. From a board point of view, a second-in-command is a potential successor in the event something happened to the CEO.

After Harrison left CN, Claude Mongeau was his successor. He'd previously been CFO and an excellent one, according to Harrison. Mongeau had been with the railroad since the 1990s, working under Michael Sabia and Paul Tellier. While highly analytical and strategic, he had not grown up in the railroad industry like Harrison. That was okay, though—not only had Mongeau learned much about railroading from Harrison, but Mongeau's COO was Keith Creel. Like the Tellier-Harrison relationship that saw Tellier running the company and Harrison running the railroad, a similar partnership developed between Mongeau and Creel.

After Harrison left CN, he and Creel stayed in touch. Creel's daughter was, like Harrison's daughter, an equestrian. At a horse show in October 2011, Creel had coffee with Harrison, who mentioned something might be in the works for him and CP. Creel was still working for CN and told Harrison that not only did he have a lot invested there, but he was also likely the immediate successor to Mongeau. Still, if the situation Harrison alluded to evolved and it was the right decision for Creel and his family, he would consider an opportunity. Harrison said he didn't know where it would lead and also said he was not permitted to solicit anyone until 2013, nor did he want to put Creel in a compromised position. For his part, Creel was not going to violate his commitment to CN. But if the time and circumstances came to fruition, they could talk.

Once Pershing reported that it had bought stock in CP, it wasn't long before Harrison's name came to the fore as the weapon Pershing wanted to plant at CP. If Harrison went there, the obvious question was whether Creel would be far behind. According to Creel, Mongeau phoned him over the 2011 Christmas break to ask whether Ackman had called him. "I said no, he hasn't called me, which was the truth. And I said, but if he does, then obviously, I've got a fiduciary responsibility. I'm going to be honest with you and I'll tell you."

Shortly after that, in 2012, when CN sued Harrison, Creel said he sat through a year of board meetings where "I'm thinking, that's the guy that essentially created all this success. I wouldn't say created it all. That's not fair to Paul Tellier. But he took what Paul had started and took it to a whole other level and created a whole lot of wealth for a whole lot of people sitting at the table. And here we were suing the guy and we essentially had forced him—not we, the board essentially forced him to retire," Creel said. "Here we are, we don't want him to work for us, but we don't want him to work for anybody else." In spite of Harrison's wealth, Creel believed Harrison had a right to work. "But CN felt otherwise, and obviously I had to respect CN because I was an executive at CN and I had a fiduciary responsibility and I kept it. And I kept my word, and Hunter never discussed me going to work for him during all that."

Still, Creel said it was hard for him not to be friends with Harrison because their "lives overlapped with the horses." After CN decided it was going to sue Harrison, Creel said he needed to speak with Mongeau. "And I said listen, I know what my job is here and I've got a fiduciary responsibility and I'm going to do it. But CN's not going to pick my friends. So, if you have an issue with me maintaining a friendship with Hunter that's clearly appropriate, then you need to let me know now."

During that interlude between 2009 and 2011, when Harrison was retired, their working relationship had evolved into a friendship.

Creel said Mongeau told him, "I'm not going to pick your friends. Just be smart about it. You know, don't be rubbing it in people's nose, people's faces, and just protect your fiduciary responsibility and I don't have any issue with it."

At the beginning of January 2013, when Harrison was six months into the job as CEO of CP, his non-solicit expired. That meant he was able to approach Creel about joining CP. On January 2, 2013, Creel was in Boston watching his son play hockey. Paul Hilal called and told him he'd had his phone number at the ready for a year, waiting to dial it. With Harrison now in charge and contractually in place through 2016, Creel could join CP as number two and be the obvious successor. Keeping his vow to inform Mongeau, Creel called his boss. "I said I made a commitment to you over a year ago and I'm going to keep it. You know, Paul Hilal just called me. He's presented this opportunity he wants me to consider. It's a significant position. It's the president and chief operating officer with line-of-sight to becoming the CEO." Creel told Mongeau he wanted to talk to Hilal about it. "And he told me, he said Keith, I understand. I don't want you to leave."

CP's stock price had already run up with Pershing's involvement and Harrison's arrival. Mongeau, Creel said, had asked him to consider whether there was much more value creation possible at CP. He also said Mongeau told him that he, Mongeau, would not be CEO at CN forever. Creel described having significant compensation awards at CN that were tied to him remaining there, a retention incentive. "All that money was on the table."

Still, Creel told Mongeau he was going to have the conversation with CP. He said Mongeau asked him to wait until CN's next earnings release came out in early 2013. Creel said he felt uncomfortable with that, knowing he was considering leaving the company. Mongeau said that's why he wanted Creel to wait before having any meetings with CP. So, Creel called Harrison and said he'd have to wait until after CN's earnings conference call. "I said I made a commitment and I'm going to keep it."

When the board meetings associated with the earnings call came around, Creel told the board he would be talking to CP, and he participated in the earnings call. He met with CN's chairman, David McLean, who he said told him, "Keith, I don't want you to leave; you know the way we feel about you. But we do understand if it's an opportunity you can't pass up and you've got a chance to become the CEO." McLean corroborated that. "I said Keith, if I was sitting in your chair I'd do the same thing. I think you have no choice."

But as Creel was in transit on the way to meet CP, he said Mongeau called and told him CN didn't want to lose him and if CP were to hire him, it would cost them a lot of money. "It's not going to happen easily," was the message from Mongeau. To Creel, it now appeared as though his retention award at CN was at risk, an amount in the neighborhood of $8 million. He felt he'd "busted his tail" as the COO and part of the team at CN and had earned that money, as well as his stock options and pension. "That was, I guess, a bit naive of me." If he left, there was a risk he might also have to sit on the sidelines for two years before starting at CP. "And I called Hunter and I said Hunter, I'm not going to go meet with these folks [the CP representatives]. And he said why? And I told him what happened."

Creel told Harrison he couldn't afford to take the risk of leaving CN to go to CP. Harrison said he'd call him back, which he did. "Keith," Harrison told him, "we're going to protect you, regardless." For many years, Creel had given Harrison his loyalty; Harrison was reciprocating. Creel then agreed to meet CP's people. It was at that point that Harrison began direct negotiations with Mongeau, which he described as three or four thirty- to forty-minute conversations on a weekend. To secure Creel, there was a confidential no-hire list agreed to by CP—sixty-four people at CN that CP couldn't poach for four years. Mongeau, Creel said, was concerned the market would want to know how many key CN people might follow both him and Harrison to CP.

Another person who spoke on the condition of anonymity said it included the whole executive team—the top five or six people, including Mongeau, not because they had expressed any interest in hopping to CP but because they were simply too valuable for CN to lose. Harrison said he never read the list. But his take was that if he was such a mean guy, why would that many of CN's top people even *think* of working for him?

It was a tough agreement and unusual, but everything with the situation had become unusual. In a country with a railroad duopoly—not to mention the wary eyes of North American financial markets—CN was protecting itself. "I can be critical of CN for locking all those people in, but the reality is," Creel said, "it's probably smart that they did it." Creel officially resigned from CN that Sunday afternoon. The next day, February 4, 2013, CP announced his appointment as president and chief operating officer, just over a month since Hilal called him. CN put out its own statement, announcing the end of all "outstanding litigation between CN and CP before the Federal Court in Chicago." In the release, Mongeau wished Creel well and said CN was "pleased to turn the page with respect to the matter of CP's hiring of CN's former CEO, Hunter Harrison."

Although Creel came aboard and the CEO's job was now his to lose, the saga of Hunter Harrison, railroad boss, was far from over.

9 NO DEAL

BY THE MIDDLE of 2015, Harrison had gone from robust to gaunt. He looked older. In July, CP announced that he had pneumonia (it was later ruled out) and had stents implanted in blood vessels in his legs to improve circulation. Traveling to a dry, high-altitude city like Calgary became a strain, particularly for someone occasionally short of breath. That month, he missed CP's quarterly conference call.

Harrison always worked hard and played hard. Until his fifties, he was a two-plus pack a day cigarette smoker and had consumed his share of alcohol. The spring of 1998 was the first time his habits caught up with him. At a horse show in Kentucky, he ate some barbecue. In spite of his large appetites, Harrison never got acid indigestion. But that day on the flight back to Montreal he had difficulty swallowing. At the office, one of his colleagues looked over at him in a meeting and said, "Is something wrong? You don't look very good."

"You know, I don't feel very good." The next thing he knew he was on a gurney being rushed to Montreal General. Paul Tellier assured him the city had excellent doctors and hospitals.

"Paul," Harrison recounted to a packed ballroom at the Queen Elizabeth Hotel in November 2009 after accepting an award, "get me to Chicago." The crowd roared with laughter.

There was a debate at the Montreal hospital about whether he was fit enough to fly, but Harrison insisted that when he got into that kind of trouble, he wanted to be home. Fine, but doctors insisted he be flown there on a medical aircraft with two doctors and a nurse. The plane landed at Midway Airport, where an ambulance and official entourage waited. "It was embarrassing. You would've thought the Pope was coming," Harrison said.

He was taken to hospital at University of Illinois, Chicago, and was looked after by a cardiologist who was from, of all places, Montreal. The doctor said he had major blockages in two arteries and needed double bypass surgery.

"That's when I said, 'Give me a couple of days [to] get my head screwed on right.'"

"You've got about eight minutes to get your head screwed on right," he was told.

The surgery was performed by a doctor who did heart transplants. While Harrison was in hospital, Paul Tellier and Michael Sabia visited and brought him a putter as a gift. His mother was in the room when they arrived. Tellier also gave Harrison an envelope, which he then handed to her. It was a check for seven figures, his bonus. Harrison slyly told his mother that it was his usual paycheck. She just about fainted. Tellier was struck by the closeness between Dorothy Harrison and her boy. "She was full of admiration for her son, rightly so," Tellier said. Sabia, however, was struck by what a personal visit by Tellier meant to Harrison. He was out of commission for three to four weeks but was soon fit to work again. Harrison lost twenty pounds, stopped smoking cigarettes, cut back on drinking, and switched from martinis to wine.

Fast forward more than ten years to his retirement hiatus—after he'd left CN and before Pershing launched its offensive—and he once again had circulation problems. This time it was in his legs, and he had two procedures at Johns Hopkins in Baltimore to clear blockages. Prior to the proxy war that would make him CP's CEO, he had been given a clean bill of health.

In the summer of 2015, however, Harrison was seventy years old and sick again. CP, meanwhile, was in the pink. The big changes—using 40 percent fewer locomotives, closing yards, and increasing velocity and train length—had already occurred. The operating ratio had dropped from 81 to 61 percent. And while Harrison was a tireless worker who could still be on the phone from six in the morning until midnight, he wasn't exactly trolling for a new opportunity. But Bill Ackman and Paul Hilal were, he maintained. Harrison argued that while Pershing had made a bundle with its investment in CP, it was ready to move on to a new deal, one that would resemble what had been achieved at Canadian Pacific. For Pershing, the active ingredient was Harrison. And while Harrison believed further consolidation in the rail industry was inevitable, he didn't think it would happen before he retired for the final time. For sure it would happen, Harrison prophesized, but on someone else's watch, perhaps Creel's.

There were only two logical targets for CP. It went from Vancouver across the Rockies and the prairies to North Dakota, Minnesota, and Wisconsin to Chicago; from Manitoba over Lake Superior to Toronto and Montreal; and as far as Philadelphia in the East and Kansas City in the South. The western US was served by two American railroads. Burlington Northern Santa Fe was privately owned by Warren Buffett's Berkshire Hathaway, meaning it was unavailable. It was also much too big for CP. The other western road—Union Pacific—was also too big. At the time CP was looking, UP was worth between USD $70 and $80 billion. The railroads on the eastern side of the continent were more of a geographical fit for CP and weren't as expensive. They were CSX and Norfolk Southern (NS). Efficiencies were there for the taking—mouth-watering for someone like Harrison.

While there were dozens of Class 1 railroads when Harrison started in 1963, there were now seven. But since the CN-IC deal in 1998, there had been no major railroad mergers or takeovers. Due to the Surface Transportation Board's moratorium after CN and BNSF attempted to combine, the prevailing view was that deals would have difficulty getting approval from regulators. Few, however, knew better than Harrison the potential of consolidation—in many respects transporting him back to Chicago, where North American railroads converge in a suffocating case of gridlock that slows the movement of continental freight by orders of magnitude. Due to congestion in the Windy City, CP said it could take a train thirty hours to make its way through Chicago.

Meanwhile, in 2014 the price of crude oil had fallen off a cliff, from more than $100 a barrel to $30 in mid-2015. Although it was not a huge component of CP's business, the transportation of crude from

Alberta and North Dakota's Bakken oil field had been growing on account of more production and not enough new pipeline capacity to handle the additional oil being produced. While Keith Creel had been hired as president of CP and was clearly the heir apparent, the board felt he wasn't yet ready to take over from Harrison, particularly with the crude market softening. The company needed Harrison to be around for another year, so in May 2014 his contract was extended from its initial expiry date of June 2016 until June 2017.

The first stab at a merger actually occurred within months of his contract extension being announced. A strategy session of CP's board had been held to discuss long-term initiatives. With Harrison sticking around longer, the CEO said the feeling from directors Ackman and Hilal was that he should be utilized to the max. That meant combining with another railroad. As a result, the board agreed that consolidation should be studied. "It was not something driven by management," said Isabelle Courville, a director since 2013. But Harrison was hardly disinterested. He told Ackman that if they were going to do it, they'd better get on with it. Not only was his tenure running out, but regulatory approvals would take time and he predicted opposition from other railroads. Beginning that spring, Hilal said he and Harrison had "multiple discussions" with the board about consolidation. With the bulk of the CP transformation already achieved and Creel running things day to day, Hilal said he thought Harrison's talents could be better used elsewhere; i.e., instituting Precision Scheduled Railroading at one of the railroads in the eastern US. "The idea had never occurred to him [while running CP]," Hilal said, who walked Harrison through the "back-of-the-envelope math" of purchasing one of them. Although it didn't really matter whether it was CSX or NS ("we would have taken either one," Harrison said) the first approach was to CSX, largely because of the price of its stock, according to CP chairman Andy Reardon. "I mean, it was in the pits compared to where it is today," he said. Harrison had also been hyper-aware of CSX for a long time.

On September 11, 2014, Paul Hilal—with authorization from CP's board—called CSX's lead director, Ned Kelly.[1] He got the number

---

1   At companies where the chair and CEO positions are held by the same person, there is often a lead director to ensure board independence.

from Gil Lamphere, the former chairman of Illinois Central who'd also been on CSX's board during a separate activist campaign six years earlier. Kelly had a distinguished pedigree—former general counsel at JPMorgan, CFO of Citigroup, CEO of a public company, and a former investment banker who'd seen his share of major deals. Kelly took the call and indicated a willingness to meet but told Hilal he would check with the board first.

The meeting took place on October 9, 2014, at the law firm Davis Polk in New York City.[2] There were five people in the room—Harrison, Hilal, and CP's chairman at the time, Gary Colter, plus Kelly and Michael Ward, CSX's CEO. "Hunter wanted to do a deal," Kelly said. "In other words, he thought a combination made sense. No discussion of terms, you know, just a discussion of why it might make sense." Kelly's view, based on experience, was that one should never say no, but "it strikes us there are some pretty serious regulatory barriers which we'd have to keep in mind. We're not going to give the firm away, but happy to talk about it."

Hilal said the purpose of the meeting had been to explore whether Ward would have dinner with Harrison to explore the merits of a combination.

Harrison's recollection was more pointed. "We can't get it approved," is what he recalled Ward saying. "He said we couldn't get it approved. I said we could."

"If you thought that, why didn't you tell us before we got here?" Harrison said he asked, irritation in his voice.[3]

Kelly said there was more to it. "In fact, I had a subsequent conversation with Hilal where I outlined terms in which we might," Kelly said. "[We] were willing to discuss things." He said that discussion with Hilal was about a week after the meeting, and Hilal told him he'd talk to the CP board about it. CSX had a robust price in mind, Kelly said, and a break-up fee in the event the deal fell apart due to regulatory issues and potential disruption due to announcing a transaction. A few days later, a *Wall Street Journal* story appeared indicating CP had been rebuffed. "I remember it vividly," Kelly said. "I was pissed." CSX hadn't

---

2   The internal codename for CP's CSX overture was "Project Orange," indicating Florida.

3   Ward and Colter declined invitations to be interviewed.

rebuffed anything. CP had not, in fact, made a formal offer that could be rebuffed.

While no specific deal terms had been mentioned, Kelly and Ward had listened to Harrison's views. Harrison had explained he could make operating improvements, and by putting the railroads together, congestion would ease in Chicago. But the two CSX men knew a lot about their company, as well as regulatory politics. Kelly had been a director of CSX since 2002 (and lead director since 2008), while Ward had been chairman and CEO since 2003 and president since the year prior. The railroad had been in a state of disrepair when Ward took over as chief executive. Its operating ratio at the end of 2003 was 91.2 percent (it improved 380 basis points the next year). Kelly said it had an aging workforce and a capital structure in need of fixing. Although it hadn't made anywhere near the strides of CN (and later CP), it had improved. By the end of 2007, the OR had dropped to below 78 percent for the first time in a decade. During certain periods during Ward's tenure, CSX's stock had performed well. In spite of the improvement, CSX was still lagging within the industry. Activist shareholders succeeded in getting dissident directors elected in 2008, pushing up the stock before they abandoned their crusade. CSX's stock dropped sharply after that and during the financial crisis. It then rose until mid 2011, and then again from 2013 until the spring of 2015 before dropping due to a collapse in the coal market, a significant part of its revenue and, as Kelly explained, "a very high margin business." The shares, though, then slowly began to move upward again.

But Ward had been CEO for more than a decade, so succession had become an issue. That fact alone made a deal within the realm of possibility. Mergers or takeovers tend to have a greater probability of occurring when one CEO is about to retire, allowing the other to take over. Those in the trade call this a "social issue." Along with the location of corporate headquarters and the name of the newly formed company, deciding who gets to run the combined entity can be highly contentious. Any one of these factors can be a deal breaker, setting aside the obvious obstacles such as price and political considerations. Most importantly, there was a fiduciary responsibility to shareholders to explore any reasonable suggestions that might enhance the value of CSX's stock. CP's overture arguably fell into that category. While CSX had concerns about regulatory issues and getting a fair price, Kelly, who as lead director said he did most of the talking for CSX in the meeting, indicated the American railroad was happy to continue discussions. Harrison got a different message. Although CP was ready to pay a substantial premium for CSX—in the neighborhood of 30 percent more than CSX's market value—Harrison said, "We would not do a hostile deal," so CP backed off. Not only was he annoyed that CSX appeared to be unreceptive—or, at the very least, concerned that it would be difficult to get regulatory approval—he was annoyed at the use of the word "rebuffed" in the press. CSX was perceived as not giving it a chance, while CP was perceived as having shut it down. Hilal said CSX believed the regulatory hurdle was "insurmountable," and Harrison and Hilal, in concert with CP's board, dropped the idea.

Meantime, there was another US railroad in the East to consider—Norfolk Southern. At one point, Harrison and Creel met with the brass of NS in a private area of a Chicago restaurant. Norfolk Southern's top tier was going to change in the fall of 2015, they were told. As Harrison sat there, he watched the body language of the NS executives. It wasn't good, he said. Harrison read it as a signal that there was "dissension in the ranks" at Norfolk Southern, a railroad that had been known for having a family-type environment.

"It appeared to us that [the] culture at NS was coming apart," Harrison said. While he had always respected NS, Harrison's original preference to do a deal with CSX was driven by the belief that it was more in need of a shakeup and presented more opportunity to create value. But something had changed at NS, he thought.

It was at that point that CP decided Norfolk Southern was a target. "We went hard after NS," Mark Wallace said. "And when NS said no, we kept pursuing," adding there was "a faction on the board that wanted to get a deal done," an Ackman-led faction. Fleshing it out, Rebecca MacDonald said, "Hunter and Bill wanted to run with it."

On November 6, 2015, Ackman indicated CP was interested in pursuing an acquisition of a competitor of CSX. There was then media speculation about CP looking to approach NS. On November 9, Harrison called the CEO of Norfolk Southern, Jim Squires, to tell him CP had a written proposal for a potential combination of Canadian Pacific and Norfolk Southern. Internally at CP, the proposed deal was codenamed "Project November."

On November 13, 2015, Squires and Harrison met face to face in the trophy room of Harrison's barn in Florida. The CEO of CP said he outlined the contours of a deal between the two railroads. Squires would still run Norfolk Southern, Creel would run CP, and Harrison would be CEO of the holding company that would contain both companies. Reminiscent of CSX's response, Squires told Harrison that Norfolk Southern expressed doubt that combining the companies would get regulatory approval. Nonetheless, three days later, NS sent CP a draft of a two-year standstill, which meant CP couldn't make a proposal for two years. CP would not sign.

On November 17, CP sent a letter to Squires indicating interest in a combination and let the market know it had done so. On November 18, CP released the contents of the letter, which included details of an offer—$46.72 in cash and .348 shares in a new company that would own CP and Norfolk Southern, with NS shareholders owning 41 percent of the combined company. The letter outlined what Canadian Pacific saw as the benefits—among them, the creation of a transcontinental rail network, operating synergies, reduced congestion in Chicago, and enhanced service. It had been written with the help of lawyers and bankers, but to Harrison it smacked of an approach that he didn't like. Harrison said the letter was condescending to NS and "pissed them off."

Indeed, Norfolk Southern's response had a sharp edge. What CP proposed, it said, was "grossly inadequate, substantially undervalues Norfolk Southern and creates substantial regulatory risks and uncertainties that are highly unlikely to be overcome." Even if it were approved, NS said it "would likely be subject to a wide range of onerous, value-destructive conditions." It said the regulatory review would likely take two years or more, leaving NS "in limbo" and "interrupting focus and momentum." A persuasively argued December 4 investor presentation by Norfolk Southern included all of this and more. During that conference call, Jim Squires said, "At any price, the regulatory risks remain the same." While Harrison had said CP wouldn't do a hostile deal to get CSX, the NS situation had quickly become unfriendly. Ackman worried that the American railroad would dredge up the question of Harrison's health.

On December 7, Harrison and Reardon sent a lettfer to Squires saying CP was revising its offer and addressing Norfolk Southern's regulatory worries by suggesting the transaction include a voting trust. Such a structure had been used previously in railroad mergers (CP said in more than one hundred instances), including the CN-IC transaction. One of the companies would be put in trust and the two companies would be run separately, pending regulatory approval. On December 8, though, CP held a conference call to announce the new proposal, and things got uglier. Ackman was critical of Squires. Norfolk Southern's CEO was a lawyer, not an operator, the activist said. The railroad, he added, had not made progress in ten years. The amended offer meant NS shareholders would now get $32.86 in cash and .451 shares of the newly formed company, giving them 47 percent of the entity versus 41 percent of the initial overture. The $28 billion offer represented less cash, but a bigger piece of the action. The revised bid was quickly rejected by Norfolk Southern.

On December 16, CP came back one more time. In addition to Harrison and CP's CFO, Bill Ackman was once again front and center. During a conference call, they unveiled the addition of a so-called Contingent Value Right. The CVR was a financial product designed to be an insurance policy should the value of the combined companies fall to certain levels in market trading. In theory, it was a simple idea, but in practice it seemed to confuse the market. In the event the stock price of the newly created company fell below USD $175 a share during a certain period, CP would pay NS shareholders the difference up to USD $25 per share. Ackman said on the call, "I've got to be able to explain this deal to my nine-year-old daughter." He then went on in mind-numbing detail about how the deal was great for Norfolk Southern shareholders.

"Nobody knew what the fuck it was," Wallace said of the CVR. After the conference call, Harrison said CP's investor relations department was swamped with calls from people who said they didn't understand it. "And I'm thinkin' this is supposed to be a brilliant no-brainer," Harrison said reflecting back in frustration. "And boom, that went and bit the dust." On December 23, NS sent a letter to CP saying the enhanced proposal including the CVR was still "grossly inadequate" and still created "substantial regulatory risks."

The battle soon went far beyond the Norfolk Southern boardroom. CP began pointing the finger at the other major US railroads, alleging they were "organizing a collective campaign to block significant mergers in the railroad industry, including CP's proposed offer for Norfolk Southern Corp." On January 19, 2016, CP submitted a letter to the US Department of Justice. It alleged "a number of the large (Class 1) US railroads appear to have begun a concerted effort to block CP's proposed acquisition through a widespread campaign of meetings and solicitations with customers, the media, and other interested parties." The letter went on to claim, "The collective communication strategy of these competitor railroads is also likely illegal because it is anti-competitive . . . Such conduct is plainly anti-competitive and unlawful." Canadian Pacific said the actions by its competitors "merit a serious and impartial review by the US government authorities responsible for antitrust enforcement." Nothing ever came of the railroad's request and its allegations went no further.

Another complication was CP's proposal to structure the deal through a voting trust.[4] The companies would combine, but the prevailing view was that *CP would be put into a trust*—not NS—and the two railroads would be run separately pending regulatory approval. "It [the trust] gives us the ability to close a transaction and to go and pay people their money," Harrison said in a television interview. "People don't like dead money laying out there. So this is just to give you a vehicle to close the transaction, subject to approval of the Surface Transportation Board."

But while Harrison had said he'd initially felt out Squires to see if he wanted to run a piece of the combined company, that was no longer on the table. If the trust structure were approved, the new proposal was for Harrison to immediately become CEO of Norfolk Southern in order to get a head start making changes. The CN-IC deal had involved a voting trust as well, but it was different. The *acquired* company, Illinois Central, was put in trust pending approval. In the CP-NS scenario,

---

4   Although Harrison said it didn't matter which company was put in trust, Wallace said there had been a debate and the sense was that it would be better for CP to be in trust because it was smaller and Canadian.

the *acquiring* company, CP, was to be put in trust. But since CN-IC in 1998–99, regulatory philosophy had evolved. And the notion of Hunter Harrison jumping into the corner office at NS right away while the STB took eighteen months to rule on the transaction was no small matter. If regulatory approval was not successful or the terms were too onerous, the companies would "simply separate," Ackman said, and no merger would take place. Creel would run CP and Harrison would stay at NS and run it. The latter fact was likely cold comfort to those running Norfolk Southern.

CP, however, kept at it. It took the next step of appealing directly to NS shareholders, asking them to vote on whether NS should engage in good faith discussions with CP regarding a business combination. In other words, "Dear Norfolk Southern Shareholders: Do you want your company to sit down and talk with CP?" There were direct letters from Harrison appealing to them. Major shippers, however, were coming out against CP—FedEx Corp and United Parcel Service Inc. "I don't know where they gained all their knowledge about railroads," Harrison poked during a TV interview.

The NS annual meeting was scheduled for May 12, 2016, but there would be no vote. On April 7, the Department of Defense in the United States raised concerns about a deal. A letter from the Army said it was too early to determine whether a merger would adversely affect national defense, but said "the potential certainly exists." Making Harrison CEO of Norfolk Southern during a lengthy review process could mean that he "must make business decisions with potentially competing interests." The next day, the United States Department of Justice also shot a hole in CP's bid, calling its voting trust proposal "fundamentally flawed." The anti-trust division of the DOJ concluded that the trust to be set up pending regulatory approval would "risk harm to current and future competition" and "create unlawful control violations." It would, the DOJ said, be inconsistent with the public interest.

Canadian Pacific had gone to great lengths to discuss the public interest issues associated with gridlock in Chicago, publishing a white paper. It made the argument that combining the railroads would shift certain operations through under-utilized hubs like Kansas City, St. Louis, and Buffalo. But while it may have sounded logical to Harrison and Ackman, once again a railroad board—and this time, major forces in Washington—didn't want them. On April 11, 2016—three days after the DOJ statement and four days after the Army's letter—CP abandoned its bid.

"NS has got a lot of pride," Keith Creel said, reminiscent of Ackman's comment about CP's board. "Historically, before CN, before Hunter, NS was always known to be the best-run railway in the rail industry. And they typically and historically always developed their own. Their succession came from within." Creel said the only way a CP-NS deal could have transpired is if NS had initiated it. The talks never got friendly. Harrison said in a TV interview nine days after abandoning the bid that "clearly" being a Canadian company was a disadvantage in Washington (CP was also smaller). The Southerner was now sounding like a Northerner.

Some associated with CP believed Harrison's disinterest in politics had an impact. Unwilling to kowtow to members of Congress and to lobby in Washington, he may not have helped his cause. Why did *he* have to lobby if he believed the deal made so much sense? It was the naive, idealistic, and impatient side of Harrison coming to the fore. To Harrison, the benefits were obvious. As a common carrier, the railroad was legally obliged to haul whatever people wanted to ship.[5] When the economy grew, more and more would be shipped, but new railroad infrastructure wasn't being built because people didn't want it in their backyards. So, if you couldn't do that, Harrison believed you were left with mergers to create efficiencies.

"You don't want to build any railroads. You don't want to have any mergers. What is going to deal with the growth?" Harrison asked. It was also ironic, given all of Harrison's considerable charm and persuasive powers, that he couldn't abide politicians and lobbying, which essentially involved the art of persuasion. But his distaste for such things was so intense that the deal was likely dead on arrival.

This may have been apparent to at least one CP board member from the outset. Rebecca MacDonald said of the attempt to buy NS, "Bill was enthused, Paul was not." MacDonald said Hilal didn't think CP was

---

5   As part of their common carrier obligations, railways have a duty to transport dangerous goods and hazardous materials, even if that could expose them to risk or potential loss.

ready to take on Norfolk Southern. "I would definitely give Paul credit that he was absolutely right. But the rest of us on the board trusted Hunter saying that he had conversations with the CEO, they are friends, and this is just going to be a nice friendly deal. And Paul's view was that there is going to be nothing friendly about it. And he was right." Andy Reardon believed Ackman and Hilal simply differed about process. Wallace agreed. For his part, Ackman did not recall differing with Hilal over process or that there was a difference in enthusiasm between them.

But it may have been more nuanced. Ackman drove the NS transaction, and while Hilal presented his views to Ackman, sometimes strenuously, his duty was to support what Ackman chose to do, which he did. The fact was, Hilal was also seriously considering what it would be like to make his own calls.

It was a complex relationship between the two hard-driving men. Deep down, Ackman and Hilal respected and relied on each other, but Hilal was thinking about going out on his own. "We're like family. He's like a brother," Ackman said. "You know the kind of brother who you also fight with every once in a while." The two had what Hilal described as a powerful, constructive tension. At the time, tensions were indeed running high between the two activists, Wallace said, even at board meetings in front of other directors, which Hilal did not deny. Wallace described an uncomfortable board meeting at the Trump Hotel in Toronto where the two "just went at it." If anything, Wallace said, "it showed that wow, Paul had a real voice." At a certain point though, according to Harrison, Hilal disengaged and decided a deal with NS wasn't going to happen. At the same time, there was a parallel track headed toward failure. While Ackman continued to drive the deal, Harrison was so convinced of the business case that he dismissed the idea of hiring communications consultants and lobbyists, much to the frustration of his communications team at CP. Not only was Hilal on the verge of splitting from Ackman to form his own fund, but the Canadian Pacific deal bus was headed toward a brick wall.

Aside from the politics of a Canadian company piercing the border to take over an American company, NS was not just any firm—it was a railroad. Furthermore, NS trains went through Washington, DC, meaning Norfolk Southern was visible to the political class. While the transaction may have had merit from a business point of view, if a deal were to be possible, it would have to include a political solution. In addition, from a corporate perspective, Jim Squires was a relatively new CEO at NS. As one CP executive intimated, Squires was fifty-four years old and had climbed the executive ladder at the company. Not long after reaching the top, it wouldn't have been particularly appealing for Squires to see Hunter Harrison's name appear on his call display. That likely meant if there were a deal, Squires wouldn't run the whole show.[6] Harrison said he didn't think this was a factor. "He [Squires] could have been CEO of either entity going forward," Harrison said. Certainly, after IC was swallowed by CN, Harrison would later go on to run the entire entity. "He [Harrison] forgets that people on the other side are very sensitive," MacDonald said. "Hunter feels that if it is for [the] greater good, everybody should be in favor."

On a December 16, 2015, conference call, Ackman did his in-the-weeds explanation of what shareholders would get, while Harrison put up his dukes, telling those listening on one of the conference calls that "if this is going to be a street fight, so be it." He brandished his credentials, telling them that he grew up "as a street fighter." Harrison got testy when someone asked a question about his health. He also criticized Norfolk Southern's hiring of what he called "hired guns," advisers who he said had "been inside the Beltway too long."

But the Beltway won the day. John Baird, a CP director and political veteran—he'd been foreign minister, transport minister, and environment minister in the Canadian government—said, "We got out-hustled." Baird said CP "approached it too much on an IQ level, not an EQ." In essence, he said, CP was saying to Jim Squires of Norfolk Southern that he was "running a shitty railroad," or more precisely, "poorly managing" it. Baird said CP "should have been better prepared" for the assault from the other side, which provided a litany of public opponents to the transaction.

"I mean, these guys [NS] had lobbyists coming out of their ying yang," Wallace said, adding that CP had "nobody."

There was the political side and there was also the price side. CP was simply not willing to pay anywhere near what NS wanted. But the

---

6   Squires did not respond to an email requesting an interview.

final straw may have been the letter from the military. Although it didn't explicitly oppose the deal, it raised questions. Simply introducing the issue of homeland security into the equation was, in some people's view, the equivalent of a death blow. "That was part of the criticism from Rebecca and the rest of the board, was that we completely misplayed Washington. It was a fair criticism," Wallace said. "Listen, the US Army did not fucking write a letter because they woke up one day and said, 'I'm going to write a letter.' They did it because someone told them to."

By then, however, Harrison said he'd lost his enthusiasm for the transaction. "When we asked him, 'What do you think?'" Courville recalled, "He said, 'Well, I think we're hitting the wall.'" It was a rare loss for Harrison, and he didn't like to lose. "I'm a driven guy, I'm a competitive guy, I'm a bad loser." And as Harrison said, he had not mellowed with age.

While the NS deal wasn't going anywhere—but hadn't yet been abandoned—Bill Ackman took one last shot at CSX. He called Ned Kelly. "I got a very warm reception." He said Kelly told him he didn't know what happened the last time CP met with CSX. "They thought, you know, things were kind of moving along and then they read in the newspaper that the deal was off." On January 5, 2016, Ackman went to Jacksonville to meet with Kelly and Ward at Ward's home.[7] According to Pershing, the meeting lasted an hour. "It seemed like they were really interested," Ackman said. "And then they ended up turning us down."

The viewpoint from CSX was somewhat sharper. To them, Ackman's tone was that CSX would be foolish to turn down a deal with CP. More than that, Kelly was concerned about potential regulatory obstacles and that CSX shareholders would get a satisfactory premium. Additionally, he found it "odd" that Ackman was reaching out while Harrison, Pershing, and CP were the still in the process of pursing Norfolk Southern. Afterward, he said he spoke with Ward and reported back to the board. CSX's directors told Kelly, "This is awfully complicated. Nothing has changed since 2014." Kelly was instructed to say no to Ackman, which he did.

---

7   Pershing's "best guess" is that the meeting took place on January 5. Ackman flew to Jacksonville that day and left the next day.

BY THE SPRING of 2016, both potential avenues for consolidation had fizzled. Harrison was also about four years into his tenure at CP, his health had slipped, and the big changes there had occurred. In approximately a year, his contract with CP would expire. His return to the horse pasture was looming large again. He loved his family dearly and enjoyed his equestrian successes, but horses weren't railroads. He'd already flunked retirement once. He wasn't sure he was ready to give it another go.

As torn as he was, with Hunter Harrison there always seemed to be one more act, and Paul Hilal would be the impresario. Hilal left CP's board in January 2016 and subsequently launched his own activist fund, Mantle Ridge LP. In the intervening months, with CP abandoning its pursuit of Norfolk Southern and CSX, Hilal did a lot of thinking, and those thoughts included Hunter Harrison. By most performance metrics, the CP turnaround had been off the charts. At the end of 2016, the operating ratio was 58.6 percent, the best on record at the railroad—and down from more than 80 in 2012. Since 2012, average train length had increased from 5,981 feet to 7,217 feet. Average train speed had gone from 18.4 miles per hour in 2013—Harrison's first full year—to 23.5 miles per hour in 2016. Average terminal dwell dropped from 7.5 hours in 2012 to 6.7 hours in 2016. Average train weight increased. While the number of personal injuries per 200,000 employee hours had risen from 1.56 to 1.64, the number of accidents per million train miles had dropped from 1.69 to 0.97. By then, all of this was occurring with 12,082 employees versus the 16,999 at the end of 2012, not including the consultants who had brought the number to 19,200 when Harrison arrived in July 2012. Could this be replicated yet again?

"I think when NS ended and he [Hilal] left the board," Wallace said, "he had visions of doing a CP 2.0, on his own, with his own name." Reardon concurred. "I orchestrated this rodeo once before," Reardon surmised of Hilal's thinking. "I can do it again." By then, Hilal knew a lot about railroads and Harrison. He knew there were other companies that could benefit from Precision Scheduled Railroading and that Harrison didn't want to go gently into the night. Hilal understood, perhaps better than anyone, that meshing CP with either CSX or Norfolk Southern wasn't really about extracting synergies between combined railroads.

Like Lamphere and Lynch knew from IC and CN, it was about parachuting Harrison into one of them so he could use his operational know-how to improve efficiencies and make another pile of money for investors.

It was sensitive, however, to talk to Harrison. Hilal had left the board, but Harrison was still running CP. Canadian Pacific couldn't buy another railroad, but it still had Harrison, whose retirement was coming up fast. Hilal believed Harrison was "the key to tripling the value of either CSX or Norfolk Southern," but the regulator had made clear it would never allow CP to use that key. He wondered if he could find a way to make it in CP's interest to sell the key—to sell Harrison to him. *Could he buy Hunter?* With that in mind, Hilal and Harrison began talking only in conceptual and exploratory terms about doing something after he was finished at CP. Harrison described the conversations as "very limited" and "awkward." He was skeptical. So was Wallace.

"I mean, I never thought it was going to happen," Wallace said. There were too many hurdles. Hilal had to raise sufficient funds, convince the board, secure Harrison's release, and get him to commit to working another four years. "I thought, you know what? He's got a lot of health issues, he's made a lot of money," Wallace thought. "Why would he want to do it again? I just didn't think he would."

Harrison, meanwhile, would only consider it if CP was willing to allow it and he didn't think the board of the railroad would. But if CP "sold" Harrison, Hilal thought, the company could save shareholders a lot of money, while only losing Harrison's services for a matter of months. More and more, Keith Creel was running the railroad. It didn't need Harrison anymore—it had Creel.

Coincidentally, in late summer 2016, Bill Ackman phoned Andy Reardon, who was driving from Hyannis airport to his house on Cape Cod. Ackman had promised to give Reardon the heads up if Pershing was selling its remaining stake in CP. It was. Pershing had made a whopping USD $2.6 billion and was divesting.[8] On September 6, there was a conference call meeting of the CP board. Ackman was also resigning, but the board tried to get him to remain a director. He politely declined, and Reardon said Ackman then left the call. Both Hilal and Ackman

---

8   In Canadian dollar terms, Pershing calculated it made 327.1 percent on its investment in CP.

were now gone from CP's board. "Given our sixth sense that something might happen," Reardon said, "the board agreed that there should be a committee of three." A sub-committee of CP's board was formed in the event someone moved to separate Harrison. After the September 6 meeting, Reardon called Harrison and told him he was sending him a letter reminding him of his obligations to CP. "Don't be upset, now. Nobody's mad," Harrison described Reardon saying to him, "but we had to write the letter." Sure enough, Hilal contacted CP about his idea. The board was intrigued. Hilal met briefly with the sub-committee—Andy Reardon, Isabelle Courville, and Rebecca MacDonald—in MacDonald's office in Toronto on October 19. Reardon said they told Hilal, "We've got a corporate asset here. And if you really want him, it's going to cost you. We don't want to know what you're going to do with him," he recalled saying, but "we'd be derelict if we didn't make you pay heavily for him." The trio promised him they would negotiate incredibly hard.

"And they more than fulfilled that promise," Hilal laughed.

10 THE TAKING OF CSX

THE WHEELS WERE now in motion for what would likely be Hunter Harrison's final encore—although with Harrison, who could predict? Because of the question of his health, by early December 2016 he was reassessing Hilal's idea. Harrison had an emergency hospital visit on December 2 when his temperature shot up sharply. It was an infection and it passed. He quickly bounced back and decided he wanted to take on the new challenge. CSX would be his crowning achievement, one last proving ground for Precision Scheduled Railroading, on a different kind of railroad than IC, CN, or CP.

"I think Hunter really felt that until he ran a US Class 1, he really wasn't validated," Laird Pitz, CP's chief risk officer, observed.[1] His family, particularly Jeannie, certainly didn't want him to do it. Earl Julo, his son-in-law, said Harrison had absolutely nothing to prove. "He's done it." But Harrison wasn't stopping.

On December 7, top executives of CP met at The Breakers in Palm Beach. Because Harrison spent so much time in Florida, the luxury seaside resort was frequently used by CP for executive conferences and board meetings. In fact, the company spent about a million dollars a year there, as did CN in the days when Harrison ran that railroad. There was something poetic about using The Breakers. Not only did Harrison

---

1   Illinois Central had been a US Class 1, but nowhere near the size of the big four American railroads, which included CSX.

love the finer things in life, which The Breakers provided in spades, but it was built by a railroader, Henry Flagler. Flagler had a been a partner of John D. Rockefeller but had split off and built a railroad into South Florida. Miami might not be what it is today without Flagler, who created a steel pathway to the tip of the state.

Keith Creel started the meeting, briskly going through the issues on his list. Harrison showed up about an hour into the session, out of breath, unattached to an oxygen machine that was plopped in the corner of the room. He talked about the painful case of shingles he was enduring on top of his other medical issues—and about what his last six months at CP would be about, giving no hint of what might lie in store.

Events picked up the following month. On January 15, 2017, CP's chairman Andy Reardon became concerned because the company's next earnings report was rapidly approaching. If there was going to be a deal, it had to be announced on earnings day, January 18. Otherwise, it would be awkward—and potentially inappropriate—to have Harrison on a public conference call if no deal had been reached but was still in the works.

"I thought to myself, I can't have Hunter giving guidance in an earnings call and going into the proxy season [in advance of the annual meeting] after it's out there and making statements and then jumping ship," Reardon said. The sub-committee he'd formed agreed and the board set a deadline. If no deal was reached by the earnings release, that would be the end of it and Harrison would have to go on the conference call. Reardon called Hilal. "Paul," he said, "if you guys are going to do something, you better do it soon."

Around-the-clock negotiations took place to finalize agreements between CP, Hilal, and Harrison. Everyone was acutely aware that things had ended uncomfortably for Harrison at CN eight years earlier. "My god," director Isabelle Courville thought, "we don't want that to happen to us."

More than a year beforehand in late 2015 at a board meeting at The Breakers, there was discussion about how much Harrison would be owed if the Norfolk Southern deal went through and he was released from CP to run NS. There was no final number, but a nine-figure sum was discussed. As well, on July 20, 2016, CP announced Creel would become CEO on July 1, 2017. The company also said Harrison committed to a three-year post-retirement consulting agreement with CP, plus a two-year non-compete. For a period of time after retiring, he would not be permitted to work for any railroad in North America. By virtue of this, his commitment to CP had deepened. "Hunter was really locked, completely locked with CP," Courville said of the five-year deal. The price to release him would be exorbitant.

Rebecca MacDonald, who along with Reardon and Courville was on the sub-committee assigned to negotiate the exit, said Hilal began by offering USD $20 million for Harrison. Hilal said it was actually in a range of $20 to $40 million, while Reardon recalled $40 million, joking that he told Hilal that CP wouldn't even pick up the phone for that amount. MacDonald, however, wanted $100 million. In separate calls with Hilal, Reardon said he had mentioned $110 million. Whatever CP's number, MacDonald and the sub-committee concluded Hilal had no bargaining power. He needed Harrison and CP had him. "The fire was under them [Hilal's Mantle Ridge, LP]," she said, "And they believed us."

The figure MacDonald chose (and Reardon roughly had in mind) was not far off Harrison's four and a half years of compensation—$114,409,036, which included part of the make-whole from what he had been owed by CN and a large chunk of what he was owed in retirement. By departing early, Harrison would be forfeiting approximately USD $88,465,000.[2] Among other things, it was in part the value of the CN pension that CP had replaced plus the value of his CP equity incentives—the latter being about two-thirds of the total. Hilal's firm, Mantle Ridge, LP, had agreed via an insurance contract to make Harrison whole for USD $84 million plus a tax indemnity (possibly as much as $23 million) to ensure he would remain in the same after-tax position as if he had not forfeited what he was owed by CP.

"The numbers were enormous. They're shocking numbers," Hilal said. "They really pressed this to the point of bleeding, right, which I

---

2   In the proxy circular, CP quoted the amount at CAD $122,890,395. In CP's earlier 8-K filing shortly after the announcement, it said the amount was CAD $118,000,000. CP said the discrepancy was due to a change in its stock price between the announcement and January 30, as well as fluctuation in foreign exchange. The proxy circular also included $3,936,000, the value of Harrison's three-year post-retirement consulting agreement with CP.

respect. And Rebecca was the tip of that spear." CP, Hilal said, knew that as he raised money for a railroad investment, it had him. "Because what am I going to do, right? It was irritating."

Even Hilal, a New York investor who'd seen a lot of big numbers, was amazed. But it was what he and his investors had to pay. Beyond the astronomical price, there was a second part to the deal. Harrison had to agree to certain non-negotiable terms laid down by the railroad. He couldn't hire anyone from CP other than Mark Wallace. If he did, he would have to step down from his new job. He also had to dispose of his shares in Canadian Pacific. The railroad wouldn't allow Harrison, or CSX, to have any stake in CP. It was a thirty-six-month standstill, Reardon said. The Canadian railroad didn't want Harrison to have "a hook into us," the chairman explained. He added that the compensation lawyer working with Harrison protested vociferously, so Reardon asked for permission to call Harrison personally. At 2:30 or three in the morning of Wednesday, January 18, Reardon phoned Harrison. Within a couple of minutes, he said, Harrison agreed to the provisions.

"I've gotta tell you, it was the most unusual transaction I've ever negotiated in my entire life," Reardon said. Here was Harrison, a seventy-two-year-old who was in high demand to run another company. The deal was uncertain until the very last hours.

On the evening of January 17 into the early hours of the next morning, Hunter Harrison was on three phones at once. By the time he was done, a press release was being drafted by Canadian Pacific. Investors and most people at the railroad did not know that the company would announce Harrison's retirement at 4:01 pm on January 18, after the close of North American stock markets. That was also when CP would release record results. Hunter Harrison was leaving five months early.

That morning in his Florida home, Harrison padded into the living room just after 9:30, not quite fully dressed. The 9,200 square-foot house, festooned with orchids, once belonged to the CEO of American Express. Harrison looked grey and groggy from lack of sleep. In blue pinstriped pants and a pink dress shirt with a white collar and cuffs, he sat on the couch, almost catatonic. Jeannie, his childhood sweetheart and wife of more than fifty years, was in her workout gear. She silently took the cuff links from his hands and put them on for him.

TOP: Harrison knew nothing about soccer, but checked books out of the library to learn. Coaching in Memphis, early 1970s.

BOTTOM: Frisco days. Harrison is in the front row, second from right.

TOP: Young executive on the rise.
LEFT: Channeling John Travolta, 1983. Credit: Gary Plowman.
RIGHT: With Jeannie, Cayce and Libby, 1983. Credit: Gary Plowman.

A bit of the Tony Orlando look.

TOP: (L to R) Hunter, Jeannie, Cayce, granddaughter Morgan, Libby and her husband Earl, 1991. Credit: John Hershey, Napierville, Illinois

BOTTOM: Illinois Central executive, 1991. Credit: John Hershey, Napierville, Illinois.

TOP: With Cayce, 1986 or '87.

BOTTOM: Hunter with his mother and sisters. (L to R) Mary, Sydney, Dorothy Harrison, Helen, Hunter, Diane, late 1990s.

TOP: With former Illinois Central chairman Gil Lamphere, instrumental in the transaction that brought Harrison to CN. At Winnipeg operations center.

BOTTOM: With Michael Sabia and Paul Tellier, 2006.

TOP: With Claude Mongeau, who succeeded Harrison as CN's CEO. ©LILA PHOTO

BOTTOM: Singing "My Girl" with Temptations' lead singer, Dennis Edwards, at Jeannie's sixtieth birthday, 2007. ©LILA PHOTO

TOP: With Jeannie and top rider Rodrigo Pessoa, 2011. ©LILA PHOTO

LEFT: Spruce Meadows, Alberta. Photo courtesy of Spruce Meadows Media Services.

RIGHT: The sport that became a passion. ©LILA PHOTO

The CEO who'd turned around three North American railroads while earning outsized profits for shareholders and himself sat there like a spent force.

But at approximately 10 am, Harrison sprang to life. He was riled up, on the phone again, this time with a compensation lawyer, finalizing his substantial settlement terms, which not only included his CN pension and CP stock awards, but also his forgone bonus and consulting contract. Although nothing like his departure at CN, it was a tense—and at times fractious—ending to his successful run at CP. Jeannie stood by as Harrison asked her for the wiring instructions so that a USD $55 million instalment could be deposited in his bank account that day (it wouldn't take place until early February). His house manager Jim and frequent driver Steve were trying to fix the fax machine in his office so he could send documents to the lawyer in New York.

At approximately 1:30 pm, Harrison got behind the wheel of a white Porsche Cayenne. He threw his oxygen pump in the back seat, the tube attached to his nostrils. It was a warm day, about eighty degrees Fahrenheit. Harrison dialed the air conditioning to high and wheeled out of the driveway of his home for the thirty-five-minute drive to The Breakers. Once in West Palm, a police roadblock forced Harrison to take a detour and he quickly got lost. As with everything else, he drove aggressively and impatiently, yelling at other cars along the way. As the clock ticked, Harrison struggled to get his bearings. It was just over two hours until CP's fourth quarter earnings would be released. Increasingly frustrated as he darted in and out of side streets, he finally stuck his head out the window to ask a young woman for directions.

He pulled up in front of the stately Breakers at approximately 2:15 pm, left the Cayenne for valet parking, and marched in to do business with CP one last time. He met the railroad's chief counsel, Jeff Ellis, and Andy Reardon. The night before, when Reardon had visited the horse farm, Harrison thought his seventy-one-year-old chairman looked pale and ill. He feared his old friend and colleague was suffering from stress and might be about to have a heart attack. He insisted that Reardon rest. He also privately called Ellis, telling him to keep an eye out for any signs of deteriorating health. Reardon appreciated the sentiment but countered that he had flown his Beechcraft Bonanza from

Naples to West Palm Beach that day. "I was just plain tired," he said. "I was probably dehydrated too."

At The Breakers, Harrison signed the documents to finalize his resignation as CEO of CP—effective January 31—a fact that would be announced to the stock market just after 4 pm Eastern Time. He was inside the hotel for about an hour. When he left the meeting room on the mezzanine floor, Reardon and Harrison hugged. "It was kind of instinctive for both of us," Reardon said.

Harrison said he did not shed a tear. Although it was not like his hurtful departure from CN in 2009, he was strangely morose afterward, odd for a man who was pocketing a fortune and being let out of school five months earlier than planned. He was, though, sour about the way it had ended. The money was great, yet he felt it was an acrimonious final curtain, entailing hard-nosed negotiation with the board over his departure package and terms. Yes, he had another opportunity he was excited about, but it felt like a hollow goodbye. He was being put out to pasture like one of his old studs, a piece of meat being sold to the highest bidder. While Harrison was getting what he was owed, CP was in fact getting off the hook and saving a bundle for something it had not initiated.[3] He was, as always, simply very hard to satisfy and in some sense denying the emotions associated with leaving. Harrison was disenchanted, feeling as though the board "kind of sold me out, washed up." Yet it's worth keeping in mind: despite these convoluted feelings, he wanted to go.

For most people, being paid out in such a fashion and at such a level would be like winning the lottery multiple times over. Not Hunter Harrison. Jeannie saw it differently. "It's like only his way is the way," she said at the time. "He's really gotten hard in a lot of ways . . . I dunno if he feels like he's special . . . he has so much to be thankful for."

She didn't dispute the characterization that he'd become bitter—nor did he—and thought it could have been due to the state of his health.

---

3   In a regulatory filing, CP said that during Harrison's tenure, after forfeitures, it paid him $55.8 million for more than $15 billion of value creation. Given what CP was paid to release Harrison from his non-compete—which he needed to be able to work at CSX—it essentially got him for free.

Pointing to the photos and awards that filled the room, she said he'd had so much recognition. "But it's almost like it's not ever enough." She said he kept saying he wanted to do the CSX deal because there was a lot of money to be made, but she asked, "Hunter, why do you need it?" It was like he was trying to prove something he'd already proved. On the other hand, she could see what the possibility of another tour of duty was doing for his spirits. He needed to work. "It's like he's willed himself to be well. And the last two weeks, he's so much better."

Still, she worried about what would happen when people saw him using oxygen, which the doctors said he should use all the time. Self-conscious about it, he wouldn't even take it when he got his haircut, she said, adding that was "not in front of 200 businessmen. He feels they'd look down at him," she said. "Make him feel weak."

IT WAS THE beginning of another chapter in Harrison's stellar career. After his successes running Illinois Central, Canadian National, and Canadian Pacific, Harrison, with Paul Hilal, now had a huge American railroad back in their crosshairs, CSX Corp. of Jacksonville, Florida. The next day—January 19—shares of CSX traded furiously. Within an hour of stock markets opening, more than 30 million shares had traded, almost four times the daily average. The stock was up 17.5 percent, increasing the market value of the company by $6 billion as investors had a night to digest the news—that Hunter Harrison might soon arrive in Jacksonville to shake up the underperforming company, a company he'd tried to make a deal with in the past. Just before noon that day, Harrison perused analyst reports that sported headlines of "Shark Attack" and "Yes, He's Back."

The night before, though, he'd had a call with Hilal, telling him, "I'm not going through what I went through before," meaning he didn't want another proxy fight like there'd been over CP. Frankly, he didn't have the physical strength for another one, likely a six-month battle that would leave him drained before he even started the job.

Jacquie McNish of the *Wall Street Journal* called, asking about his health. "My health has improved and doctors have told me I'm fine to work ... I'm much improved." That was true, but Harrison was dealing with a variety of ailments. A lung condition necessitating the use of oxygen afflicted him with a persistent cough. Due to other conditions, he required a special diet and wasn't supposed to drink alcohol, even though he'd broken the rule the night before with a three-figure bottle of 1996 Bordeaux (Château Léoville Poyferré, Saint-Julien) to quietly celebrate his departure from CP. But Harrison lived by that golden rule—he who has the gold, rules. When his chief of staff Mark Wallace gently chided him for imbibing, Harrison brushed him off.

"Let me get my first $55 [million] in the bank, then I'll be back on training again." He ate a New York steak with fries and an iceberg lettuce wedge.

As if the list of medical issues wasn't enough, since 2015 he'd been hospitalized approximately a dozen times, the last instance in December 2016 when his temperature spiked and left him hallucinating. He'd also had his gallbladder removed during the battle for Norfolk Southern, endured a bout of shingles in late 2016 and early 2017, and had two "sun spots" removed from his face.

"I do think that he's walking a fine line," his daughter Cayce said in the first half of 2017. "I know my mom is scared of this, that it's to the detriment of his health. But I think that if he didn't work, it would be to the detriment of his mental health."

His various conditions required him to take ten pills a day—six in the morning and four at night. If Jeannie wasn't there to supervise his medications, he would forget to take them. She also ensured that he ate properly. Jeannie worried who would attend to these crucial daily needs if he had to stay in Jacksonville or was on the road for CSX and she wasn't there to help. Harrison was clear that he would not work if it jeopardized his health. He said his doctor had told him, "If I thought this was bad for your health, I'd tell you to stop tomorrow."

Meantime, Harrison told McNish, "If the shareholders don't want to do this, I'm fine to go home." But in truth, he really wanted to keep working—part of him seemed to believe it would keep him alive. He was excited again—and he was talking to the reporter, in spite of protests from Hilal, who wanted him to remain under the radar. He was asserting his control and letting out the story like an expert fly fisherman casts a line. By being his own man, he was putting Hilal in a corner. Hilal had already amassed more than a billion dollars in commitments from investors and had fully deployed it, and Mantle Ridge owned almost

5 percent of CSX. Without Harrison, Hilal's plan was empty. When Hilal lobbied to be CSX's chairman and to nominate a slate of seven of directors, Harrison barked back. He privately complained that Hilal's ego was getting in the way of getting the deal done. Harrison also believed Hilal, whom he described as a northeastern intellectual, didn't understand the CSX board. Hilal, however, had many strengths. He was a relentless researcher and investor who'd raised a lot of money. He'd shrewdly uncovered the CP opportunity that allowed Harrison to come out of retirement and he now thought CSX was ripe for turnaround too. Had he and Ackman not lured Harrison back to work in 2012, the railroader's career as a CEO may have ended with CN, leaving him frustrated.[4] The fact remained that Hunter Harrison needed Paul Hilal as much as Hilal needed him.

Although the spike in CSX's shares showed the value of Harrison to the market, he was frustrated watching the stock go up from the sidelines, unable to profit from the rise that was tied to his name. While he and Hilal would soon strike a deal on what he would get, he insisted on a package that took into account the value that had already been created by the mere mention that he might be CEO, as though he were a railroading messiah. Many believed he was.

In spite of the big payout and the leap in CSX shares, Harrison was low key, slightly down. By his own admission, he wasn't very good at exits. He didn't conceal his sensitivities or his hurts. It may also have been a mild case of seller's remorse—and part exhaustion. He had thrown every particle of himself into CP. While he enjoyed adoration, at the same time he compartmentalized any warm emotions he may have harbored for his past chapters. When the job was done, he was done. The cowboy had left the saloon, blown into the end of his pistol, and slid it back into his holster. There was smoke, dust, and broken glass, but what remained was also refurbished, highly efficient, and money-making.

Harrison preferred the excitement of entrances and proving quick results. When he started a new assignment, he was like a meteor, a bright streak no one could stop watching. Despite everything, he was

---

4   Harrison alluded to this in his acceptance speech for Railroader of the Year in 2015. "If it hadn't been for them [Hilal and Ackman]," he said, "I wouldn't be standing here tonight."

about to fire up one more time. Minutes after the news broke that Harrison was resigning as CEO of CP, Paul Hilal dialed Ned Kelly's cellphone. After CP's first overture to CSX fell through, Hilal made it his business to stay in touch with Kelly. Indeed, they had lunch on April 15, 2015 at Marea, an upscale Italian restaurant in New York known for its "power lunch" clientele. Now, as CSX's shares were moving up in after-hours trading, Hilal was telling Kelly what a great CEO Harrison would make.

"Paul," Kelly said, puzzled, "isn't he still at CP?" Kelly hadn't heard the news. When Hilal informed Kelly that Harrison was resigning, Kelly responded by saying, "That's interesting," and told Hilal he'd circle back. Kelly, in his many years working in and around Wall Street, had never seen a market reaction like what happened to CSX's stock after the news came out. By the close of trading the next day, the stock was up 23 percent—adding $8 billion to the company's market value in twenty-four hours. CSX had also just reported disappointing earnings, depressing its stock some 3 percent prior to the news about Harrison. CSX shareholders were ready for a catalyst. Snagging Harrison was tantalizing, but there were issues for the CSX board, Harrison's health among them.

There were also issues between Harrison and Hilal. It was not an easy relationship. Mind you, what relationship of Harrison's was easy? Hilal, too, had a demanding persona and he wasn't the type to relent. It was a marriage of convenience. For Harrison, Hilal was a lifeline to a new gig and possibly another fortune. Harrison also believed a new challenge might jolt his body back to better health and vigor. For Hilal, Harrison was his ticket to show Wall Street that he could do his own deals. CSX would be a marquee transaction, and he needed Harrison to put the bums in the seats.

It would not, however, be a chummy path. In fact, the phone calls between them on January 18 and 19—when CP announced Harrison's resignation—were not what you would expect from partners looking to close a deal. The grenades were principally being thrown by Harrison. Hilal seemed intent on muzzling him with the press. From the railroader's point of view, talking to reporters was the way to get the story out and put pressure on the CSX board. Hilal said he "begged him to stop talking to the press." Hilal's approach and request for a large number of board seats also didn't sit well with Harrison. He thought a deal could be done quickly and that Hilal's jockeying could jeopardize everything.

Hilal reasoned that overwhelming influence on the board would mean Harrison would have the support and latitude to do what he needed to do for shareholders. During a call on the morning of January 19 from his home in Florida, Harrison told Hilal they had to sit down with Kelly to find out what they had to do to close the deal.

"You exhibited a whole lotta balls," Harrison said to Hilal, playing to the activist's ego by praising his audacious plan. Mantle Ridge—a.k.a. Hilal—had taken a huge risk assembling investors on just the prospect of a deal. "You're on the cusp of making a whole lot of money," Harrison advised. "Don't blow it." While Hilal was preparing for war, Harrison wanted a friendly deal. The call ended.

That afternoon at 3 pm, with CSX shares up sharply and the company saying it and the board would "actively evaluate Mantle Ridge's views," the two spoke again. Once again, Hilal tried to persuade Harrison not to speak to the media in the hope that the CSX board would open up and be receptive to finding common ground. Harrison disagreed, clearly satisfied that the previous day's press report had lifted CSX's stock considerably. He worried that if the deal wasn't done expeditiously, the current CEO would have time to exert influence over the board and the company might mount a negative campaign focused on his health. There was nothing more powerful, in Harrison's view, than a swift market reaction to persuade a board and shareholders—and the media coverage helped. Harrison was also a truth piñata, only you didn't have to hit him for it to come spilling out. If a reporter called, he spoke his mind. "When in doubt, default to the truth," was an oft-repeated credo.

Hilal told Harrison he would call Kelly—whom they both respected—and explore whether there was a way to expedite a deal, given the noise in the media. That was fine, but Harrison wanted to meet with the full board and say, "Here's our plan. It's in your shareholders' interest . . . quicker we do this, the less it costs . . . If you want to take this to a proxy fight, we'll see you at the proxy fight." That, however, was clearly not what Harrison wanted.

The call then took a turn. Harrison dredged up a moment of tension between himself and Pershing prior to taking over at CP—when Ackman announced there would be a search for CEO. Hilal protested that Harrison was being unfair. Whether it was bitterness in his voice or a performance, Harrison then complained to Hilal that he had received no compensation for the several months he was on the road selling the Pershing deal. Harrison griping about his CP pay package (which included 650,000 options) was an exhibition of maximum chutzpah.[5] Hilal, meanwhile, continued to defend himself and Pershing's announcement about the executive search. Only a board was authorized to hire a CEO, he explained later; independent directors were not. Had Pershing tried to subvert governance procedures, it would have lost support of shareholders and ISS. ISS was important, Hilal told Harrison, whether the railroader liked it or not.

"If you want me to run the railroad, I'll run the railroad, and I think I can make all of us a lot of money," Harrison said, frustrated. "If you try to get cute and drag this thing on, you're going to blow the whole thing."

Hilal would not back down, arguing that time was on their side. As each day passed, more of the shareholder base swung to support Harrison as CEO. But they'd only make money if he got the job. The case for change, Hilal said, was getting stronger, and he continued to press for seven board seats, which Harrison still viewed as excessive. While Hilal had good reason for doing it—to provide backing for Harrison—it didn't matter to the railroader. He paid little heed to boards. Harrison was perhaps forgetting that at IC, CN, and CP he had significant board support. He would need it at CSX.

Harrison then laid out what they should say to Ned Kelly—that they admired how he treated Michael Ward, the CEO, but this was about shareholder value. Harrison's track record at three other railroads had proven to be a legitimate model. He didn't want to make Kelly, Ward, or the board look bad, but shareholders had voted with their pocketbooks. The company was suddenly worth a lot more. Harrison suggested he and Hilal ask Kelly how they could be helpful. For a man accustomed to using the blunt edge, he advised the gentler approach.

Hilal had another view. He didn't want to fight with Harrison but was convinced their bargaining power had increased. Harrison, the master psychologist, then changed his tone. "Well, you got their ass," he said,

---

5   Harrison's option grant was part of the compensation package he and Pershing had agreed to in October 2011.

stroking Hilal. "Good job." But he also couldn't resist one last jab. "I'm a better dealmaker on the street than y'all give me credit for." The Tennessee brawler was tired of New York tactics. He wanted a deal and he wanted it soon.

The call ended when Harrison's cellphone battery died at 3:50 pm. At the close of trade ten minutes later, CSX had traded 98.5 million shares, more than ten times the daily average. The market value of the railroad had jumped from $33 billion to more than $41 billion in twenty-four hours. "Nice move," Harrison said—another understatement—as he looked at the share price.

Sixteen minutes later he was on the phone to Keith Creel, who was on CP's jet approaching Calgary. Harrison sniped about how Hilal was trying to tell him what to do. There would be more arguments between the two of them before CSX would make a deal. In spite of his sour feelings, Harrison would credit Hilal with getting him out of his non-compete at CP. Harrison didn't think it would fly, believing CP wouldn't want to do it. "I was wrong," he conceded. "Paul was right."

While he respected many facets of Hilal's business acumen, the younger man plainly irritated him. If they were cartoon characters, Harrison would be the crotchety bulldog while Hilal would be the excitable terrier. That said, Harrison was easily irritated. The New York investor was bringing Harrison to a deal that could earn him hundreds of millions of dollars, yet the railroader had little patience for him. "I try to be very scrupulous to a very annoying level," Hilal admitted, "and I'm proud of it." Ultimately, though, Harrison and Hilal—a combustible confection of Memphis and Manhattan—would get past their differences and prevail at CSX.

On Sunday, January 22, Harrison would use one of the CP jets (the Gulfstream 450) for the last time, flying to the Mayo Clinic in Rochester, Minnesota. He would undergo a battery of tests to try to get to the bottom of what had dogged him for eighteen months and required him to be hospitalized on several occasions. The results, he said, were inconclusive. However, in spite of having more money than he could ever spend, the prospect of running yet another railroad—and a big American one—was what rocked his world. Even though he now relied on an oxygen tube for most of the day, creating a sucking and hissing sound with each breath, the five-star general of railroads was now in his last campaign. And he'd been told by investors that despite whatever health problems he had, they'd be happy to have him as CEO for just thirty days, even if he was on a respirator.

Very quickly, a meeting was arranged for January 27. Harrison and Hilal flew to Atlanta on Harrison's jet to meet Kelly and another director, David Ratcliffe, at DeKalb-Peachtree Airport, northeast of the city. They dined on Chick-fil-A, a popular fast-food offering. Harrison, Kelly said, spoke most of the time, but governance issues were an obstacle. Hilal still wanted seven board seats, certain incumbent directors to depart, and the responsibilities of the newly constituted directors to be defined (Hilal indicated the chairmanship was something he had always been willing to concede). The answer was no to all of the demands. As Harrison had tried to tell Hilal, he wanted too much. Kelly, meanwhile, reported back to the full board. The other directors, he said, shared his and Ratcliffe's reaction to what Hilal wanted, adding that it still made sense to try to hire Harrison.

The next step, according to Kelly, was to have the whole board meet Harrison. That meeting took place February 1 at the Ritz in Atlanta and lasted more than five hours. The board was not unaware of the market response either. "Our view was that given the market reaction, we should do our level best to retain Hunter, if we could do so, under any reasonable circumstances." It was clear, however, that it would be expensive, but Kelly said, "That wasn't regarded as an insurmountable barrier given the upside for our shareholders." While Hilal wanted a lot, so did Harrison.

Initially, CSX appeared to blanch at what Harrison wanted compensation-wise, estimating his total ask at more than $300 million for the four years—with only a portion of it including performance metrics—calling the request "extraordinary in scope" and "exceptionally unusual, if not unprecedented."

Not only had Kelly never seen such a market reaction in his lengthy career, but he'd also never come across a major publicly traded company hiring a seventy-two-year-old CEO who came with health-related questions. Kelly confirmed that at the meeting at the Ritz, the board had watched closely for indications about the state of Harrison's health, having heard reports that he used oxygen. He said Harrison did not use oxygen at either that meeting or the earlier meeting at the airport in Atlanta in late January. CSX soon said it wanted Harrison's medical records to be examined by an independent physician designated by the board. He refused but did provide a short letter from his physician. Kelly said that gave him pause. "I didn't read anything nefarious into it [Harrison's refusal to provide the records]. But I would rather have it." Kelly added, "Harrison was always open with the board about his health, his need to use supplemental oxygen, and in fact did use oxygen at later meetings."

Kelly had also never seen a buyout the size of Harrison's—what Hilal had agreed to cover to release Harrison from his non-compete obligations to Canadian Pacific. "You know it's $84 million in actual, plus a tax indemnity. And that's cash up front with no performance, irrespective of whether he lives or dies." In Kelly's mind, it all added up to about $100 million. Hilal's firm was protecting Harrison via an insurance contract that would only pay him if CSX didn't hire him. If CSX did hire Harrison, Harrison insisted the railroad reimburse him.

Kelly said he had three concerns—the dollar amount, that Mantle Ridge would be the beneficiary, and that Harrison was seventy-two with health issues. While the money involved and associated issues were somewhat vexing, they paled in comparison to the jump in CSX's worth since Harrison's name had been mentioned as a possible CEO. "There are people who have sometimes extreme talents," Kelly said. "That's Hunter and railroads. He's been doing it for fifty years. I think he understands them probably better than anybody on earth."

When Harrison and Hilal left the meeting with the board at the Ritz, they exited into a dimly lit stairway. There, Harrison said they bumped into CSX CEO Michael Ward, the man who would be replaced by him, "which was kind of awkward." At first, Harrison didn't recognize him. "Oh, Hunter, how are you?" Ward asked him, and offered his hand. After the brief encounter, Harrison and Hilal got into a waiting car.

"Take the deal," Harrison said he advised Hilal. The bird in the hand—two or three board seats—was enough, in his opinion. He was fine to let Hilal bring him to the table, but once the deal was done, he said he didn't want to hear from him and didn't want him having the power of seven board seats or overseeing an operating committee. Harrison already knew how to operate a railroad.

In fact, a hot-tempered Harrison was forgetting Hilal had assumed significant risk to get them where they were. Hilal, meantime, asserted in a letter to CSX that it was not a "battle for control," that Mantle Ridge only wanted what was in "the best interests of the company."

There were many times during the six and a half weeks from his resignation to appointment when Harrison blasted Hilal for not appreciating the Southern culture of the CSX board. The activist investor needed to give a little, Harrison believed, to win over the CSX directors. And he did. In the summer of 2017, Hilal reflected that he eventually realized that the CSX board was different than the unfriendly CP board that needed taming through a proxy contest. Unlike at CP, CSX's directors were welcoming Harrison and willing to cut a deal. While Hilal settled for five directors, his initial concerns about the board support Harrison required would later be vindicated.

Ultimately, the board determined that shareholders should be allowed to vote on whether CSX should make the substantial payment promised to Harrison. Meanwhile, the railroader said publicly that if CSX didn't reimburse him, he would resign, triggering the protection he'd been promised by Mantle Ridge. ISS, the shareholder advisory firm, recommended shareholders vote in favor of CSX paying what Harrison had forfeited at CP. Ironically, ISS had raised concerns in the past about Harrison's compensation. In this case, although it was potentially a "troubling governance precedent," ISS supported the payment because the threat of Harrison's resignation could lead to "the loss of market value that accompanied his arrival." The old fox had everyone in a box.

"Not a shareholder in the world is going to turn it down," said Mark Wallace.

That was pretty much the case. But after shareholders voted at least 93 percent in favor, the board then had to vote on reimbursing Harrison.[6] Before that took place, Kelly went the extra mile. While Harrison had refused access to his medical records, Kelly asked Harrison if he could speak with his physician. Harrison agreed, and Kelly heard what

---

6   The result was announced June 5, 2017.

he needed to hear—that Harrison was fully able to continue to perform his duties. Hilal also spoke with the doctor several months earlier, adding that he did so before raising money. "If you want him to live forever," he said the doctor told him, "feed him a broken railroad every five years."

In the end, other than Ward departing, it was a relatively peaceful coup. On Monday, March 6, 2017, at just after 5 pm Eastern Time, Harrison signed a four-year contract to be CEO of CSX—forty-seven days after CP Rail announced his resignation.[7] The Florida-based company released the news to the market at 5:36 pm ET, trumpeting Harrison's successes at CN and CP respectively. "I just started about fifteen minutes ago," Harrison said by phone shortly after 5 pm. "It's done." In the background, Jeannie Harrison was picking up other phone lines in the house, ringing with people wanting to talk with him.

The CSX board had come to terms with Hilal and Harrison. "I give them credit," Mark Wallace said. "At least they listened to them [their shareholders]." He was comparing CSX directors to the board of CP Rail, who lost the bitter proxy fight. The CSX board, though, had the benefit of learning from history. Wallace particularly gave credit to Kelly, who would become chairman, while Hilal would be vice chairman of the board. Wallace gave Hilal kudos as well, while clarifying that the deal didn't happen via "brotherly love" with Harrison. "He [Hilal] may be difficult, but certainly I tell ya, he can get a deal done," Wallace said. "To pull off what he did, it's miraculous." In fairness, the railroader did say to Hilal on more than one occasion that the investor had exhibited "balls" by raising money and promising to make him whole before he had a deal in the bag. That was high praise from Harrison. Hilal's extreme attention to minutiae also made other advisors sharper, said one involved in the CP battle.

As the smoke cleared, Harrison's chief of staff was already taking charge in the new CEO's name. A CSX jet was sent to pick up Wallace in Calgary. Nothing signified a change in power more clearly than the ability to summon a company aircraft. "How would you like to be me

---

7   This settlement occurred unusually quickly. According to a 2017 Columbia Business School study of 250 activist settlements between 2000 and 2011, the median amount of time from an activist initiating a position in a company to a settlement was 198 days.

walking into their corporate offices tomorrow afternoon?" he joked. His wife Josée asked him whether he was "going to be wearing a bullet-proof vest."

Some of the key executives at CSX wanted to talk to Harrison that night. He reckoned he would show up in Jacksonville "Wednesday or Thursday for the first time." But he wouldn't spend much time there, he said. Harrison would direct the transformation from his study at home, not from the field. If they want that, he said, "they got the wrong people." Truth be told, his health would not allow it. Besides, the mere presence of him at the top of the organizational chart would start change in motion.

His compensation would be "what I asked for." The cash would be a base salary of $2.2 million and an annual target bonus of $2.8 million, not including perquisites and benefits, such as housing in Jacksonville. But 9 million options would be the pot at the end of the rainbow, which amounted to 1 percent of CSX's outstanding common stock.[8] The strike price[9] would be the closing price of the stock the day of his appointment, $49.79. The day he resigned from CP, CSX's stock was $36.88. Harrison said that if the stock went to $80, he would reap $270 million from the options alone.[10] "I'm pleased," he said, in what could only be described as massive understatement. Was he pumped? "Haven't got pumped yet. They'll get me pumped in a day."

HUNTER HARRISON WAS taking control of CSX just three days after an investigative story appeared in Canada's national newspaper, the *Globe and Mail*, chronicling a so-called "culture of fear and intimidation" at CP and the human cost of the Harrison turnaround at Canadian

---

8 The CEO of a major Canadian pension fund said his team would not buy into the deal, in part, because it viewed Harrison's compensation as "ridiculous."

9 The strike price is the fixed price at which the owner of the options can exercise them. In Harrison's case, he received the right to buy 9 million CSX shares at $49.79 each.

10 In a February 16 release, Hilal put Harrison's compensation at approximately $32 million per year for four years, of which approximately $20 million was explicitly performance based. The option grant was worth $78 million because it did not include the first $10 of share value creation; i.e., the "Hunter rally" price.

Pacific. The same phrase had been used in a 2007 government report when he ran CN. The article cited examples of employees being summarily fired and then having to fight via lengthy arbitration hearings to be reinstated.

Wallace emailed that the article was a "Piece of SH&T!! Total hatchet job!" He wrote that the union had led the reporter "down the garden trail," calling the piece, "Very unfortunate and unfair." One could imagine, however, the story making the rounds at CSX as employees tried to get a bead on the new boss. "I don't think it'll come as a surprise to anyone that Hunter is tough and demanding and slashes costs—assets, people, etc. Unions hate that. They can throw all the grievances they want at him," Wallace said. "They call it fear and intimidation—we call it accountability and doing your job. Do people really think the CEO gets involved in all minor firings or grievances?"

After the news was announced that Harrison was going to CSX, Doug Finnson, president of the Teamsters Canada Rail Conference, the union representing thousands of CP workers, sent a message to the American railroad's employees via a quote to the Globe and Mail: "Thank god that you're unionized." When Harrison was at CN, the issue of iron-fisted discipline also arose, particularly when it came to older workers. "You know, he can be belligerent at the best of times, and when it's the worst of times he can be really excessive," Buzz Hargrove recalled. "I just told him he's got to do some things on discipline." The union, Hargrove said, didn't seek to eliminate discipline, but "we did set out to put some more fairness in it and we did resolve a number of grievances."

Reacting to the article, CP executive Tony Marquis, a self-described Harrison disciple, allowed that the railroad had been too tough on some people while trying to transform the culture. "I made some mistakes. We all made mistakes," said the senior VP of operations for eastern Canada. "But it had to happen to change the course of this company. And Hunter didn't want to ever see us treat an individual wrong." Distinctions, however, had not been made, Marquis said, between innocent errors and conscious choices to violate rules. That had now changed, and CP had become a much safer railroad than before the turnaround.

Paul Tellier, who was plenty tough himself and had cut thousands of jobs, also felt Harrison was too harsh at times—not just with workers, but executives. "Best railroader in the world," Tellier said, "but there were very few people that didn't have their ass kicked by him." Aside from himself, Tellier could think of only two people Harrison didn't scream at—Keith Creel and CP director and former senior vice president at CN Gordon Trafton—both long-time protégés.[11] When asked why, Harrison told Tellier he didn't have to yell at those two.

His granddaughter Mackenzie remembered waking up as a kid hearing the screaming on the phone—"the Harrison scream," she called it. Laird Pitz, who spent several years working with Harrison at CN as VP of Risk Mitigation, recalled executive committee meetings there could be brutal. Another former CN executive said you could tell how the meeting would go by how hard the door slammed. "If he didn't like what you had to say, there wasn't any meeting afterwards," Pitz said. "It took place right then and there," much like Pierre Berton wrote about Van Horne. When Pitz didn't agree with Harrison, however, Pitz would say so. He said "the whole damned room" would look at him, then look at Hunter, wondering what would happen next. When Harrison would say "we can agree to disagree," the other executives were even more flabbergasted—how come Pitz can get away with that? Harrison respected people who stood up to him, although Pitz added—as only an old friend could—that Harrison never really agreed with you no matter what you said. He had to be right and he hated to wait for anything.

"I always had the pleasure of working with Hunter, never working for Hunter," Michael Sabia said with the trace of a smile. "I think those are probably very different experiences." As amazing as Harrison was, Sabia said—the intensity, the leadership, the inspiration, the vision—"sometimes Hunter can go too far." Pitz echoed that. "How much is enough when you're in a public corporation?" There is a point, he argued, where you *could* go too far. So, had Harrison gone too far? "He's come close," Pitz said.

CP director Rebecca MacDonald doesn't think he ever went too far. "Business is a living, breathing organism of people. That's all business is. And if you have to cut down some people for that organism to keep on living, you better be prepared to do it," she said. Harrison worried about

---

11   Trafton had also worked with Harrison at Illinois Central and Burlington Northern.

people and was compassionate, MacDonald added, but "You needed someone like Hunter to clean up." While Keith Creel said nine times out of ten he and Harrison would make the same decision, the younger CEO said, "Hunter's always the wartime general." Creel said natural leaders aren't born every day—"There are not a lot of Hunter Harrisons out there," people who have the intestinal fortitude to make the tough calls.

MEANTIME AT CSX, it would be Harrison and Wallace against the world. Their relationship was complex. Age-wise, there was a generation separating them. Wallace is a Montrealer and Canadian, although Harrison described him as "the most Americanized Canadian" he'd ever met. Their relationship went back to CN, where Wallace worked prior to Harrison's arrival. He'd joined the railroad's treasury and tax department in January 1995 as the company readied for its public offering in the fall. Later, Wallace moved into investor relations, and during his first week on the job, his boss asked him, "Have you ever heard of IC?" Of course, Wallace said. "Well," his boss said, "we're buying them."

The deal with Illinois Central hadn't been announced, but Wallace worked through Christmas getting ready for it. He first encountered Harrison in early 1998, when Paul Tellier brought the IC chief around to meet people. "You kind of felt [Harrison's] presence when he walked in. The drawl. A very imposing kind of guy. Very intimidating guy. I was scared shitless of him," said Wallace, who was not quite thirty years old, while Harrison was in his early fifties. They ended up sharing a common wall on the sixteenth floor at CN. "I could hear the pounding on the desk and the yelling." It wasn't what they were used to at CN, certainly not from Paul Tellier. "I'm not going in that office," Wallace thought. "Shit, he'll eat me for lunch."

Over time, however, he got to understand Harrison. It was the commitment, the passion, Harrison's encyclopedic knowledge of the industry, and the explanation of how things would change at CN that turned him. "The scariness eased away over time." Being on the road when they did earnings announcements helped. Those were the days when it wasn't simply a conference call. The executive team would fly to New York and then fly to Toronto to release the financial results and meet directly with analysts. Wallace would have drinks with Harrison in hotel bars. When Tellier abruptly resigned to go to Bombardier and Harrison was made CEO, the phone rang in Wallace's office. "Hey, what's up?" Harrison always started his calls with "Hey."

Wallace became Harrison's chief of staff, followed by other key jobs at CN. After Harrison left CN, Wallace did as well. He had a few jobs post-CN, but in 2011, Wallace's father, who'd been a mechanic, took sick in Montreal with viral encephalitis. His father-in-law had just passed away a few months earlier. Wallace took the remainder of the year off to look after his parents. His father died in September at seventy-eight, which Wallace described as a shock.

Soon after, reports began surfacing that Bill Ackman of Pershing Square had bought CP stock and was looking to recruit Hunter Harrison as CEO. In 2012, Wallace was brought back into Harrison's sphere at CP, where again he became number one gatekeeper. A CEO who did business with CP during that period said nothing got done at the railroad without Wallace. The chief of staff spoke for Harrison. In fact, he went to CP having such faith in his boss that he didn't know what his salary would be and hadn't asked. His wife Josée kept asking how much she could afford to spend on a house in Calgary. The subject came to a head a couple of months into the job when Wallace, Harrison, and the head of HR, Peter Edwards, went to dinner in Calgary. Harrison asked Wallace if he was happy with his compensation. There was an awkward silence. Wallace didn't have any compensation yet. It hadn't been resolved.

"It wasn't really about the money or how many options you were going to get. It was about the experience of going in and doing this whole thing again," he said, although he confessed to having second thoughts, probably every day initially. "Even sometimes today, what the fuck am I doing?" he asked himself in the winter of 2017, but "I knew I was involved in something important. And the experience of being that close to a senior executive at that young age and learning, despite the pressure, despite the responsibility... despite the harassment. Listen, he's a demanding guy."

For Harrison, there was no Canada Day or Fourth of July. He didn't believe in holidays and thought there were too many statutory holidays. He told one executive he'd never taken two weeks' vacation. He figured if the company could do without him for two weeks, it could do without

him, period. In the middle of opening presents on Christmas morning 2016, Wallace was on the phone with Harrison for an hour and a
half. "It's always been like that." Saturday mornings, Sunday mornings,
the Wallace family called it "Hunter time." When Harrison was ready
to work, Wallace worked. If he was at a horse show, the Wallaces went
grocery shopping. The rewards for Wallace have been immense. But the
risk was high—he knew he'd hitched his wagon to one man.

"The risk part is unfortunate," Wallace conceded, "[but] he has given
me more, not just monetarily and professionally, than I can ever repay. I
owe him a debt of gratitude." That said, it was an agonizing decision to
join up for one more tour of duty, this time in Jacksonville, particularly
with one of his children attending university in Alberta and protesting
the move. He could have stayed at CP in a good position. "That's not
who I am," Wallace said. "I owe him. And if there's an opportunity to
do this again and be successful, then I want to take that risk." He also
felt Harrison couldn't do it alone, that he would need help. "He's not
going into CSX friendly," Wallace said. "He's going to need me to take
some bullets."

But why did he feel indebted to Harrison? Wallace pointed to the
opportunities, the mentoring, and the coaching. He also did not rule out
the notion that Harrison had cast a spell on him, particularly during the
beginning of the CP stint. Wallace had just lost his dad and Harrison was
"kind of that fatherly figure, a little bit," he said. "It was therapeutic for
me, working with him again, getting over the loss." He felt deep loyalty
to Harrison and knew that because of his health, he would "probably
struggle" at CSX if he was alone. "In a profound way," he explained, "it's
almost like you don't want to have that loss again. You want to stay in
the guy's life. You want to keep helping him." He said that if he hadn't
talked to Harrison for a while, he'd "get withdrawal."

Once again, Mark Wallace had no idea what his own compensation
would be and wasn't paid for two months at CSX. "Put something down
on paper and we'll take care of you," Harrison told him. It would most
certainly be more than he was paid at CP, given the risk he assumed.
But typically, Wallace said his boss was uncomfortable talking about
other people's compensation, except when Harrison was handing out
bonuses—when he was generous to those who performed.

Expectations were now set for Harrison to beat down CSX's operating ratio from 69.4 percent in 2016. RBC's Walter Spracklin, who
had been a non-believer during the early part of Harrison's tenure at
CP, wrote that by 2020, Harrison could more than double CSX's 2016
profit of $1.714 billion and suggested he could get the OR to 58 percent
in that timeframe.

In advance of Harrison's appointment, Wallace already had a menu
of priorities from Harrison for the first month or two. "You should see
my to-do list," Wallace said. He was soon in Jacksonville. The first order
of business, according to the new CEO, was to let the CSX team know
what was expected of them. A lot, was the answer.

11 ONE LAST THING TO PROVE

TO ANYONE WHO'S played Monopoly, the B&O Railroad is a familiar name. The roots of CSX can be found in that company, the Baltimore and Ohio. While Canadian Pacific Railway was born in the 1880s, CSX Corp. is older, dating back to the establishment of the B&O in 1827. The CSX of today, with 21,000 route miles, began with just 13 miles of track and once used horses to pull its cars.

Between 1830 and 1860, numerous other railroads with long-forgotten names were chartered east of the Mississippi. The industry grew in lockstep with the rise of the steam engine and the advent of the American-built locomotive. A small coal-burning locomotive was built specifically for the B&O in 1830. The term "horsepower" evolved as a marketing tool—a comprehensible yardstick to compare the work that could be done by horses to that of a steam-powered engine.

During the Civil War, railroads were integral to moving supplies. They were also targets. In May 1861, the B&O was attacked by Confederate troops. By the late 1800s, electric locomotives appeared, as did the air brake—invented by Westinghouse—that could be applied to all cars at once. This allowed for longer trains, with more than 100 cars. The industry grew to the point where the US government decided it needed federal regulation, and in 1887, President Grover Cleveland signed the Interstate Commerce Act.

The modern CSX took a century and a half to coalesce. It's the amalgam of several lines that evolved through the 1800s and early twentieth century—the product of a dizzying number of mergers starting in 1900. In 1973, the Chessie (Chesapeake) System was incorporated— the parent of B&O, C&O (Chesapeake & Ohio, which included lines in Michigan and Illinois) and the Western Maryland Railway. These lines cut through, among other areas, the Carolinas and coal fields of West Virginia and Pennsylvania. The current CSX was then born in 1980, the same year as the BN-Frisco merger, an inflection point in Hunter Harrison's career. CSX's formation was the meshing of the Chessie System and Seaboard Coast Line Industries (which included lines in Tennessee and Georgia)—the C was for Chessie, the S for Seaboard, and the X for the multiplication expected by combining.

In the late 1990s, CSX and Norfolk Southern each took a piece of the Consolidated Rail Corporation. Conrail was established by the American government in 1976 to take over half a dozen bankrupt railroads in the east, plus Penn Central. In its deal with Norfolk Southern, CSX picked up 42 percent of Conrail's track. It had lines throughout the northeast, stretching as far west as St. Louis and Illinois, as far south as West Virginia, and as far north as New York and Connecticut.

If you look at CSX's route map, you'll see a dense, spaghetti-like network covering much of the eastern seaboard of the United States, stretching to Chicago and Montreal in the north and New Orleans and Miami in the south, illustrative of the intensity of the traffic east of the Mississippi to the Atlantic coast. It touches twenty-three American states, two Canadian provinces (Ontario and Quebec), and some seventy ports—ocean, river, and lake—and the most populated geographical regions of the United States and Canada.

That, of course, is good and bad—good because of the tremendous flow of goods throughout the area; bad because trains have to keep stopping at terminals, the spots where the network slows down. A twenty-six-year veteran of CSX, former senior vice president Asok Chaudhuri spoke to the *Daily Record* in Jacksonville, Florida, a few weeks after Harrison took over. He said the densely populated eastern seaboard is vastly different from the wide-open spaces of Canada where trains can run long distances before hitting major terminals. Chaudhuri argued that geography created a potential challenge for Harrison's efforts to lower the operating ratio at CSX in the same fashion as he had at CN and CP. CSX also relied heavily on revenue from shipping coal. With the long-term shift away from coal (in spite of President Donald Trump's stated wishes), a major source of revenue for CSX would likely be in decline. Harrison didn't disagree. Yet within three weeks of his arrival at CSX, he was already predicting the turnaround there would be more dramatic than the one at CP.

"It'll be historic," he said on the phone, forecasting that it would be bigger than any of the previous railroad transformations he'd orchestrated.

Over the four years of his contract, he said thousands of employees would go. CSX would close eight of its twelve hump yards, calling them "major cost centers." As for employee reaction, he reckoned 50 to 60 percent of the staff had jumped on board quickly. Another 30 percent, he said, were in wait-and-see mode, while 20 percent would never be onside. To him, they were "mud."

"They're going to bitch no matter which way you go," he said, adding that "shareholders are going to make a ton of money. Billions."

As for talk that CSX's network through large population centers would create an obstacle to the turnaround, Harrison countered that in Canada, you had to run trains all sorts of places even though the business case wasn't there to service small, underpopulated areas. Then there was the secular move away from coal to cleaner forms of energy, for years the bread and butter of CSX. But Harrison refused to get bogged down in conventional criticism about the issues any individual railroad may or may not face. He had to swat away those salvos during the proxy fight for control of CP. Many said that because of its network through Western Canada and the Rockies, CP faced issues that were more challenging than on CN's routes—weather, tougher grades—and that he'd be unable to match his record performance at CN. He proved them wrong. Harrison argued that each of the Class 1's had opportunities to be the best.

"Nobody has the structural issues that says they're the dead solid winner."

The plan would be to not only cut what he considered fat, but also simplify the network. By eliminating two-thirds of the hump yards, he would be putting CSX into a simple shape, with the four corners of the network being Selkirk, New York (near Albany); Willard, Ohio (60 miles south of Toledo); Nashville, Tennessee; and Waycross, Georgia. Stripped down, CSX wasn't spaghetti; to Harrison it was more or less a square. His was a trimmed-down, cost-conscious approach to capture the bulk of rail shipments east of the Mississippi. It was deceptively clear-eyed design—simplicity that captured the complexity. Overseas, there was also a big cut planned. There were 250 information technology and customer service people based in India. He couldn't imagine how the company managed them from afar.

But as Harrison talked about his assessment of the landscape at CSX and his plans for getting the railroad into shape, he struggled physically. During the week of March 27, just three weeks after grabbing the rudder at CSX, he had a bladder infection. The following week, on April 6, he was scheduled to receive a general anesthetic at a Jacksonville satellite of the Mayo Clinic so polyps could be removed from the area. The bladder issue was just one more health obstacle in an already crowded course he'd been facing for almost two years. Such problems, however, brought out Harrison's wit. The left tire goes flat and we fix it, he said. The right tire goes flat and we fix it. "The car's still runnin'." By the end of a half-hour conversation, though, he was short of breath.

On Sunday evening, April 2, Harrison sounded like his old self. A horse he owned, HH Azur, an eleven-year-old Belgian Warmblood, had just won the Longines FEI World Cup in Omaha. Ever the competitor, Harrison was thrilled. The rider, McLain Ward, was now number one in the world. Adrenaline had washed away the symptoms of Harrison's various afflictions, at least for the moment. He'd be back at the office in Jacksonville the next day for two days. CSX would soon buy a 4,000 square-foot condo there where he could stay. Although he said he wouldn't be in the field, he'd gone a few times, including to Jacksonville and Waycross, Georgia. "All you have to do is smell. Things just start jumping out at you."

He'd also observed what he considered to be wasted space. "They've got waiting areas everywhere," he said. He went to see the executive vice president of operations and discovered she had her own waiting room. "What the shit?" he said to himself. "We've got more waiting rooms than we've got offices here." He took issue as well with what were known as

"CSX holidays," listed on the calendar at corporate head office. "This is *boolshit*," he protested. "These aren't holidays. What do you think about the trainmaster who works New Year's Eve night? You think he gets a holiday?"

On Wednesday, April 5, Harrison went to the Mayo in Jacksonville to be prepped for the bladder procedure scheduled for the next day. When it came time, Jeannie said his oxygen level was too low because the machine he was using wasn't adequate. The procedure was postponed and he flew home that day. Coughing sharply, he described the situation two days later: "I'm not doing my best." The medical team rescheduled him for May 2 but would not use a general anesthetic.

"The prognosis is not great," Harrison said. The medical team was disturbed that he hadn't made progress, although he was quick to add he hadn't exhibited a lot of degradation.

"They just don't have a great plan at this point. They're being very candid that they're frustrated I'm not improving." He was also getting a range of opinions. One doctor told him he had patients who were worse off than he was and they'd been that way for four or five years, while another thought there should have been some improvement. Jeannie, however, said she "never got the impression" he was going to get better.

Harrison was philosophical. "The worst is not the worst," meaning he believed he was mentally prepared for death, if that's what he faced. "[It's] not something I'm scared of," he said, "We're all going to go through it." Harrison never argued with facts. If his health was done, his health was done. "I have very few regrets. There's nothing special about me that I get to dodge death."

Just a month after Harrison was appointed CEO of CSX, Jeannie was shielding him from calls. Six days later, on Good Friday, the two were scheduled to fly to Kansas City to be with Libby and her family. But Libby's clan would instead fly to Florida for Easter because her father was in no mood to travel. And what of the railroad? The previous CEO was already gone and a successor to Harrison had not yet been chosen. If something happened to him, who would take over?

No one had yet been identified as the go-to person. A newly named president of the company, announced just two weeks before the change in CEO, had been the board's anointed successor. But he was not

Harrison's choice. An executive who was in synch with him still needed to be groomed or recruited. Wallace, meanwhile, had left his job at CP to join Harrison and had already bought a house in Jacksonville. He was living in the Omni Hotel near company headquarters while his wife Josée was in Calgary clearing out their old house, getting ready for the movers who would be there mid-April. Wallace was unaware anything had changed with Harrison's health. In fact, they had spoken that morning at nine o'clock, one of the four or five times they'd talk most days. "Are you in the office yet?" the CEO demanded to know.

"It's Saturday morning. I'll be there in half an hour, give me a break," Wallace said with a combination of laughter and exasperation. "He was barking all sorts of shit," he said. "He's definitely got his pedal to the metal now... and patience is not an asset of his." Wallace wondered if Harrison simply thought he was short on time to make the changes he wanted to make. Meanwhile, the chief of staff was the one in the office seven days a week. The senior executives were mostly career CSX people, and although they were polite and kind on the surface, Wallace said he knew they were huddling and talking. Whether Harrison's condition had worsened or not, were investors aware of his situation? Wallace believed Harrison had been forthcoming with both Hilal and the board. But because there had not yet been a board meeting since the transition on March 6, other than Hilal, he said the directors had not seen the oxygen equipment. Wallace said Harrison considered sending them a note prior to the meetings that were scheduled for April 17 to 18, the two days prior to the next earnings release. Wallace worried that if the news about the oxygen got out in an uncontrolled manner, it wouldn't be good. "It is what it is, he needs this, it's supplemental, it's not a big deal," Wallace suggested saying publicly.

He admitted that "when you see him with it the first time, it's kind of shocking." He added that Harrison had been in the office two or three days a week with the oxygen on, working ten or twelve hours a day. Senior executives had seen him using it, as had other staff and operating people, perhaps hundreds of people, Wallace said. But when Harrison sermonized for literally ten hours straight (some of those close to him would jokingly call it pontificating), Wallace said everybody realizes, "Shit, this guy's fine." Certainly, after a session like that Harrison was tired. Anyone would be. "I'm exhausted just listening to him," Wallace said, laughing.

There's no question, however, that the circumstances were highly unusual for a major corporation. Its CEO did not want to be out in public. "It's a little hard to manage," Wallace said. As for investor meetings when Harrison would have to make a presentation, they were targeting a date in late fall, allowing time to make major changes that would impact the stock. If people were making money, they'd be more willing to overlook a CEO carting around an oxygen tank. CSX could not, however, avoid the company's annual meeting scheduled for June 5 in Virginia. Wallace hoped they could just do a fifteen- or twenty-minute "in and out" affair, which was highly unlikely. Earlier that week, someone suggested to Harrison that he should stop working and relax.

"Absolutely not," was the answer.

As for the oxygen, he said whenever there was any reaction, he explained it. "I think they [CSX people] probably leave the room [and ask], 'Why is he taking that oxygen? Is he going to die on us?' It's no secret." They know "he can't run a 5K," but they also witnessed him working a couple of twelve-hour days in Jacksonville. "He's a good guy, he's going to be helpful, let's use him while we can. If we replace him now, what's the difference if we replace him in six months?" According to his contract, the board couldn't let him go for health reasons unless he failed to perform his duties for "180 days in any 365-day period."

He loved the example of Oscar Munoz, who'd been at CSX and was in line to be CEO but had left to run United Airlines. Thirty-eight days after arriving at United, Munoz had a heart attack followed by a transplant almost three months after that. Munoz was back, though, running United. Harrison also cited Jim Collins's famous business book, *Good to Great,* which tells of Kimberley-Clark CEO Darwin Smith turning around the company while dealing with nose and throat cancer, diagnosed just two months after he became CEO in 1971. As Collins wrote, Smith was told by doctors he probably had less than a year to live. They were wrong. Smith was CEO for twenty years. In politics, Franklin Roosevelt was elected to the presidency four times—confined to a wheelchair due to the effects of polio, not to mention having heart disease and severe hypertension. Somehow, he and a senior citizen named

Churchill managed to lead the allied effort against Germany and Japan. Dwight Eisenhower had a heart attack in 1955 during the first term of his presidency—in an era when heart attacks frequently killed people— yet he was re-elected. JFK was hopped-up on drugs to battle Addison's disease, not to mention for chronic back pain that led him to wear a corset-like brace. The truth is, investors in most companies have little knowledge of the health of top executives—which ones are alcoholics, receiving chemotherapy, or taking heart-related drugs or anti-depressants. Still, it's highly unusual and hardly ideal in today's light-speed business world for a CEO to require supplemental oxygen.

When pressed about it, Harrison downplayed it. In more reflective moments, though, he was planning his memorial service and giving instructions to Jeannie. He wanted to be cremated. For a man who made his name on cost savings and efficiencies, an expensive casket was a waste. "Just put me in that urn up on the mantle," he wisecracked. "If you want to say something, just tap on the side of it."

He'd also decided on people he wanted to say a few words at his service—among them, Mark Wallace, Keith Creel, Nadeem Velani, and Laird Pitz. From the equestrian side, he wanted the two championship riders he'd worked closely with, McLain Ward and Rodrigo Pessoa. As for his sons-in-law, Earl Julo and Quentin Judge, he wanted them to do it only if they felt able to get through it. In certain of these cases—Julo, Creel, Wallace, and Ward—there were echoes of a father-son relationship. All were mentored by a man who was the only boy in his family. In addition to his two daughters and three granddaughters (Morgan, Mackenzie, and Hunter), in 2016 a grandson (Harrison Rhodes Judge) arrived "in a family that doesn't produce boys."

Harrison's patience for talking about his health and possible demise, like his patience for many things, was limited. He wanted to talk about it—privately he *needed* to be heard—but then didn't want to talk about it. In the spring of 2017, his granddaughter Mackenzie judged Harrison was "a lot more scared about his health than he leads on. He's kind of the tough man." She felt she could read his anxiety and that he had a lot of it—enough to keep him up at night. He joked about it, which was a signal to her that he was anxious, so he focused on the railroad. It was hard to ignore, however, that the following week the company would report first quarter earnings. Prior to that release on April 19, there would be two days of board meetings in Jacksonville. Most of the directors had not yet seen Harrison on oxygen. "They don't have a lot of choice," he said.

In a call with Wallace, he instructed his chief of staff to ensure there were oxygen machines everywhere he'd be—in the board room and in his office, as well as a portable one available for when he was on the move. Jeannie Harrison, however, expressed worry about the strain of the meetings. Normally, there would be a board dinner one evening. She couldn't envision how her husband would muster the energy to do what was usually required.

In fact, on the night of Tuesday, April 11, Keith Creel paid a visit to his former boss's home. Moving around the house, Harrison was tethered to an oxygen machine but didn't realize that it wasn't powered up. Technology was not his strong suit—he had trouble with a cellphone and a PC—so for an hour and a half, he thought he was getting oxygen but wasn't. As a result, he had a fitful night. At about 7:40 the next morning, Jeannie Harrison called me.

"Hunter isn't feeling very well this morning." She thought he wouldn't be able to continue our interviewing until he rested some more. I asked if I could come to the house anyway so I could begin making my way through his plump scrapbooks she'd laid out.[1] When I arrived at 9:30 am, I didn't want to knock in case I woke him, so I let myself in. It was instantly clear he was not asleep. I could hear him yelling into the phone at some hapless CSX person. Harrison had rallied again. In the past, I'd wondered if he was putting on a show because he knew I was scribbling notes. This time he didn't know I was there. The doors to his office were closed, but his high-volume assault gushed through the crack. Was he an Oscar Munoz or a Darwin Smith, able to get past extreme physical adversity that others would consider career-ending?

For a publicly traded company, though, there is the question of when to disclose material information that would cause a reasonable person to reconsider the value of the company. "I don't know why you would. I don't know what it would accomplish or what it does," Harrison said.

---

1   The scrapbooks had been compiled by staff at CN, followed by his late sister, Sydney.

In his view, it would only result in speculation. Besides, he said, with several medical opinions on offer, "which doctor does the market take or believe?" If, on the other hand, there were suddenly a severe setback—if he were bedridden and given a life expectancy of a matter of weeks—"that would trigger" disclosure. Certainly, this question arose in coverage of Steve Jobs's medical condition. Clearly, Jobs was sicker than the market knew. While his passing was a profound loss, the continued strong performance of Apple shares in the years after his death showed the company did not suffer financially or valuation-wise. Au contraire. Jobs had also carried on (he took medical leaves) for seven years after revealing to Apple employees in 2004 that he had been diagnosed with a rare type of pancreatic cancer. He died in 2011. But in the case of CSX, how many of the new investors in the company—investors who had bought in because of Harrison—knew the particulars of his health? How much did they have a right to know versus Harrison's right to privacy?

"We're not going to lie," Harrison said. If somebody asked if he was taking oxygen, the company and he would say "yeah."

Meantime, Harrison worked at home—at all hours—coughing, while dressed in his pajamas and robe. The man who had taken the reins of what was now a $43 billion company, the third-largest railroad in the United States—atop 31,000 people—was frequently running it in his nightclothes. In spite of his health, he was plowing through and blithely predicting the CSX turnaround would "probably be the grand slam" of the companies he'd improved as CEO. A little more than a month in, he claimed he could see victory in sight. In addition to the one thousand people the company had cut just prior to his arrival, he vowed to cut another thousand by year end. By the end of the four years, assuming normal growth patterns, CSX's workforce would fall to between 21,000 and 22,500. "The deal is not to get as low as we can go. The deal is to grow the bottom line."

The upcoming first quarter report would not show much change in operations, given he'd been just six weeks on the job. Looking ahead, though, Harrison calculated that in the second quarter report in July 2017, "we'll have to show a little leg as to what's going on. We can't just say we're still looking." When analysts and investors heard the number of hump yard closures, head count numbers, or estimates about the number of locomotives and railcars CSX would cut, "there'll be a run" in the stock. He reckoned such a run could result in another five or six billion dollars added to the market value of the company, about a five or six dollar gain in the share price. "You'll see plateaus. It'll be in steps rather than some direct trend line."

As for locomotives, initially the number could be reduced by 450 to 500 out of 4,300. In the end, "it'll be 30 percent of the locomotives" and 20 to 25 percent of the freight cars. At the same time, he predicted a dramatic improvement in service. "That's what people don't have any appreciation for," he said, forecasting a two- or three-day improvement in shipping time from Chicago to the Gulf.

"People say 'I don't know how y'all do it.' I say, 'Just don't go in a hump yard.'" Every time you go into one, he explained, the dwell time was twenty-seven hours. By the fourth quarter of 2017, the OR would be 65 or 66, down from 69.4. That's where CSX had aimed for a decade. "We're finally going to get there." It could be 66, it could be 64, "but in that tight mid-60s range."

Asset sales would also come. There were seven company locations in Jacksonville. A building adjacent to headquarters, he said, would be vacated and sold. That alone, he estimated, would generate $25 million. But with a plan that called for cutting ten thousand people—most of whom were management—"you need office space for ten thousand *less* people." The goal was to get from seven locations down to two or three. In all, Harrison ball-parked perhaps a billion dollars–plus in asset sales. In the Chicago area alone, given CSX's large stakes in the Belt Railway and the Indiana Harbor Belt that circles the city, as well as various yards, there were tracts of land that could be sold to developers.

No detail was too small for Harrison. Even the company ball cap got a makeover. Instead of black with white letters, it shifted to company colors, blue and gold.

ON THURSDAY, APRIL 13, he awoke around 7 am and wandered into his home office, again in his housecoat, pajamas, and slippers. He started reading the internal company "clips," press reports compiled by the PR department. By 7:15 he was on the phone, snarling. He'd learned a train had blocked a public crossing the previous Monday in a small town in Florida—for eighteen hours. Staff had gone home rather than fix the problem, gumming up the network, creating a public nuisance, and putting a dent in average train speed, a holy number for Harrison. Meantime, the PR person was quoted in the local media as *an emailer*—someone who didn't return phone calls. A train inexplicably stuck on a public crossing for eighteen hours was bad enough, but someone who preferred emails to picking up the phone was dire. Harrison had a point. Frequently, it can take several emails to accomplish what can be done in a two-minute call. Although he looked at email, Harrison rarely responded to it in kind.

Like many effective leaders, Harrison took the path of simplicity. On the relatively clean desk in front of him, there was a large index card with his name printed at the top. Written in his own hand were the key telephone numbers (land line and cell) he needed—his chief of staff, the COO, the general counsel, and his doctor. On the back, he had another fifteen numbers, including those of other key operating people at the railroad, as well as Hilal's.

On April 19, the railroad reported first quarter results. The period ended on March 31, less than a month after Harrison arrived, so he couldn't claim much responsibility for what the company announced, a record operating ratio of 69.2 percent. However, the stock rose after hours and again the next morning when CSX announced a quarterly dividend increase of two cents and a $1 billion share buyback that would reduce the amount of stock outstanding. Before the market opened on the 20th, the shares pointed to a 7 percent increase.

On the conference call for analysts and investors, Harrison had his first opportunity to publicly answer critics, including analysts, who'd raised concerns that CSX's network was spaghetti-like versus linear Canadian railroads. Harrison said, "The way to handle it is to eat the spaghetti and get rid of it." He meant get rid of the hump yards and terminals allowing trains to get through faster. He also said that Precision Scheduled Railroading, in a complex network, would provide more opportunities than at a linear railroad, thereby turning the criticism on its head.

"We're going to get bigger in the rearview mirror" of the competition and then "pass them on the left," he said. When asked, however, if competitors would up their game and perhaps try to copy what he was doing, he said they could buy the books he'd written at CN. "[They're each] on eBay for a thousand dollars," he cracked, adding that he hoped they would try to emulate his operating methods, because he viewed his competitors as partners, since railroads depend on each other's lines to get their cars to where they need to go. Like an old rocker playing oldies to an adoring crowd, Harrison gave the market what it wanted to hear (the railroad didn't need nine dispatching offices, for example). He said CSX would curtail bureaucracy, and he adorned the basic melody with classic Harrison riffs like "Don't spend one dollar in precious capital until you've explored every operating alternative." He was beginning his farewell tour and they were loving it.

While the number of locomotives and freight cars would be reduced, four Atlanta yards would be consolidated into one super yard. That brought up real estate, so he mentioned a parcel in Atlanta "that's going to be worth a good deal of money." But real estate sales would be "gravy." It would be a big number, he said, but wouldn't drive the business. Nonetheless, it would be considered when making operating decisions.

"The real opportunity I see is on the highway." Harrison was telling them that CSX was aiming to steal market share from trucks, which still hauled most of the freight in North America. CSX would be better than trucks, he promised. You could also hear a message to Washington, suggesting IT jobs in India could be repatriated. Although not a fan of Donald Trump, he even used the phrase "Made in America." (The jobs in India were indeed eliminated.) He sounded realistic about coal, long CSX's core business. "Coal is not something the rail industry should depend on."[2]

As for Chicago, he reiterated his belief that the congested swamp there was unsustainable, something he'd argued when CP tried to buy Norfolk Southern. This time, though, he had more of a seat at the table. CSX was a much bigger player in Chicago than either CP or CN. Although he said he had no intention of trying to merge with another railroad during his term at CSX, he couldn't resist saying that "one stroke of

---

2   With politics, Cayce said her father considered himself an independent. In December 2017, a CSX employee asked him about the Trump tax cuts. He predicted that, long term, they would put the US in financial peril.

a pen" would shift traffic away from Chicago. A merger between an eastern and a western road could route traffic through underused infrastructure in Kansas City, he reminded analysts, just in case they'd forgotten since he'd made the case for the CP-NS deal. Alas, he reiterated it would not be on his watch. "There's no such plan," he said. "I don't have time."

He told them he had just four years (he would be lucky to have that, given his health). "I want to go out at CSX in blue and gold, running through the goal posts," he said. He barely coughed through the call, although in the last half hour of the two-hour session, there were a few hacks in the background. Those on the other end of the line would have been hard pressed to know they were listening to a man on oxygen who could barely leave his home the previous week. Throughout the call, there was not one question from analysts about his health. In fact, one of them said, "Hunter, you sound well." He made it through his first test. The next day, Friday, April 21, the stock was up another 2.44 percent to $50.77. Since the earnings were released after trading on April 19, the stock had added $4.14 or 8.88 percent. It was the run he'd predicted.

The week before the first quarter earnings report, though, Harrison had a series of phone calls with senior executives in the company. In a peculiar way, phoning in his orders from a distance seemed to create more of an aura of authority than he already had. They could only hear him, which left the rest to their imaginations. It was the railroad god on the line. Had they seen how rough he looked, their anxiety level might have been considerable going into their first earnings release with him.

On the call with chief operating officer Cindy Sanborn and her direct report, Jermaine Swafford, Harrison defaulted to his tried and true— early quits. It was not enough, he said, for a supervisor to simply say, "Well, we told 'em . . . I've done my part here." If supervisors couldn't confront those leaving work early, supervisors would be confronted. He queried Sanborn and Swafford about pushback, knowing full well it would happen, as it had at CN and CP. He said some would resist, figuring they could fight the change and it would go away. They didn't know Harrison.

"This is not without risk, to push back or resist," he said. There would be pushback in Atlanta. Selkirk, New York, however, was working well in his view. "Life is going to be good in Selkirk."

Shortly after, however, there was another call, which included three top executives plus Mark Wallace. It was a headcount discussion, and the volume rose. Harrison spoke specifically about taking a component of the New Orleans operation from eight people to two. "What in the hell would we be doing with eight people at the New Orleans ramp?" suggesting two clerks would do. The six excess workers meant three thousand dollars a day, eating up all the profit at the location, he explained. This micro example led him to sketching the macro picture (the ramp was closed).

"Two thousand people come out this year, starting with the restructuring. Does that give anybody heartburn or any problem?" There was silence on the line. If I start to look at my earnings curve, he said, or free cash flow, "that's where I am." He was trying to clarify the goal for them—how the market could evaluate the streamlining. He was going beyond railroading—playing the financial market game and teaching them how to play it. Then, he got to the three- to four-year target.

"If I had to make an educated guess," he said, "over the four-year plan, the number is like in the eight and a half to ten range." There was silence again. He was telling them that as much as a third of the workforce would go—8,500 to ten thousand staff. "The bottom line is we got too many people around here." Cutting that many wasn't something he was proud of, but he gave examples of reading the organizational chart and coming across a person's title yet having no clue what the person did.

He wasn't finished. Then came the assault on the monthly "outlook." He growled that compiling it was simply busy work, again adding no value. The team already drew up a budget for the year in the fall. Unless something changed drastically, he didn't want high-priced employees fooling with spreadsheet updates. "Shit, we ain't nuthin' but statisticians . . . I want to move boxcars" and serve customers, he added. "I want to know who in the shit you do this for?" Again, silence.

The tirade went on. "I didn't want to get on my pedestal today, but it's too late." Wallace, who'd seen Harrison in table-pounding mode for years, tried to play good cop. He suggested an outlook was perhaps useful once a quarter, rather than once a month. Harrison took the cue from his chief of staff and changed tack. He allowed that he wasn't so concerned about the month as he was the quarter and year-over-year comparisons "cause can't nobody manipulate that."

"I know one thing. I know how the street [analysts and investors] looks at it. That's the most important to me." Railroading wasn't about being a train aficionado. It was only a route to shareholder value creation. That was everything. It had nothing to do with outlooks or PowerPoint presentations. Harrison put it plainly—it was about hitting significant targets. "Whatever comp I get is what we achieve." Railroading, shareholder value, compensation—one, two, three. Get it?

On April 27, he called from Florida. According to Harrison, his first board meetings had gone well—supportive, complimentary, candid exchanges. "They just want to make some money and make some good headlines, which I can do." There were all kinds of things that the company had simply overlooked, he said, that he learned about every day—simple things that were an opportunity to save a hundred million here and a hundred million there. "This thing is a gold mine," he gushed. "It's unimaginable." While he could see where the nuggets lay, they would soon prove to be more difficult to grab than he anticipated.

One issue continued to come up at CSX—coal. More than 18 percent of the company's revenue—the biggest segment—came from coal. Given environmental pressure on the industry, how would that impact the railroad's prospects? "Has it hurt? Yeah," Harrison said, but "in my view, fossil fuels are dead. It's not going to be a base for the company to build on." This wasn't an environmentalist talking. This was a realist. He'd said something similar in 2016 while CEO of CP, acknowledging climate change and drawing praise from Greenpeace. Harrison reckoned that in fifteen, twenty, or twenty-five years, coal would fizzle out. "If you care anything about the environment, you're not going to burn coal." He also said that eventually Trump would not be in power and there would be regulations that would make it very difficult for the coal industry.

"They [CSX] have used it as an excuse." Yes, it was 20 percent of the company's business and it was down 10 percent, but Harrison said he was making up for it elsewhere. As he put it, "It's the simple ass stuff." Like the early quits—not just a Canadian phenomenon; that's what differentiated companies, he said. "That's the difference in CN before and after. That's the difference in CP before and after." Roughly quantifying it, he said that's 50 percent of it. "It's execution and make people get off their ass." It's training and selling the supervisor, he said, convincing them "that they're not mistreating people when they ask people to work eight hours."

He recalled a labor meeting in Toronto where a supervisor in the back had raised his hand.

"I can't do this," the man said. "I can't make these guys change what they're doing. And they're my friends."

"Well, you can't be a supervisor," Harrison said.

"What do I do?"

"Go back to work."

Harrison said the employee gave up his supervisory position and went back to being a mechanic. "We take great mechanics and make them piss poor leaders," he said. "Don't do that."

Harrison was like a drug-sniffing dog when he started working at a new railroad. Thumbing through the CSX employee rulebook, which resembled a phonebook from a mid-sized city, he shook his head. There was a section about the rules allowing for napping on the job, just the thing Hunter Harrison wanted to see. "We ain't nappin' on my watch. No more naps." As of April 2017, naps were out at CSX. Holding up the manual, he said that the more of *this* you have, the less safe you are. He argued that voluminous rulebooks give people a false sense of security. He planned to eliminate it and have a new one written that would fit in a pocket and not tell people "how to walk." He also planned to get rid of the two or three so-called safety crews. His view was that the company had supervisors. If supervisors did their job, the company didn't need safety specialists. With safety specialists, he said supervisors think they don't have to worry about safety.

Health issues, however, were ever present. Although the surgical procedure to remove polyps from his bladder had gone well and he claimed to be feeling better when we spoke three days after, there was an incident the following week. On a flight from Florida to White Plains, New York, to the airport closest to his Connecticut farm, Harrison felt unwell. His oxygen wasn't working properly, and the plane made an emergency landing in Philadelphia. I was slated to arrive a few days later to continue interviewing him and the family. Jeannie emailed that "Hunter is not doing great but wants to get to work on the book so it is good you are coming."

On Monday, May 15, as I sat in Toronto's Pearson Airport waiting for my flight to LaGuardia where I'd get a shuttle to Connecticut, Jeannie texted. She said she'd taken him to the hospital in Greenwich, but that I should still come. She didn't know how long he'd be there, but if possible, she would bring me to the hospital to speak with him. Even there, Harrison wanted to work. By 1:40 the next afternoon, though, he was back home walking slowly in a blue track suit. His medication had been increased to help calm his coughing, and it worked.

It turns out the company-operated jet they were on did not have the oxygen Harrison required. Aside from the standard emergency masks, "We only had my little portable unit," Jeannie said (CP's aircraft had been outfitted for his needs). He was close to losing consciousness but revived quickly after receiving oxygen from emergency medical personnel. In spite of the disturbing episode, shortly after arriving back at the farm, he was driving around the property in an ATV, showing a visitor the vast facilities.

By 3:30, he was ready for interviews again and the sparkle returned. Over dinner, he was lively, then watched the NBC hit *The Voice* with Jeannie and his granddaughter Mackenzie after eating (he also enjoyed *Judge Judy*). Then after 9 pm, he took a call from the *Wall Street Journal*. The paper was getting calls about his health and stories about him requiring oxygen. He told the reporter, Jacquie McNish, that yes, he used oxygen to mitigate his cough, but that his doctor had said it was okay for him to work. But how often was he going into the office? He said he wouldn't get into specifics, but he told her he asked the board not to judge him "on attendance," but on results. He also said that independent counsel had deemed his condition did not require a public disclosure of a material change at the company. Harrison tried to persuade McNish that his health was a non-story.

"Tell them to buy Burlington Northern," he said defiantly and facetiously, an indication that if shareholders were worried about their CSX shares, they could vote with their money.[3]

When the call ended around 10 pm, he phoned Mark Wallace. Harrison was adamant that there should be no public release about his health.

---

3   The only way they could buy BNSF was to buy Berkshire Hathaway, its owner.

"I don't think we do anything about the health," he said, adding that counsel's view was that once you released something, you were in Harrison's words a "dead duck." The issue would never go away. Wallace was less sure about it, saying that it "will be introduced" at the annual meeting—i.e., a large number of people would see him with oxygen. Harrison seemed outwardly unconcerned.

On the morning of May 17, 2017, he held a conference call with Wallace, CSX's chief counsel Ellen Fitzsimmons, and David Baggs, the treasurer and head of investor relations. They talked about how to answer questions about his health, given upcoming investor meetings and media inquiries. Fitzsimmons's advice: "In a proxy solicitation—given an upcoming shareholders' vote—any communication about a CEO's health had to be 'fulsome and accurate,'" she said, adding that health is nobody else's business in the "absence of a performance issue. When there is a performance issue, we'll talk about health."[4]

"I haven't been hiding it. I haven't been wearing a Halloween mask," Harrison said. "The doctor says I'm okay to work." Certainly, much had already been done. In addition to the reduction in hump yards, locomotives, and real estate opportunities, "train starts" had fallen by at least 25 percent. With longer trains and not as many locomotives, there weren't as many engines to start. This was a data point he'd begun watching at Illinois Central, and the reduction was "huge." A drop meant the same amount of volume was traveling on fewer, longer trains, saving on crew costs. That was almost $100,000 a day right there, which was about $35 million a year. On top of that, with fewer people required, it was not only the wages but the savings on benefits, a domino effect.

At 12:30 pm, Harrison had a conference call with one of CSX's biggest shareholders. Harrison said the firm had been a shareholder in other major railroads but had not participated in the CP turnaround.

---

4   A CP spokesperson said when Harrison had health concerns at the railroad, "he did not feel like his faculties were diminished to the point that he could not run the railroad." However, the spokesperson said there was an ongoing internal debate with CP's legal team and everybody else who needed to know to ensure "all of the necessary steps and conversations were being had to decide whether it was material." Laird Pitz said when Harrison's health problems arose, Creel "was running the company in many respects" so "I never felt that the company was at risk."

Now, it had bought into the CSX-Harrison story. The market, investors, and pundits, he maintained, also frequently missed a key factor—the people who make a difference at companies, the Hunter Harrisons or the next ones coming up.

The portfolio manager led the discussion, but he had colleagues on the line from the UK to California. Harrison rose to the occasion, answering all of their questions without coughing. Still, there was a question about his health. He told them he wouldn't work if his doctor said it put his health at risk, adding that the doctor recommended that he work because not doing so would put more stress on him. His response did not elicit a follow-up. The participants would not have guessed that he was talking to them while wearing his pajamas, white terry cloth bathrobe, and slippers.

The work had begun in earnest, but Mark Wallace had been notified that morning that the *Wall Street Journal* would be publishing a story about the CEO's condition later that day. At first, Harrison seemed blasé about it. But later, he worried that he might now have a battle at the corporate level, with directors who would become uncomfortable with his health. If you set yourself up as a "rock star and a one-man show" and something went wrong, what happens? he asked hypothetically.

It didn't stop him, however, from having a glass of wine at dinner a couple of hours after the story was published. His wife and granddaughter had gone out, so Harrison and I dined alone that night. He sipped a cabernet from a silver wine goblet. Jeannie would have been upset about him having a drink, but he was still making his own rules. The stress and emotion, however, were weighing heavily on her. That afternoon in the family room off the kitchen of her home in Connecticut, with her granddaughter Mackenzie sitting nearby, Jeannie Harrison began talking about her husband's condition, unprompted. She fretted about his resistance to hiring a dedicated nurse to look after his needs. "We just disagree on that," he said. That morning his oxygen alarms had been sounding. As he worked at his desk, the tube got caught under the door to his office, restricting the flow. Jeannie fixed it. She was now his principal caregiver and left the house infrequently.

"I don't want him to die on my watch," Jeannie said. She began to cry, a rare sight in public, according to her husband, who said he was more prone to outward displays of emotion. "This is all he wants to do in life," Jeannie said. "I think he thinks it's his purpose in life." He was still the kid from Memphis who needed a focus.

When the *Wall Street Journal* story came out, it was arguably a good thing. The article quoted Harrison confirming that he used oxygen—but that he was "having a ball" running CSX. It was information from the source himself. Seeing him at the annual meeting wouldn't be such a shock for investors. The day after, shares of CSX rose 1.5 percent.

The next morning, he was on the phone to three of the company's railroaders in the Jacksonville area, ripping into them for poor service. A customer had emailed him directly with a complaint that he viewed as valid and was letting them have it. The fact that the customer felt the only way to get satisfaction was to reach out to the CEO reflected badly on them, he told them. But day by day, the CSX troops were learning General Harrison's way. Merit is what mattered. He didn't care if you were black, blue, transgender, or Martian. If you got the job done effectively and you were honest, he didn't care what or who you were.

ALMOST SIX MONTHS after he resigned as CEO of CP, Hunter Harrison was at The Breakers again. A dozen people, including certain former and current directors of the railroad's board, gathered for an intimate retirement dinner for him. Among them: Bill Ackman, Paul Hilal, Andy Reardon, Keith Creel, Rebecca MacDonald, and Gordon Trafton. It was a candle-lit, flower-adorned, black-tie event. A six-piece band played soft, pop-style dinner music. There was a tiered cake for the honored guest, complete with a silhouette of a black horse. Those in attendance said a few words, with Creel making the wry observation that this was Harrison's retirement dinner—*again*. When asked why Jeannie wasn't there (she was in New York City with friends), Harrison quoted her as saying she'd already been to five retirement dinners "and you haven't retired yet." (She called that "another embellishment.") Harrison spoke and said a few words about everyone around the table. For some, it was bittersweet. They'd worked with a living legend and they didn't want it to end. But once more, Harrison had moved on. It was a legacy dinner, but he wasn't finished crowning it. He was still closing yards, including a relatively new one an hour north of Nashville. Based on his study of the

CSX network, the Casky yard was in the wrong place. It was also where he discovered trains delayed for up to two and a half hours so they could be refueled to travel from Chicago to Jacksonville. Harrison was puzzled and went directly to the man responsible in the yard, asking why he thought the refueling was required. The employee told him, "We can't make one thousand miles," the approximate distance between the two cities. He was challenging the wrong person. Harrison knew the train could make it on one tank of fuel.

"Just fill 'er up tonight in Chicago," he instructed. "Call me when it quits." Harrison soon got a call, but not because the train ran out of fuel.

"I'm sorry," the employee said. "You're right again."

"How many gallons did it have left?"

"Three hundred."

It was hard to get around Harrison's granular knowledge of railroading. At the same time, Cayce says her father was not "a railroad buff" or a "foamer," as they're referred to by railroaders. The shelves of his offices were not cluttered with model trains. As Jim Gray put it, Harrison was not nostalgic about railways. "He cared about today and tomorrow," Gray said.

As for the here and now, Harrison was also thinking about the competition. CSX's biggest competitor in the eastern corridor is Norfolk Southern, the company Harrison tried to combine with CP. Harrison's contention was that by not agreeing to the deal, NS would pay for it for the next couple of years while he ran CSX. "I'm going to bust their nuts," he vowed (so much for him wanting strong competitors). Harrison predicted CSX could take about 10 to 15 percent of NS's business. He said CSX would get its costs lower than NS's and then price more aggressively. "It won't take me long and I'll catch the rabbit." Indeed, on CNBC, Jim Cramer raved about Harrison, calling him "the train whisperer" and the "new darling of Wall Street." By July 12, CSX's shares topped $55, up from $36.88 when the news broke in January that Hilal and Harrison had teamed up, a 49 percent gain. The company's value had risen $16 billion. In an interview earlier that month, Ned Kelly said Harrison was "very engaged. I think people's reaction has been that he's improving the railroad."

Each time Harrison took over a new railroad, however, investors wanted more and wanted it faster. After the market closed on July 18,

CSX released its second quarter results. The reaction from analysts was lukewarm at best. The stock was down in afterhours trading. Harrison and Wallace complained about it over dinner that night in Jacksonville, anticipating the conference call with analysts and investors the next morning. The stock had already run up so much since January that large expectations were already built into the share price. The railroad had to deliver stellar results to live up to them. Once again breaching doctor's orders not to drink, Harrison sipped a 2010 Bordeaux at dinner, followed by a double Hennessey to go with a piece of key lime pie for dessert. He got back to his hotel around 10:30 pm. To Jeannie Harrison's irritation, Paul Hilal phoned their room—Harrison's cellphone—at 11:38 pm that night. It never stopped.

Amazingly, Harrison's health and energy seemed better than in the spring. A late evening meal didn't prevent him from being in the office at 7:20 the next morning. He was revved up for the second quarter conference call, which lasted two hours and fifteen minutes. His strategy was to "needle" the analysts a bit, which he did. He told them he hoped they'd read the same earnings release he'd read, reminding them, "We had a helluva quarter." But they weren't buying it and neither was the market, which rightly or wrongly expected more. On July 19, CSX's stock dropped more than 6 percent by mid-session—even though profits were up, the operating ratio was better, and the company announced an increase to the share repurchase program, which can often be a positive catalyst for the share price.

Harrison observed on the call that what used to be an all-star performance didn't even make the cut anymore. When he went to CP, people doubted he could do what he promised in four years. At CSX, the analyst community seemed to expect everything in his first four *months*. Near the end of the call, he sharpened his comments. "I haven't missed one yet," Harrison boasted about his multiple turnarounds. He told those listening that he sure as hell wasn't going to miss the last one, being CSX. He wasn't going to give analysts the opportunity to write things that would frustrate him when he was no longer there.

After the conference call, he did a few brief phone interviews with the media. To a reporter from the Associated Press, Harrison got the last word. "They don't get it. That's why they're analysts." By the close of trading, the stock recovered slightly, closing just below $52. Harrison said he wasn't worried. The impact of the changes he'd made, he said, would start to materialize in subsequent quarters, perhaps even by October, when the company reported third quarter results and just before an investor conference at the end of that month in Palm Beach.

What did worry him was the focus on service disruptions and relationships with customers, a raw nerve for Harrison going back to his days at CN. He didn't like the criticism and wanted specifics—which customer, when, and where? When a reporter for the *Wall Street Journal* mentioned a document containing such details, Harrison challenged him to produce it. Suspicious by nature—his granddaughter Morgan said that she didn't think her grandfather liked "anybody at first"—that afternoon Harrison wondered aloud whether there was an orchestrated effort to bring customer complaints about CSX to the fore. He said that never before in fifty-plus years in the business had he felt what he'd felt on that particular day. "Don't get in a piss fight with a skunk," he told two of his top executives, a warning to whomever was drumming up the campaign he imagined existed. There was no mistaking who the skunk was—the man sucking on an oxygen tube 24/7, just months away from his seventy-third birthday.

Harrison showed no signs of fading away. If anything, he was more invigorated. He never "punched out" from the job. Days before, he'd kept CSX's chief legal counsel and his chief of staff in the office until past midnight. Aside from the options he'd been granted, he had another motivation for working hard. He told a reporter "I spent $15 million of my money—cash—bettin' on it, okay? I'm not going to miss any meals, but I don't have that kind of money to throw away." Wallace confirmed their back of the envelope prediction was that the OR would be sub-60 by 2020.

In spite of the frustrating conference call, that afternoon Harrison was onto other matters. He'd violated his own "no consultants" rule to bring in a former senior VP from CN, Sameh Fahmy. Fahmy knew how to save money. He was also another Harrison loyalist, and he gave an example of why, which went beyond the work. In 2009, at an executive committee meeting at CN with more than twenty people in the room, Harrison noticed Fahmy was very quiet.

"Sameh, what's wrong?"

"Nothing, Mr. Harrison."

"No, no, no. Something's wrong," Harrison said. "You're not yourself."

The CEO kept pressing him. Fahmy was indeed troubled. His daughter was undergoing a cesarean. Her first delivery had been harrowing and Fahmy was tense. "The only person who noticed was Hunter," Fahmy said, sitting in a conference room at CSX in Jacksonville.

At sixty-five, Fahmy still wanted to work—and he wanted to work with Harrison again, where "things get done fast, decisions get made fast." Not only did Fahmy still hold 50,000 CN shares, but he'd loaded up on CSX since Harrison came on the scene, so he had a direct interest in the railroad earning more money. He owned 10,000 CSX shares and was convinced he could find savings for his old boss (he'd bought several thousand shares that morning when the stock dropped during the conference call). In one year alone, he reckoned he could ferret out $35 million, which would have amounted to about 7 percent of the latest quarter's earnings. Fuel was a no-brainer to Fahmy. The key to using less, he said, was balancing horsepower to tonnage. "You don't want too much power for the tonnage that you are carrying, because if you do, you are going to burn fuel for nothing. So that would be one of the first things I would look at."

AMONG THE FACTORS highest on Harrison's list was culture. CSX, he said, was the sum of putting together more previous railroads than any of the other Class 1's. "We don't have a culture," he said. "We have about nineteen." As a result, he said staff "don't know where they belong." To enact cultural change, Hunter Camps would be revived. He hadn't done them since CN, but he would at CSX in mid-summer 2017 at—where else—The Breakers. Harrison would speak to the troops for hours on end, just like the old days, oxygen be damned. Jeannie texted me while he was there, saying he was "loving every minute of it."

By August, however, there was more pressure. A thirty-two-car CSX derailment in Hyndman, Pennsylvania, forced the evacuation of hundreds of people. Liquefied petroleum gas and molten sulfur had leaked and there was a fire. A little over a week later, the last of the residents were allowed to return to their homes. But it was a chilling reminder of how edgy the public had become about rail accidents since a runaway train carrying crude oil derailed and exploded in 2013 in Lac-Mégantic, Quebec, killing forty-seven people.[5]

Around the same time, customers were rearing up again as service complaints had become a bigger issue since the July conference call. The campaign Harrison had imagined was for real. In a letter to key members of Congress, the Rail Customer Coalition called for US regulators to investigate what it called CSX's "chronic service failures." It was signed by forty-six groups representing, among others, farmers as well as the forest and chemical industries. The letter said that major service changes had been imposed with little advance notice, and CSX's response had been "woefully inadequate." It went on to say that it had put rail-dependent businesses "at risk of shutting down," threatening the health of the economy. The disgruntled customer issue was haunting him once more and threatening to become a political issue— double trouble.

Harrison didn't hold back. "CSX was greatly disappointed with your many unfounded and exaggerated statements in your letter of August 14 related to the service experienced by some customers." He wrote that CSX was in the midst of "transformational changes" and would work with the Surface Transportation Board, which had written a letter in late July about customer complaints. The STB had requested weekly service performance data from the railroad. Harrison followed up with an email apologizing to customers: "The pace of change at CSX has been extremely rapid, and while most people at the company have embraced the new plan, unfortunately, a few have pushed back and continue to do so," he said, adding, "This resistance to change has resulted in some service disruptions. To those customers who have experienced such

---

5   A CP train initially transported that cargo, but handed it off to another railroad, Montreal, Maine & Atlantic (MMA) in Montreal. The accident occurred with an MMA crew on an MMA train, locomotive, and track. The investigation reported there were eighteen distinct causes and contributing factors that led to the accident. Among them, "a weak safety culture" at MMA "that contributed to the continuation of unsafe conditions and unsafe practices." The Transportation Safety Board went on to conclude that "employee training, testing, and supervision were not sufficient" and that "the company's safety management system was not effective." The TSB also said that Transport Canada Headquarters "did not effectively monitor the Region's activities" and the company required more frequent inspections.

issues, we sincerely apologize." The juke box was once again spinning that familiar tune, "The Customer Blues," featuring Hunter Harrison. If there were ever any evidence that anti-Americanism toward him was a red herring in Canada, this was it. *His own countrymen were anti-Harrison.*

ON THE NIGHT of August 18, 2017, he had another high fever. This time his temperature was approximately 102 Fahrenheit, he said. He was close to going to the hospital before it broke. On the 19th, he was tired and short of breath on the phone, at least for the first fifteen minutes. If he could just complete two years on the job, he said, he'd have CSX turned around. As for when the turn would begin to show, "if we're not already there [by Q1 2018], we'll get there by the second quarter." For the first time, though, he allowed this one was tough—tougher than his previous three. At Illinois Central, it had been a private equity scrubbing. At CN, the railroad had already been through the first turnaround with Tellier and it was clear there'd be a second, Harrison's. At CP, most of the employees wanted better performance. They were sick of being the worst railroad. But CSX was different. His son-in-law Earl said, "I hate to say this, but in a way, they're more set in their ways in the southeast." As a result, the resistance put an additional strain on Harrison. "He's fighting that," Julo said. Harrison was not quite six months into the job and admitted that he'd thought it would be easier. This was also going to be his last act, so there was more pressure. "It's going to be the hardest one by far," he said. It was giving him nightmares.

The next morning, Sunday, August 20, Harrison held a three-hour conference call with the key operating people at the company. He showed his determination to succeed by applying more pressure. More disruption was coming, he warned. Instead of two thousand employees cut by the end of the year, he said on the phone it would more likely be double that. On September 6, CSX cut its financial guidance, adjusting a previously expected operating ratio in the mid-60s to the high end of the mid-60s, the kind of subtle change market participants obsess over. The company cited operating challenges in July and August. A public hearing was also scheduled for September by the Surface Transportation Board in Washington. Harrison was supposed to attend to hear customer grievances, but the meeting was postponed until October due to Hurricane Irma bearing down on Florida. The storm felled three trees on Harrison's property, while Wallace's home in Jacksonville lost power for several days. CSX headquarters sustained minor damage. South of Orlando, the railroad was out of service for a few days, resulting in minor losses. The hearing, when it occurred, was expected to be "a bit of a gong show," with Wallace anticipating he'd have to keep Harrison calm while the CEO sat and listened to complaints, "some deserved, some not." While the hearing, according to Wallace, went better than expected, Harrison said later it was "frustratin' as shit." He couldn't contain himself, however, when reflecting on one of the complainant's gripes.

"You know what we've had to do?" he said, mimicking a complaint from customers who had to find alternatives to CSX. "Pay these exorbitant truck rates!" Pause. "*Well, kiss my ass,*" he said, relishing each word.

On October 9, 2017—three weeks before the company's first investor day since Harrison took charge—the stress level was stratospheric. The CEO wanted to make changes in senior management but was experiencing resistance from certain members of the board of directors.

"We've got this major, major investor day. We've got this 2020 plan to lay out to the street," Wallace said, explaining the scenario. "We've got to be able to give some confidence to them that we're going to hit those numbers—with a guy on stage on oxygen."

To give comfort to the investment community, they hoped the plan would involve announcing a surprise hire of a major senior railroad executive, someone who could carry out Harrison's plan and be a backstop in case anything happened to him. Harrison and Wallace wanted to show bench strength. But some directors were not yet onside. It brought to mind the concern Paul Hilal had expressed during negotiations. He'd fought for more directors on the Mantle Ridge slate to give Harrison the carte blanche he needed to carry out the transformation. What Hilal had fretted about—and Harrison had minimized—had materialized. Harrison always said he'd told the board that if it wanted him to make dinner, it had to let him buy the groceries. But he was now feeling constrained.

"That's why activists want control," Wallace said, "so they can do whatever they want." It wasn't getting any easier.

TOP: With Bill Ackman, Pershing Square town hall, Toronto, February 2012. Credit: Fred Lum/The *Globe and Mail*.

BOTTOM: Mother and daughters, 2007. ©LILA PHOTO.

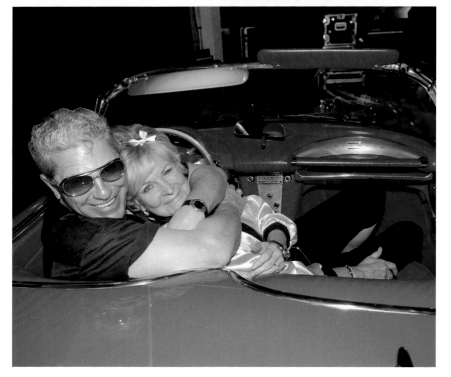

LEFT: He never missed a chance to cut a rug, 2007. ©LILA PHOTO.
RIGHT: His seventieth birthday party, 2014. ©LILA PHOTO.
BOTTOM: Hamming it up with Jeannie, West Palm Beach, Florida. ©LILA PHOTO

TOP: On his own jet with Lucy, the family dog.
BOTTOM: With championship rider McLain Ward, Old Salem Farm Grand Prix, 2014.

TOP: Cayce's wedding at the farm in Connecticut, October 2011. Credit: Elisabeth Millay
BOTTOM: Father of the bride, October 2011. Credit: Elisabeth Millay

TOP: Author interviewing Harrison in Florida home, December 2016. Photo by Mark Wallace.
BOTTOM: In home office preparing to leave CP, January 2017. Photo by author.

TOP: CP retirement dinner, June 2017. (L to R) Paul Hilal, Andy Reardon, Gordon Trafton, Keith Creel, Hunter Harrison. ©LILA PHOTO.

LEFT: Entering The Breakers in Palm Beach, Florida, to do business with CP for the last time, January 18, 2017. Photo by author.

RIGHT: With Paul Hilal at CP retirement dinner, June 2017, The Breakers, Palm Beach. ©LILA PHOTO.

LEFT: With long-time friend and colleague, Laird Pitz, December 6, 2017, Palm Beach, Florida. ©LILA PHOTO.

RIGHT: Keith Creel, Harrison and Mark Wallace. ©LILA PHOTO.

BOTTOM: The last Hunter Camp, CSX, December 6, 2017, Palm Beach, Florida. Photo by author.

TOP: With Jeannie at his seventieth birthday party, 2014. ©LILA PHOTO.
BOTTOM: With grandson Harrison Rhodes Judge, 2017. Photo by author.

On October 17, less than two weeks before the October 30 investor day, CSX reported its third quarter results, Harrison's third since becoming CEO. Earnings were 1 percent better than the comparable quarter in 2016. The operating ratio was also marginally better—68.1 versus 69—even though the railroad did not run smoothly during July and August while Harrison's drastic measures were being instituted. On the call with analysts, he admitted to "some slippage" service-wise in the quarter that "we're not proud of" and "embarrassing situations" that were rectified. In the latter case, certain employees were found to be falsifying records about car movements "so they wouldn't be criticized about cars being delayed. We can't tolerate this," he said. He did admit, however, that "we've got maybe a little ahead of ourselves on the hump yard closures, maybe I am pushing too hard."

This was classic Harrison. The change-agent had swung the bat several times in the first six months. Some china was shattered in the process, but the message had been sent and received. There were 2,116 fewer employees, a high percentage of them management people, he said. In total, there were now some four thousand fewer people on the payroll if contractors and consultants were included.

While velocity was flat and dwell time was up slightly, trains were now averaging about three hundred feet longer than the first quarter, when Harrison started. By September, the last month of the quarter, Harrison believed the railroad was running like it should. By October, there were 850 fewer locomotives, a 30 percent reduction and 40,000 fewer railcars, 25 percent less than when he started. The company, he said, was now ready to "go forward at what I might describe as breakneck speed." Perhaps the most significant question on the call, however, was about the hunt for a successor. Harrison responded by telling those listening that it was an issue the board was "very sensitive to." He said that he too, "both as CEO and a shareholder," shared the questioner's concern. "Until we receive an answer, we will stay on top of it," he said, "in [a] grand way."

Unbeknownst to those on the call, Harrison was in the midst of an internal dust-up about that very matter. A week later, CSX answered the question with a news release. On October 25, it announced the hiring of a new chief operating officer, James Foote. Foote had been executive vice president of sales and marketing at CN during Harrison's tenure there. He had joined CN as head of investor relations in 1995 and played a key role in taking the company public. If Claude Mongeau had not succeeded Harrison, Foote was next in line, Harrison said. CN announced Foote was leaving in late 2009, not long before Harrison himself departed.

But the days leading up to the hiring of Foote were tempestuous. Harrison said he had battled with certain board members about being allowed to pick his own team. Two days before the announcement, Harrison was worried that if an agreement couldn't be reached, the October 30 investor day would have to be postponed, which would raise questions in the market. He'd flown to Jacksonville for eleventh-hour meetings and indicated in a voicemail on the evening of October 24 that the situation had been resolved. Foote had been interviewed by the board that afternoon and was already working at CSX the next day when the announcement was made public.

While Foote arrived, two executives—Cindy Sanborn and Fredrik Eliasson—would simultaneously resign "to pursue other interests." General Counsel Ellen Fitzsimmons would retire and be replaced internally.[6] This was the first major change at the top. Rail historian H. Roger Grant told *Trains* magazine, "I can't think of another example of such a sweep of top executives." With Foote, Harrison was betting on an executive he'd worked with in the past. Foote knew Precision Scheduled Railroading and could conceivably step into the CEO job if Harrison were unable to continue or when his contract ended. Things seemed to be looking up again for Harrison. Presumably now, Foote could be presented as a trophy catch just days later at the investor event. But late on October 25, CSX canceled the meeting and said it would present the new team at a later date, likely early 2018. Concurrently, the company announced a second $1.5 billion share buyback. The buyback announcement was a bit of a shock absorber. It meant the company thought the stock was cheap and the repurchase reduced the number

---

6   In January 2018, SunTrust Banks, Inc. named Fitzsimmons general counsel and corporate executive vice president. In February 2018, Sanborn joined Union Pacific as an operating executive. In March 2018, Eliasson was appointed executive vice president and CFO at Change Healthcare.

of shares outstanding, theoretically making them more valuable. If shareholders had any concerns about why the investor meeting was postponed, at least they got a buyback. But there had been an argument at the board level about doing it. Sophisticated investors like Hilal wanted it, Harrison said, but many other investors wanted dividends—cash in hand. Although Harrison had advised Hilal to "just let it go" for the time being, the activist's view prevailed.

On Sunday, October 29, Harrison sat on the sofa of his home office, feeling sluggish, covered in a blanket. The boardroom tussles of the past few weeks had left him drained. Among other things, he'd been criticized for his tone of voice. He was told that "my tone was too mean and it ran down through the organization." It was 25,000 of them versus him, he felt. He said the internal view of him was, "One week I'm no good. The next week they need me." One senior executive was upset at being yelled at by Harrison, telling him he was dangerous and unqualified. Unapologetic, Harrison confirmed the yelling, saying he did so "at the top of my lungs," adding that he probably wouldn't change. In an indication that it was no longer the Bill Thompson era of the 1970s and 80s, there was a view by some inside CSX that Harrison needed "sensitivity training" (it didn't happen).

Any successes he'd had at streamlining the company and the multiple billion-dollar increase in market value had only created jealousy, he believed, and intensified attempts to get back at him. He confessed to having been naive about how he'd be received at CSX. "I got there and there was a desk and a telephone," he complained. "There was no 'Welcome to Jacksonville.' I was the enemy and you could feel it and see it." He didn't hide his bitterness. There were echoes of Montreal, but compared to his arrival at CP, when the office was virtually empty because executives were at the Stampede, "this was ugly." But what did he expect? He was the incoming missile, just like he was at CP. Harrison had thought about packing it in, but as much as he said he'd mulled leaving, he felt responsible to others—shareholders, large and small, who'd stuck with him, not to mention Mark Wallace, who had come with him to CSX.

Harrison also conceded that Hilal had been correct in asking for more board seats at the outset. "Paul was right, there." It was another case of Harrison versus boards—oil and water. He harkened back to Illinois Central's relatively tiny board: "We had seven [directors] and didn't have one problem." That was, however, in the bygone days before strict corporate governance became the theme du jour.

Despite the unpleasantness, he was unbowed. With the company having booked 300 rooms at The Breakers—more than half of the hotel—in lieu of an investors meeting on October 30, CSX decided to use the day to mount the equivalent of a Hunter Camp for the company's thirty-odd vice presidents. Also present was the new COO, Jim Foote. Harrison would speak to the group, calling it a "restart." By then, he'd already led three Hunter Camps for some seventy-five to eighty employees (there would be a fourth in early December). With the emerald-blue Atlantic crashing in the background, Harrison held forth for five and a half hours on his reception at the railroad ("People don't like you shoved down their throat"), the board ("There was a coalition to get me. I'm still standing, okay?") the market (the shares "maybe double"), safety ("We can't turn our backs on [the safety risk of] cell phones and their use [by rail workers]"), his health ("I'm going to live, I think"), not to mention railroading, leadership, and how to completely transform CSX. There was only one bio break, and no one was looking at their smartphones. He finished in top form with the yarn about Thompson spinning the pistol in front of him and his old BN colleague, Earl. "You think this is tough, wait till we get the pistols out," he said to laughter.

It wasn't until just after 5 pm that he barely touched the ham sandwich that had been put in front of him at lunch. After being driven back to his home in a chauffeured Maybach, he barely ate dinner—a cup of bean soup followed by key lime pie. Reflecting on the session with the VPs earlier in the day, he estimated he'd probably persuaded eighteen of the thirty in the room. Although he'd encouraged them to ask questions a number of times, there were few. "They're scared of me."

Every day he worked, though, he believed the company would be better. He still had lots in store for them, and the market. By the fourth quarter report in January, he predicted the OR would be less than 65, and in Q1 in April, it would be 64. At the end of 2018, it would be "62-ish." By 2020, in the high fifties. Big things were coming, he said. A yard in Montreal and CSX's Canadian lines would be sold due to insufficient business, and possibly one in Ohio called Northwest, 220 miles due east of Chicago. Added to the Casky yard north of Nashville he'd already closed, there was perhaps $2 billion that could be realized from selling the properties. He'd also identified 300 miles of unused track that ran from Vincennes, Indiana, to St. Louis, as well as a stretch from Jacksonville to Tallahassee. "Why do you have three hundred miles of railroad sittin' there generatin' nuthin' for you?" Someone would buy it. Harrison spied these excess lines on a ratty, torn map that he had in his home office, not by looking at Google Maps. "Every segment is going to be under scrutiny," he said. The company had too much railroad—but he also said he would buy lines if they made sense. If the group wondered how he was going to get to a 58 OR, "There's how we get there."

On November 29, Jim Foote had his public debut at CSX, at a Credit Suisse investor conference in Palm Beach. A strong communicator, he sounded every bit the potential successor, and obviously not afraid of Harrison.

"There's only one genius in the room at all times that knows the railroad business like nobody else does," Foote said, adding that at times, he and Harrison agreed to disagree. "He's meaner than I am, but I'm bigger than him," he joked, "so we're usually able to work it out."

But Harrison was still center stage, fully in control, doing most of the talking for the hour. There wasn't one query about his health. Sitting in the audience next to Mark Wallace was CP CEO Keith Creel. With those two, along with Foote and Harrison, it was a miniature CN reunion. Harrison waxed poetic about his former CN team, calling them the "finest group of railroaders that have ever been put together,"[7] and how he'd now discovered four or five "rock stars" at CSX, indicating he was building yet another team.

Harrison said that although "we got egg on our face" in the summer, CSX was now operating "as good as it's been." OR and free cash flow "look more encouraging, potentially," predicting it would be "as much or more than CP's" and that "yeah," CSX could be the next CN, in answer to a direct question. Privately, he'd told Hilal that the activist would need a "bigger safe" because of all the money he'd make. The turnaround was happening.

---

7   In his office in his Florida home, a large painting portrayed his time at CN.

He alluded to the issue of succession, that he would be "trying to stay back a little bit" to let Foote and others do what they had to do. "It's [CSX] going to be ready to deal without Hunter Harrison." In the afternoon, after the webcasted session, he spoke one-on-one with three different investor groups. By the time the market closed, the stock was up more than 4 percent.

A week later, nine months after taking over at CSX, Harrison was leading his fourth Hunter Camp for twenty-seven non-operating employees. Next to being with his family, he seemed at his happiest there, explaining railroading, taking questions, and regaling the room with his stories. Hailing from the trenches, most sitting in the Magnolia Room at The Breakers had never had such a close encounter with a CEO. They were thrilled to have been selected, given a chance to learn leadership from the legendary character they only knew from what were mostly scary headlines. They saw another side to Harrison, the teacher. Outside of his "classroom," they played golf, fished, and visited the spa. In the evening, they were treated to gourmet dining, fine wines, and a jazz trio. Laid out on a high table, cigars waited for them when they departed the elegant Circle Room, frescos adorning its ceiling. "He's not cheap," one of them said, clearly awed and excited by the experience. More than that, by being chosen to spend several hours with him over a couple of days, they had been sent a signal that *they were important.* Yes, fewer people would work at CSX when Harrison was finished, but he rewarded and invested in those who could bring value to the company. Near the end of the Camp, the group was told the company was planning to institute an employee stock ownership plan in 2018, permitting them to buy shares at a 15 percent discount.

EIGHT DAYS AFTER the Camp, events took a sharp turn. Just before 9 pm on December 14, 2017, Mark Wallace called to say CSX had announced Harrison was on medical leave. The company said "it was due to unexpected complications from a recent illness." The board named COO Jim Foote the acting CEO.

The previous week, when I was with Harrison in Florida to do more interviewing and observe the Hunter Camp, Jeannie had said he wasn't doing well. He was sleeping a lot, and she wasn't sure how much longer he could do the job (I was at the house speaking with her in the kitchen on Thursday, December 7 from about 10 am until noon—he was asleep). He also ate very little while I was with him—some crackers, a bite or two of a sandwich, although he had dessert. On the morning of Saturday, December 9, Harrison was on the phone with the operating team for a lengthy call. But that night, he didn't feel well again, and Jeannie went with him to the hospital close to their home. One of these days, she had told me earlier that week, he's not going to be able to go to work.

Indeed, that happened the following week on Monday and Tuesday, December 11 and 12, when CSX's board met at The Breakers. Harrison did not attend. Wallace had received a text from Jeannie saying, "Hunter told me to tell you to take care of everything."

On Sunday the 10th, Wallace flew from Jacksonville to visit Harrison in hospital, describing him as "groggy." He was getting medication to fight an infection. Typical Harrison, he was soon up, talking and "complaining about the nurses," Wallace said.

On Tuesday night, December 12, he got a text from Jeannie saying, "He's not good." Wallace called Jim Foote, who said let's not panic. Foote was in South Florida and drove to the hospital on Wednesday morning to see Harrison. According to Wallace, Harrison didn't say much to Foote and didn't acknowledge him. Late that afternoon, Wallace and Foote phoned chairman Ned Kelly and Paul Hilal, asking, "What do we need to do?"

On Wednesday, Keith Creel visited Harrison and called to say he was doing better (he visited a number of times). On Thursday, December 14, Wallace went to the hospital again. Harrison was awake and stuck out his hand for Wallace to shake. He said Harrison was groggy again and it was "pretty damn scary" to see him in such a state. He then stayed with Jeannie for about two hours. She was crying, saying, "I want to bring him home. I've called hospice." He said she was pretty adamant, but the doctors convinced her to keep him in hospital. Cayce was also there, in tears. When Wallace left the hospital, he thought to himself, "Oh my god. It didn't look good. I thought that was going to be the last time I was going to see him." Wallace "said goodbye" to his long-time boss and "was pretty upset." Harrison had not been responsive.

Wallace flew home and got a message from Cayce's husband, Quentin, saying, "He's actually feeling better." Creel visited again that night until the early morning hours, reminiscing and talking with Harrison about railroading.

That evening, there was a board call. The directors decided, given all the information—which Wallace said was changing every couple of minutes—that Harrison should be on medical leave. "Clearly, he's not showing up at work," Wallace said. "He's not able to perform his duties."

After speaking with Wallace, I sent a text to Jeannie, expressing my concern. She responded immediately. "I hope you got all Hunter's stories."

The next morning, December 15, in pre-market trading, CSX shares indicated a drop of 12 percent, representing a decline in value of about $6 billion. Once the market opened, they recovered ground and finished the trading session down 7 percent. Meantime, Wallace texted that Harrison was "awake and eating and drinking coffee. Meds seem to be working. No one is declaring victory just yet but he seems better than he has [the] last few days." Creel said Harrison wanted to see the newspaper and complained about the wallpaper in the hospital room.

That day, Wallace spoke with him on the phone for about five minutes. Although he was hard to understand, Harrison told him "we'll talk over the weekend." That was the last time Wallace spoke with him. Harrison had a bad night. The doctors were doubtful he would make it through the next day.

At 12:08 pm on Saturday, December 16, Hunter Harrison died at Wellington Regional Medical Center. That afternoon, CSX said in a news release his death was "due to unexpectedly severe complications from a recent illness."

Canadian Pacific announced it would lower its flags to half-staff in tribute. Keith Creel issued an emotional statement from CP, calling Harrison "the best railroader ever, plain and simple . . . and an even better person." CN sent a statement to the media calling Harrison "a giant of the railway industry for decades and a transformative figure at CN." David McLean, CN's former chairman, who'd squared off with Harrison at the end of his tenure there, went on television to say Harrison "understood railroads like nobody I ever worked with," and was a man who loved his employees and who had "a big heart."

On a conference call the day before he died, Jim Foote told analysts Harrison had already done the "heavy lifting" at CSX and assured investors the railroad would continue implementing his plan. On Monday, December 18, the first trading day since Harrison's death, CSX shares held steady and even rose a bit. They continued to rise the rest of the week (Foote was named CEO on December 22) and hit new highs in January. In February, in spite of a broad-based stock market decline, CSX announced an increase in its dividend and share buyback. On March 1, at a long-awaited investor day presentation, the company detailed more of Harrison's blueprint to get to an OR of 60 percent by 2020. On April 17, CSX reported that its operating ratio in the first quarter had dropped to 63.7 percent. The next day, the stock rose 7.85 percent to more than $61, a new high. By June, it was $67. The company was worth $25 billion more than in January 2017. Aside from the stark reality of his passing, there were confident signs that the turnaround he had initiated had taken hold and would continue.

As per his wishes, there would be no funeral. Instead, there would be a celebration of life, and at a later date, Hunter Harrison's ashes would be scattered in the Memphis rail yard where it all started.

12 COMING TO TERMS

THE PASSING OF a figure like Hunter Harrison leaves much to ponder. In his case, his professional legacy and personal legacy are intertwined. Untangling them is as complicated as he was.

With Harrison's career, there are two legacies: overwhelming success as a railroader—some would call it genius—coupled with controversy wherever he'd been. The latter stems from the former—how much he pushed to attain his railroading achievements, which reflect his hard-edged methods and personality. But for a man who believed in the power of measurement, controversy is difficult to quantify. Sensitive and acrimonious issues can be debated, while success can be tracked via many yardsticks. There's no question Harrison's scorecard is bountiful when it comes to the people he nurtured, the practices he pioneered, and the number of awards and trophies he won, not to mention the staggering turnarounds he effected.

For CEOs, though, one of the key columns on that scorecard is compensation. That too is bulging and reflects elements of both his success and his controversy. Without a doubt, Harrison was richly rewarded. Between CN, CP, and IC he tabulated that he was paid approximately $500 million. Had he lived to see CSX play out the way he expected, there was the possibility of another few hundred million.[1] With an

---

1   In the end, "the company received staggering benefit," Hilal said, "vastly out of proportion to the millions" Harrison "captured for a service that he was uniquely capable of providing." Because he passed away before the one-year anniversary of his hiring, his estate was not eligible for even the first instalment of the option grant from CSX.

average annual income for an American or Canadian household of between USD $50,000 and $60,000 a year, it's hard for the majority of people to comprehend such numbers. Most have a sense of what's fair—what you should get for what you accomplish or sell. What many view as unfair is when certain people receive hundreds of times the average.

Yet Harrison was not average. He was exceptional, even compared to other CEOs. The railroads he ran all became better operators, by orders of magnitude. The shipment of goods and commodities by rail in North America is arguably better because of him. At the same time, he directed teams that created billions of dollars in value for shareholders at four railroads—some $50 billion.[2] He could cite train schedules from memory. He could call up an obscure railroad rule from just a number that someone mentioned. A refrain among operating executives at another major US railroad was WWHHD: what would Hunter Harrison do? Essentially, Harrison may have been one of the highest paid repairmen in the world—the consummate outsider called in to make things work. And when the repairs were done, directors held their noses, paid the fat bill, and were ready for him to go.

It will surely inflame many of those he fired—and there are many—but he also sacrificed on a personal level. Few CEOs have the job over a span of decades or have lived with the stress or endless hours for as long as he did. As a result, Harrison admitted he had few close friends. "I think for most people, Hunter [was] kind of a hard guy to get close to," said Laird Pitz.

In addition, Harrison and his family moved so frequently they didn't put down roots anywhere for long. A sense of community was perhaps sacrificed. When asked about that, Harrison was dismissive. But on another occasion, when confronted with a question about compensation, with gritted teeth he shot back saying that his family had endured moving *eighteen times*, a factor that, for him, in part justified what he'd been paid. The anguish was transparent. So, which was it? All of us, if we're human, contradict ourselves.

---

2   CP reported its market value grew by more than CAD $15 billion during Harrison's tenure. According to Bloomberg data, at CN, its value increased CAD $19.2 billion during his time as COO and CEO. At Illinois Central, the increase was close to USD $2 billion. When Harrison died, CSX was worth approximately USD $16 billion more than when it was first suggested he might go there. Separately, Hilal calculated Harrison created $54.4 billion in value.

"They have no life," his sister Mary says of CEOs. When the family got together at Christmas, it was "nothing for him to spend hours pacing on a conference call because there's been a derailment. There's no day off. There's no vacation. There's no downtime."

As for the stress and pressure, some thrive on it. Certainly, few can tolerate it. "Sometimes I think he handles the pressure well, sometimes I think he covers up a lot," Mary said in April 2017. "I definitely wouldn't want to be in Jeannie's position. I'm sure she feels a lot of frustration." Indeed, in spite of all the excitement of his many career moves, just days before his death, Jeannie said she envied people who remained in one community among neighbors and lifelong friends.

As strong as Harrison was, he was also fragile—and somewhat hapless on his own. Like many men of his era, he would have been lost without his wife. He became virtually unhinged during the period when his marriage broke up, waking up in a pool of blood after being beaten by three men in a bar brawl. Libby had visited him in Mobile when her parents were divorced, finding crackers covered in peanut butter in the bed of her father, the hopeless bachelor. Cayce fondly recalled him badly typing an essay for her in the fourth grade and bringing it to school with a lunch he'd made for her—a sandwich wrapped in a Lays potato chip bag, the sandwich lying amongst loose chips, an apple, and a juice box.

Such stories about crackers in the bed and disorganized lunches, of course, are part of his charm and part of family lore. He was loved not only for his many triumphs, but also for his imperfections. While Harrison was surely the CEO, his granddaughter Morgan described her grandmother Jeannie as the COO of the family—overseeing their large and complex properties and their staff and paying the extensive bills. Jeannie added that her husband was always incapable of looking after his own finances. People flew him, drove him, fed him, and cleaned for him. Fortunately, he was in a position where he'd made enough money that he could afford such luxuries and staffers to free him up to do higher priced work.

Harrison was blessed with the steady, loving presence of Jeannie in his life for more than half a century. Sometimes, he didn't know how to hook up his oxygen properly. She did. And she was one of the few not afraid to talk back to him, sometimes sharply. About a month after being appointed CEO of CSX, Jeannie let him have it in graphic terms.

"Most of it has been related to this health deal," Harrison conceded, confirming the confrontation. "It's been frustrating for both of us," he said, adding, "Jeannie's been a real trouper, but it's kind of put a crimp in her style." It fell to her to make sure he took his medications properly. "We've done very, very, very well. But every once in a while, it builds up in both of us," he said.

On another occasion during our interviews, she came by his office and asked if we'd like something to drink. She meant a water or a coffee. Harrison went into wise guy mode and requested a cabernet. Jeannie's response was tart. "In your next life, Buddy." (It seemed she was one of the few people he feared crossing.) Mostly, though, he didn't like people "hovering," including his loved ones. Later that month, though, not long after his first conference call at CSX, he described having balance problems. Walking down the long hall of their Florida home, he started to keel over. Jeannie broke his fall. Harrison got lightheaded, woke up on the ground, and didn't remember anything in between. He'd also begun to fall in a hotel lobby in Roanoke, Virginia, the night before CSX's annual meeting, but someone caught him. The next day he was fine for the meeting.[3]

His health issues couldn't help but raise the issue of mortality. He professed on more than one occasion that he had come to terms with the fact that he didn't have much time left. Dying didn't scare him, he said. "Is there some anxiety, apprehension, what's it going to be like? Yeah," but not fear. What he worried about was his family, Jeannie, his children and grandchildren—a tight family unit. Would they be okay? What he meant was would they be properly provided for, almost an absurd question given the accumulated wealth. But the tradition in the family was that there was always a Big Daddy, going back to his great-grandfather. Big Daddy meant being the protector and the provider, a role that fell to him. No matter how much money he'd made, it was an emotional mindset he took seriously.

His daughters and granddaughters—all articulate, grounded, and thoughtful—worried that he was still working on their account. They

---

3 CSX now requires its CEO to have an annual medical examination, the results of which will be reviewed by the board. The exam will be performed by a doctor approved by the board.

had enough, they told him. Both daughters cried easily speaking of him—a larger-than-life presence, provider, and protector.

"I've tried to be a little light about it," he said, and mentioned a book by a pastor at Libby's church in Kansas City. At one point, there was reference to how "it was the Lord's way." Well, Harrison said, "What am I worried about this shit for if *He's* already got this worked out?" His comment mirrored the incredulous thoughts he'd had as a child after the sudden death of his grandmother when adults had told him it was *part of God's plan.*

"All things considered, it's been pretty good," he said, in uncharacteristic understatement. "I haven't lied to people. I haven't cheated anybody. I held the kids to high standards." And he certainly did not believe that people's lives were pre-determined. Some people blew it, while others solved their concerns. "It's not pre-determined or destiny."

If someone had told him he could smoke cigarettes early, smoke cigars late, and consume the amount of alcohol he did and live a pretty good life until seventy-five—versus not having any wine, alcohol, cigarettes, and cigars and live to eighty-five, "I'm going to take the seventy-five every time," he said, smiling.

WITH ALL THE money anyone could ever want, in his last year, Hunter Harrison was leashed to an oxygen machine and taking medication to combat myriad conditions. Doctors suspected his years working in a rail yard that likely had hazardous particles in the air had permanently damaged his lungs. But how much of his ill health was caused by stress or the things he did to cope with stress? He drank a lot and he smoked a lot, for many years. Yet in spite of the pressure and medical problems, he insisted on working. He was considered indispensable for so long, it was as though he couldn't stand the idea of the alternative. As one person who respected him and worked closely with him for years said, he had to be "the man." He had a talent, he told Jeannie, and wanted to work. She said he also felt a responsibility—that he'd let a lot of people down if he didn't continue. He'd mentioned shareholders and the company. But for her, it wasn't worth it. "All the things he's had to give up? To run this railroad? I'm sorry," she said nine days before he passed away. "I have a resentment there."

The price was high in other respects as well. He and his family endured death threats, one of the reasons he wouldn't fly commercial. Harrison estimated he'd faced fifteen or twenty death threats in his career, most of which he kept to himself and didn't share with his wife and children. One, though, launched in the spring of 2017, targeted Harrison's family and involved repeated calls to his home.

"When is it going to be enough? It's not money," Mary said during the last year of his life. "It's the satisfaction, it's a challenge . . . We're thinking 'when are you going to enjoy life?' And I guess to him that is enjoying life." She was torn, because she knew he was a phenomenon and said there was no one she admired more. "It's either going to give him a kick to keep him going or it's going to be the death of him."

MENTION HUNTER HARRISON to business people—other non-railroading executives—and some raise the issue of safety, whether they're qualified to comment or not. Did his relentless quest for efficiency impact safety at CN and CP? "I was never of that opinion at all," said Jim Gray, former CN director and member of the safety committee. "I didn't believe that. I didn't see that." Hunter, Gray said, "personally and emotionally was committed to safety." Another former director, Ed Lumley, concurred. "The priority for safety substantially increased [under Harrison]," Lumley said. "Keith [Creel] was always harping about safety. Well, he wouldn't have harped about safety if Hunter hadn't supported him." Charlie Baillie, a CN director for a dozen years, was in the same camp. "I don't think the CN board during his tenure or after felt that he made shortcuts on safety," Baillie said.

One suggested that his record had to be looked at over time, in the years after he left, to determine whether there was an increase in the number of accidents attributable to changes made during his tenure. Harrison himself said there can be a lag effect, although by the same token his period as CEO could have included accidents that may have had nothing to do with *his* tenure. More than that, not all accidents are a railroad's fault. The day after Harrison started at CSX, there were two. In one tragic instance, a busload of seniors stalled on a track. The driver did not evacuate the passengers. A train came along and crashed into the bus, killing four people. The same day in New York State, a truck went off the road, resulting in a derailment. Neither accident had any-thing to do with how the railroad operated.

For his part, Harrison didn't enjoy having to haul hazardous sub-stances. But that was the business and railroads had to adhere to the law—the common carrier rule, which requires railways to carry materi-als they might otherwise prefer not to transport. Obviously, given what occurred in Lac-Mégantic, Quebec, crude oil, or at least crude in a more volatile form, would fall into that category. Chlorine would be another. If citizens and policy makers are concerned, Harrison argued they should rewrite the law. Railroads in Canada and the US carry freight right through the center of highly populated areas—major cities and residential neighborhoods. The people who live in those places don't like it. But the reality is that cities grew up around rail lines. The con-nectivity provided by transportation routes is a major reason why cities evolved in the first place—think rivers and ocean ports. Changing the routes of the major carriers would require an enormous effort. In spite of trucking, businesses also want the convenience and economics of shipping goods by rail, but cities would find it very difficult to permit new tracks to be built through other areas, and perhaps less econom-ical routes. Approving large infrastructure projects today is arguably much more onerous than it was when the railroads were initially built. Everyone wants it both ways, Harrison said. Yes, there were risks to running freight trains through cities. Harrison didn't like it either. But he was a realist. Until citizens and populations provided an alternative—and that alternative in his view was *not* an increase in dangerous goods being transported by trucks on highways—people had to accept the risks of living near railroads. If people wanted to pay billions to build railroads away from population centers, that would be a beautiful thing, he said, "but I don't think people will pay the price."

After Lac-Mégantic, Harrison spoke out about railroads continuing to use what he and many others viewed to be an inadequate tanker car, the DOT-111, which was prone to rupture on impact. Most of the cars were not, in fact, owned or leased by railroads but by customers. Harri-son thought—and said—that they should have been banned and taken out of service, given the safety concerns surrounding them. If a passen-ger airliner was deemed unsafe or had a flaw that needed immediate attention, he said, it was grounded. Why not railcars? A prime example is what happened to the Boeing 787 Dreamliner, which is now in service all over the world. In its early days, however, there was a battery issue that led to fires. The aircraft, which is an excellent and popular product, was grounded until the problem was rectified.

Aside from the moral imperative of running a safe railroad, accidents are expensive and bad for business. If safety were an issue with Harrison, why would Paul Tellier have insisted he join CN? Would Bill Ackman, then the largest shareholder of CP—not to mention so many other institutional investors such as Ontario Teachers' Pension Plan and Canada Pension Plan Investment Board—have voted out the board and CEO at Canadian Pacific and supported Harrison to run it? Why also would the proxy advisory firms have supported the Ackman slate? Presumably, if there were safety questions connected to Harrison's tenures at IC, CN, and CP, why would the board of CSX have hired him? If any shareholders had concerns about safety, they certainly set them aside in exchange for share price appreciation.

If you read Harrison's manuals, safety was in fact one of his core principles. "Don't get anybody hurt" was his simple way of saying it. He wrote about a chilling and moving episode that saw a man die when trapped and impaled between two railcars. Meaning well, the worker had darted between the two cars to fix a problem, but he had broken the rules. The man was still alive immediately after the incident, but uncoupling the cars to free him would kill him. If the cars were not uncoupled, he would still die, but it would be prolonged. The man's family was called to come quickly to the rail yard to say goodbye. They did, and the cars were uncoupled. Within minutes, the man was dead. Harrison himself had worked in between railcars as a young laborer. He knew the risks. For him, the rules were written in blood and he said so.

"My memory," recalled Jim Gray, "is that safety was number one with Hunter. He cared about safety. He cared about the railroaders."

When an engine derailed on a bridge over the Mississippi and the crew was trapped, his sister Mary said that her brother, who was afraid of heights, crawled along the bridge to tell the crew that the railroad would get them out. When their mother asked Hunter, given his acrophobia, why he didn't get someone else to do it, he said, "I can't tell somebody else to do something I wouldn't do myself." When there was a derailment, he was known to load workers onto the company jet and take them to the site. On the plane, it would be an airborne Hunter Camp. "They talked about what happened, what do we need to do next time? What did we do wrong?" As for technology to enhance safety, he didn't think that was the magic potion.

"All this [high] tech ain't going to fix any of it," he maintained. "There ain't nuthin' like a safe man or woman."

A case that practically had Harrison jumping out of his chair involved cocaine use. According to a ruling by an arbitrator at the Canadian Railway Office of Arbitration & Dispute Resolution, in December 2012 a CP locomotive engineer was found to have used coke within twenty-four hours of being available for duty. The train he operated ran through a main line crossover switch which derailed a locomotive. The engineer was dismissed, which the union said was excessive. The ruling stated that at a hearing before the arbitrator on July 10, 2014, the union did not deny the person had a dependency on cocaine. But because of the engineer's rehab efforts, the arbitrator ruled that it was appropriate "to give the grievor another chance," although he would be subject to random alcohol and drug testing for two years. Harrison was livid. "The arbitrator's decision is an outrage and, as a railroader, I am appalled we would be forced to put this employee back in the cab of a locomotive. On my watch, this individual will not operate a locomotive." For him, it was simple. If you use coke, you can't be an engineer. You give up that right by jeopardizing the public. Multiple court cases followed, with CP and the union fighting it out. The union had requested that the Supreme Court of Canada hear the case, but on November 23, 2017, the country's top court dismissed the union's last chance to appeal. For a period, the man remained a CP employee doing non-operational work, but he is now no longer at the company.

At the time of the arbitrator's ruling, Harrison called for further public debate about allowing Canadian companies the ability to conduct random drug tests where issues of public safety are involved. The union—the Teamsters Canada Rail Conference—downplayed the incident involving the engineer, calling it "a minor little screw-up" and said Harrison was personally attacking the employee. As for Harrison's call for random drug testing, the vice president of the union, Doug Finnson, was quoted in the *Toronto Star* saying, "We have an American CEO, criticizing Canadians for our laws and the way we do things in Canada."

CP director John Baird—also a former Canadian transport minister—was struck by watching Harrison up close. "This guy does not fuck around with safety," Baird said of Harrison's immediate, strong response. "It wasn't just a chief executive. He was a railroader."

After Lac-Mégantic and other oil-related derailments, Harrison said he'd never seen the public so tense about train accidents. With railways obligated by law to carry hazardous goods, CP argued it must also have the freedom to terminate employees who didn't comply with safety rules.

Harrison was also a firm believer in having cameras in locomotives to monitor crew behavior—a "black box" to record video and voices. Highly controversial with workers who deemed it an invasion of privacy, Harrison was unmoved. "So, we put a supervisor out there riding with you. You feel better?" He believed people gave up the right to privacy when they took the throttle and had hundreds of lives in their hands. His point was that at work, if you were watched, your behavior changed.[4]

The investigative piece in the *Globe and Mail* chronicling ruthless discipline and firings at CP hit a nerve with Harrison. While he, Wallace, and Creel questioned the fairness of the article, his longtime colleague and friend Laird Pitz described Harrison as a spiritual person who, at a certain level, had to be "conflicted" about what he had to do to whip companies into shape. At the same time, Pitz argued that it wasn't Harrison's fault that he was the one who had to come in and make railroads more efficient when others didn't have the will required to do it. Above all, Pitz said Harrison would be long remembered by the railroad industry for his outstanding achievements. At CP, one-time communications head Marty Cej said in July 2017 that he relished working for one of the great industrialists of the era. But he also said that while Harrison made CN and CP the two best railroads in North America, the former CEO had not acknowledged the high internal cost of his changes and the

---

4   In May 2017, Canada's transport minister introduced legislation to amend the Railway Safety Act, requiring locomotive cabs be equipped with voice and video recorders, while limiting the use of the data to investigations, detecting safety threats, and developing policies.

emotional turmoil it caused employees. The grinding change could be harrowing for many, and "there are times when no matter where you are in the company under Hunter where your decisions on any given day will either lead to you getting promoted and a bonus or to being walked off the railroad," Cej said. "And you don't get over that level of anxiety quickly." It's as though his focus always gave him the power to see things others didn't, while at the same time he was blind to—or at least dismissive of—some of the effects. As the *New York Times* wrote about New England Patriots' quarterback Tom Brady, comparing the football player to other superstar athletes who at times have borne the weight of public disapproval, "there is sometimes a blemish that goes with the brilliance . . . he is a human being, with flaws . . . their great gift is a tunnel vision that lets them focus only on being great while others wring their hands over the rest. Maybe that is why just as many people seem to despise them as love them."

Harrison admitted he was very sensitive to criticism and frequently complained about the media. There were still vestiges of the "rabbit ears and red ass" that the St. Louis Cardinals scout had observed so many years ago. But on balance, Harrison was the beneficiary of his fair share of glowing press. There are scrapbooks full of magazine articles from his tenures at CN and CP that paint him in iconic terms. And for someone who complained about the news media, he was not one to say "no comment." He talked to reporters—unfiltered—and didn't believe in media training for executives. He was particularly negative about Canadian media.

"If it's management [talking], they [the media] don't believe anything they say," Harrison maintained. But "you get some bogus ass, lyin', labor leader, they'll print anything they say." He maintains he never once went to the print media and said anything about a labor leader, "but they could talk about us as liars, no goods, cheats, it was all okay."

I was personally on the receiving end of his barking. During the research for this book, when presenting him with other peoples' points of view, he quickly got angry with me. In fairness, due to his health at the time, he was perhaps more easily irritated. But his reaction was in character. In 2012, during the CP proxy fight, he fumed over the phone about journalists in Canada. He mentioned a newspaper reporter and then mentioned me. What did I do, I asked? "You baited me." I replied that "I didn't have to" and that I had no idea what he was talking about. I also said that it was a bit rich for *him* to be so sensitive about media coverage given that he and Pershing were the ones who'd busted into town and started a proxy war. He backed down, and before the call ended agreed to come back on the television program I hosted. As well, he rankled at a question he said he was asked by another Canadian broadcaster upon joining CP: How do you feel about what you've done, taking Fred Green's job? "I didn't take Fred Green's job," he protested. He's right. Nine out of ten shareholders of CP voted for change, and then the company hired Harrison.

The truth is, he didn't have a lot of experience with media prior to coming to Canada and working at CN. Illinois Central wasn't big enough, nor was it a national company; therefore, it didn't garner the same kind of public attention as CN. And at CN, ironically, he was criticized for taking *too much* credit in the press for the turnaround. Paul Tellier, Harrison said, raised it with him, and Tellier confirmed he had concerns about this, particularly when Harrison went to CP. Harrison said he told Tellier that he'd never told reporters he'd done everything at CN. "Paul," Harrison said, defending himself, "I didn't write the articles." So how bad could the Harrison coverage be?

He liked to be unpredictable, to keep people on their toes, and simply couldn't help himself. Besides, as you would expect, he happily used the media to his advantage and was a magnificent communicator—a quote machine and gifted speaker. While Paul Hilal was leading the charge to make him CSX's CEO, Harrison gladly took calls from the *Wall Street Journal*. Every utterance he made put more pressure on the directors at CSX and he knew it. "Let them have a fuckin' night in Jacksonville worryin'," he said to me with a mischievous smile after speaking with the *Journal* from his SUV on January 18, less than an hour after his resignation from CP was announced.

WITHIN WEEKS OF Hunter Harrison's departure from CP, in the wake of the *Globe* article, Canadian Pacific announced policy changes, quoting Creel, the new CEO. On the surface, it appeared to be a shift from the Harrison doctrine—not unusual when the baton is passed—to portraying more empathetic leadership. For sure Harrison made

Canadian Pacific hugely efficient and made a ton of money for share-holders including himself, but the article threatened to be an asterisk on his championship stats. He came down hard on people who weren't accountable, didn't do their jobs, or broke the rules. That was a strength, but did it create a culture of fear for some? How could it not when he reveled in being the tough guy? Nonetheless, it didn't stop him from complaining about criticism, while he blithely described Bill Thompson as a "kick ass, take names, culture-of-fear kind of guy," the man who became his mentor at Frisco and BN. He admired Thompson greatly, therefore tacitly approving of Thompson's culture, under which he, Harrison, and the railroads he ran prospered. Laird Pitz, who expressed deep fondness and respect for Harrison, said he "would be surprised if most people who knew Thompson and knew Hunter wouldn't say that Hunter was a clone of Thompson," given how much Harrison enjoyed, even revered, the stories of his shared past with the man. He undoubtedly absorbed a strong dose of Thompson's approach. Harrison himself said the bond between them was "just never broken." It was cemented at Frisco, where Thompson was hired—just as Harrison has been—to knock a railroad into shape. Frisco, Harrison said, was too family-oriented; there was too much nepotism. It was too *nice*.

Harrison was also a true believer in the "significant emotional event" for employees. If that required a culture of fear—or the label of it to highlight emotional events that change behavior—so be it. *Nothing* would get in the way of Harrison making a railroad more efficient and more profitable. That was always the end game. And he was all about the end game, what you're trying to achieve. Looking back, the Thompson era was surely nastier than Harrison's era. Pisser Bill didn't hold Hunter Camps.

"I modeled myself along a lot of his principles," Harrison said, but "from a style standpoint, no." That may be true. But it may also be true that Harrison may have been simply unable to believe that his style came from anywhere but himself. His daughter Cayce said during his last year, "He has a huge ego and he needs his ego stroked and he needs people to listen to him and to need him." Nevertheless, Harrison also took pride in viewing himself as an original, which he was. Like all great operators and great performers—*and he was a performer*—Hunter

Harrison was an intricate brew. While he was sensitive to criticism, it never stopped him from doing what he thought he should do.

The truth, however, is that all the criticism took a piece out of him emotionally. He was a rich, successful businessman with much to show for it, but he was wounded. Part of it was the "rabbit ears and red ass," part of it was his health, and the other part was that he *just didn't get* why people slapped at him. He had mentored so many people, changed so many lives, made so much money for so many shareholders and employees. He couldn't understand why certain other people didn't see that.

Almost a decade afterward, he was still embittered about CN telling him he was no longer needed, yet he himself presided over thousands of job reductions in the name of efficiency. When confronted with that polarity, within days of his death, he stood his ground. "I did the job. Nobody was mistreated, in my view, unfairly. If I felt empathy for them, I felt it because they were misled by others before. And they had been allowed to do X, Y, or Z and they shouldn't have been," he said. "I don't think I have anything to apologize about." He said without people like the Hunter Harrisons who get black eyes for making unpleasant decisions, what happens when the company "goes into depression"? "Why do you think CN brought me? Because they fuckin' thought they could make a lot of money," he said. "Sorry, I can't find guilt. When I do, I'll let you know. I lay awake at night about some things, not about that." Then there was a pause. "And I'm not a mean man," he said softly, one of the last things he said to me.

In fact, his kindness could be life-saving. In 1994, Tom Caldwell, an IC employee, was in liver failure due to hepatitis C. He needed a transplant or he would die. Unfortunately, at the time, the Illinois Central Hospital Association would not provide insurance coverage for transplants, in his case $300,000. Somehow, Harrison found out and phoned Caldwell, telling him that he would get the transplant even if Harrison had to pay for it himself. Caldwell got the surgery and didn't have to pay a dime. After that, all IC employees were covered for transplants. Almost twenty-four years later, talking about it brought Caldwell to tears.

When it came to his life and career, Harrison claimed to have few regrets. "I'm pretty demon-free," he said a number of months before, pausing and then grinning as he added the perfectly timed, self-directed punchline. "People say you *boolshit* yourself pretty good." The one that he admitted he still carried, though, was that "I was a little bit of a bully as a child and I regret it." He said he was "ugly and mean to people" during that phase, analyzing it as an immature stage of his life. But during his lengthy tenure as a CEO—more than two decades—he said he always tried to do the right thing and be true to himself. Managers, he frequently repeated, do things right—while leaders do the right thing. "My mandate in these jobs has never been to be Mr. Popularity."

Indeed. Shareholders of four railroads hired Mr. Un-Popularity to turn around their flagging fortunes. The willingness to not be loved was the price he paid to get things done. Illinois Central was on the verge of bankruptcy when he was hired. CN knew precisely what it was getting with Hunter Harrison and *insisted* he come to the company as part of the deal. CP's board fought to keep him out, but nine out of ten of the company's shareholders had a different view. And CSX surrendered to shareholder pressure and hired Harrison as CEO, in spite of an exorbitant sticker price. To those who criticized and badmouthed him—even board members—one wonders how many made money on the back of the turnarounds he achieved? All of these companies and their shareholders were greatly enriched by his unpopularity. He did exactly what he was hired to do. David McLean, the former chairman of CN who headed the board that told Harrison he was done, said he bought shares in CSX when he found out Harrison would run it. (During the writing of the book, Rob Ritchie, the former CEO of CP, also held shares in CSX while Harrison was running it.)[5]

"I've been around a lot of CEOs who would rather be loved than be successful," said Matthew Paull, a CP director and former CFO of McDonald's. "That's not a good idea."

As for Harrison being tough on labor, that's where *he* started, smeared in oil. And from there, he scaled the heights without attending an Ivy League school or coming from the one percent, an accomplishment that is becoming more and more rare.

---

5   McLean and Ritchie were no longer with CN and CP when they bought CSX shares.

While he was widely hailed, a cursory search of social media turned up plenty of unfavorable, anonymous, and vicious commentary. Harrison said he was aghast when his daughters and granddaughters discovered it. Although they knew he could be intimidating and unflinching when it came to rules, they'd go online to refute the nasty remarks. Morgan, reconciling the public criticism of her grandfather as being part of the market system in which he worked, said "leaders will always be criticized for whatever they do on one side or the other." Cayce remembered one comment that said, "Hunter Harrison would sell his daughter on the streets of Mexico if he could make a nickel." The family joked about it, but at some level it hurt. It was one of many comments by people she said who had never met her father and had no idea who he was.

Views of him are surely kaleidoscopic. Idolized and villain-ized in equal measure, there's no question he was a polarizing figure—both extremely successful and extremely controversial. "Most successful people are," reflected Andy Reardon. Most of them have also, he said, spent many sleepless nights. In spite of his enthusiasm for tough decisions, Harrison was also a believer in giving people second chances. "If people hadn't given me second chances, where would I be?" he once said to Reardon.

Few can argue about Harrison's accomplishments in the arena of railroading and his encyclopedic understanding of transportation. Given everywhere he worked, he may have known the pathways of the North American continent better than any other human being on the planet. Going back to industry clippings from the 1980s when he was in VP roles at BN, he was saying the same things he was saying in 2017: focus on service, safety, costs, assets, and especially the people—putting them in the right spots at the railroad. He could see that running a more efficient operation meant lower costs and improved what could be offered to the customer. His philosophy was already in place thirty years earlier, but he had articulated, honed, labeled, and preached it since then.

"Can you think of any CEO who has gone from company to company to company to company within the industry and had success at every one?" asked Paull. "There's nobody. Nobody like that." At many successful, big companies, he said, CEOs think it's all about them. Then they move on to another company and end up a miserable failure—because it wasn't them, it was the company. Paull said, "In Hunter's case, it was him. It wasn't the company."

When I told Harrison in the fall of 2017 that I was reading Walter Isaacson's biography of Steve Jobs, he expressed simpatico feelings with the late CEO. "People thought he was crude, rude, insensitive, and you could make a case I guess that he was all of the above," Harrison said, but "he was a hell of a leader."

Although Harrison and Jobs were different, there were commonalities. Both had problematic relationships with their fathers. Both staged comebacks. Both disliked boards. Both could command a room and hated PowerPoint. Both worked while sick. Isaacson, however, portrayed Jobs as off-putting in the extreme. While Harrison was hardheaded, brusque, and curmudgeonly, he was also charming, funny, and generous. The Southern manners he learned as a boy kept him from being intentionally rude like Jobs. And they had zero in common when it came to how each dealt with the arrival of a child. Jobs abandoned his daughter. Still a teenager, Harrison woke up to his new reality and accepted it.

But both were revolutionaries, ahead of everyone else and not afraid to tell them, feelings be damned. One of Jobs's manifestos—written with two teammates—was about people like himself, and it could easily apply to Harrison. "Here's to the crazy ones," he wrote. "The misfits, the rebels, the troublemakers . . . the people who are crazy enough to think they can change the world are the ones who do."

While there is little doubt Harrison was the not-so-secret ingredient, he would also point to the teams he developed at each stop along the way. Aside from his family, there's no question he was proudest of the people he coached who, along with him, created enormous shareholder value—and what he described as a vastly improved transportation system. Trains that once took several days to get from Chicago to Vancouver now take fewer. Freight gets to where it needs to go faster, on time, on schedule.

Thirty years ago, he said, no one dreamed what railroads could be or do. In his estimation, the importance of the industry couldn't be overstated. People are addicted to Facebook and their smartphones but have no idea how goods that form the backbone of the economy get shipped from A to B. He truly believed the work he and his teams accomplished made both the Canadian and US economies more competitive. If the railroads slipped, economic transactions were delayed and GDP could falter. Not only did the railroads he ran become more efficient, but so have others as they've tried to catch and match the roads over which Harrison presided. His competitors improved because he raised the bar. There was, according to John Baird, a difference between a chief executive and a leader. Harrison was a leader, he said. "I know the way. Follow me."

"How many living legends have you had an opportunity to know or work with?" Pitz asked. Knowing him for more than thirty years, he said Harrison was not someone you would define as a modern-day CEO—he was archaic, a throwback to the pre-tech era of heavy industry, someone who started out as a worker. "Look how many people have come and gone and he's still the guy," he said in July 2017. That was true. It's highly unusual to have a multi-decade span as a CEO. According to data at the end of 2017, the average tenure of an S&P 500 CEO was five years. And who did all the other Class 1's in the US hate? That hard ass Hunter Harrison, said Pitz. They were jealous. "Suffice it to say that Ewing Hunter Harrison will not be a forgotten part of history, particularly in this industry."

Bill Ackman, who spoke with Harrison the night before he died, lamented not working with the railroader again on CSX. There are plenty of other investments, Ackman said, but there was only one Hunter Harrison. Rebecca MacDonald described him as "The Gruffalo," the character in the children's story who is the world's most loved monster. "He barks and sometimes bites, but all for the benefit of the end result. And that's Hunter."

"He's like the exception to the rule," his sister Mary said, still incredulous all these years later that the brother she grew up with made his way from a carman in the yard to becoming the CEO of multiple railroads. "He's something people strive for. Look what he did. He's kind of like the impossible dream."

In his last years, Cayce and Libby were painfully aware that time was running short with their father. I told him this in our last interview, ten days before he died. Harrison began to cry. He couldn't guard them and Jeannie from what was to come, knowing how much they relied on him.

"I literally talk to him every day," Cayce said. "There is no major decision we make in our lives without consulting him." They realized he'd pushed and challenged them as a way to prepare for life without him. His grandchildren, too, thought about what they'd miss—the endless stories, for one. "I could listen to him for hours," Mackenzie said, while Morgan spoke of his unlimited generosity.

In the twilight of his life, by most people's standards, Harrison lived in a state of great material comfort, even excess. For that, he was also unapologetic and was a self-described "flaming capitalist."

"I didn't have a lot growing up," he said, allowing that there was love and that there was always food on the table. Jeannie's family didn't miss meals either, he said, but as a second daughter, "she probably never had a new dress that was hers till she married me." They both liked nice things, he said, and were not inhibited about spending on themselves or their family. At Jeannie's sixtieth birthday party, held in Key Biscayne, Florida, Dennis Edwards, the former lead singer of the Temptations, performed with his Review. Hunter Harrison even sang "My Girl" with them. Although Jeannie kept an eye on expenditures and wasn't afraid to declare something ridiculously priced—like the utility bill at their Connecticut estate, which resulted in a switch to geothermal power—they enjoyed the money that they never imagined having and generously shared it with family, friends, and strangers.

In the last days of his life, he and Jeannie were thinking more about philanthropy. Harrison's approach to charity was to funnel money to people who needed it in the most direct way. He told his minister (Harrison had critical questions about God, but he indicated he believed in God) that if there was a family in serious financial difficulty to let him know. Such a family might end up with $100,000 out of the blue. He and Jeannie gave $1 million to help fund his sister Diane's ministry, which assists female prisoners. They planned on a similar donation to support his sister Helen's work with hungry, low-income schoolchildren in Tennessee. Jeannie said they also set up a foundation in Greater Kansas City but had not decided where the funds would be directed, perhaps for college educations. When severe flooding hit Calgary in the summer of 2013 and a couple hundred CP employees' lives were severely impacted, Harrison quietly had the company spread a couple of million dollars around their bank accounts to help them get through the trauma.

CN and CP also contributed significantly to heart-related research while he was CEO, a high percentage of the money going toward pediatric care. People whom he judged needed money got money, care, whatever. In business, he had teeth of steel—in life, a heart of gold. His teams revered him. And while he said he had few close friends, Laird Pitz said, "If you're his friend, you're his friend for life."

One thing is certain. For better or for worse, shareholder value is the ultimate arbiter of the system within which Harrison toiled. Businesses, he argued, would not exist in the first place without the owners—the shareholders. And he or she who makes the most for shareholders wins. If you didn't think like an owner, Andy Reardon said, Harrison didn't have much time for you. Bill Gates, whose investment vehicle profited in the billions by being the biggest shareholder in CN, once scribbled a note to him: "I do hope you stay even longer as CEO! You have done an amazing job." That was the game. And he never played any game halfway—not golf, not show jumping, not railroading. He had to be the best. His dad, Tank Harrison, always told his son, if you can't go first class, don't go. Hunter Harrison not only mastered railroading, he mastered the game. And his father was right. "Bubba" would run the railroad. Four times.

EPILOGUE

HE WANTED IT to be a party that he would have liked to attend. On January 7, 2018, some 700 people gathered by invitation (he had friends, after all) at the Harrisons' Florida farm to give a rousing send-off. His favorite foods were on offer—fried chicken, pulled pork sliders, catfish, and coleslaw—prompting jokes about how he would sneak off to KFC to escape the Mediterranean diet to which he'd been sentenced. Under a huge white tent, a seven-piece R&B band played Motown and a gospel choir with celestial voices sang "Lean on Me." Hanging from the ceiling was a silhouette profile of the man himself holding forth at a microphone. Outside the tent, photos of childhood, family, and career adorned panels, a mini-museum to his life. His blue Bentley convertible was parked on the grass with the top down, the barn in the background.

Milling and reminiscing were old colleagues from Frisco, BN, IC, CN, and CP and his relatively new team at CSX. The heads of three of the continent's biggest railroads were there. Among the CN contingent were former director Ed Lumley, as well as Mike Cory, the chief operating officer whom Harrison had once demoted to teach a lesson. Also present was Sean Finn, CN's chief legal officer. Much of the Canadian Pacific board was there as well—Andy Reardon, Rebecca MacDonald, John Baird, Gordon Trafton, Isabelle Courville—as well as Bill Ackman and Paul Hilal. Harrison's sister Diane, a United Methodist minister, led the proceedings, clearly another Harrison gifted in public speaking. The majority of those who did speak were those he'd chosen or "ordered" to do so, as son-in-law Quentin told the gathering.

Most choked up and spoke of how Harrison coaxed them to be their best selves. There were teasing references to screaming, yelling, and fear, but coaching, mentoring, and love were the thematic streams. Above all, the leitmotif was family, with Diane telling everyone that the best thing her brother ever did was marry Jeannie.

Cayce Harrison needed time at the podium to compose herself, but she overflowed with eloquent emotion about the father she spoke to every day, sometimes five times a day, not shying away from noting his temper and know-it-all side. But she recognized what he was doing, pushing her. "Don't half-ass it," he'd implored her. Nearing the end, while hospitalized, she said her father became so frustrated with the medical facility that he told one of the doctors he was going to retire from the railroad and come back as a hospital administrator and "whup all your asses."

She told me afterward that her father knew his time was up. Leaving the Connecticut farm in the autumn, he reflected it would be his last time there. Acutely aware of his situation, in the hospital a couple of days before he died, Harrison himself had requested hospice—although just thirty-six hours before he passed, he wanted to watch CNBC, read the paper, check CSX's stock price, and have a Starbucks. Two of his granddaughters, Morgan and Hunter Julo, also spoke, the former describing visits with Harrison to every toy store in Chicago, his convertible's top down, tunes blasting. The latter, his namesake Hunter, recited a poem she'd written, "Is That the Chattanooga Choo Choo?" It was Tennessee, trains, and Harrison all wrapped in one, even alluding to the asbestos that had ruined his lungs.

When the speakers were done, the band launched into the Temptations, followed by Sam and Dave. As the musicians belted out "Soul Man," the dance floor was full.

APPENDIX: **CHRONOLOGY**

Born November 7, 1944, Memphis, Tennessee

Class of 1962, Kingsbury High School, Memphis, Tennessee

Married Jeannie Day, 1963 (birthdate: February 26, 1947)

Carman Oiler, St. Louis–San Francisco Railway Co. (Frisco), Memphis, December 1963

Dropped out (twice), Memphis State University, 1963 and 1964

Birth of daughter Elizabeth "Libby" Harrison, February 12, 1964

Safety Supervisor, St. Louis–San Francisco Railway Co., Springfield, Missouri, 1968

Divorced, 1969

Car Foreman, St. Louis–San Francisco Railway Co., Mobile, Alabama, 1970

Remarried Jeannie, July 10, 1970

Assistant Trainmaster, St. Louis–San Francisco Railway Co., Memphis, 1971

Trainmaster, St. Louis–San Francisco Railway Co., Memphis, 1972

Assistant Superintendent, St. Louis–San Francisco Railway Co., Memphis, 1973

Superintendent, St. Louis–San Francisco Railway Co., Memphis,
1974–77

General Superintendent, Transportation, St. Louis–San Francisco
Railway Co., Springfield, Missouri, 1977

Superintendent, KC Terminal, St. Louis–San Francisco Railway Co.,
Kansas City, Missouri, 1978

Superintendent, St. Louis–San Francisco Railway Co., Memphis,
1978–80

Assistant Vice President, Burlington Northern (BN), Seattle
Region, 1980–82

Vice President, Terminals, Burlington Northern, St. Paul,
Minnesota, 1982

Birth of daughter Cayce Harrison, October 3, 1983

Vice President, Transportation, Burlington Northern, Operations
Department, Overland Park, Kansas, 1983

Vice President, Chicago region, Burlington Northern,
November 20, 1985

Railroad Man of the Year, presented by the St. Louis Railway
Club, 1987

Vice President, Service Design, Burlington Northern, 1988

Vice President and Chief Transportation Officer, Illinois Central
Railroad Company (IC), Chicago, Illinois, May 1, 1989

Senior Vice President, Transportation, Illinois Central Railroad
Company, November 27, 1991

Senior Vice President, Operations, Illinois Central Railroad Company,
July 1, 1992

Acting Chief Executive Officer, Illinois Central Railroad Company,
February 4, 1993 (when CEO Edward L. Moyers hospitalized)

President and CEO, Illinois Central Railroad Company,
February 17, 1993– March 29, 1998

Executive Vice President and Chief Operating Officer, Canadian National Railway Company (CN), Montreal, Quebec, March 30, 1998–December 31, 2002

Railroader of the Year, presented by *Railway Age*, 2002

President and CEO, Canadian National Railway Company, Montreal, January 1, 2003–December 31, 2009

B'nai Brith Canada Award of Merit, 2006

Honorary Doctorate, University of Alberta, 2007

CEO of the Year, *Report on Business Magazine*, 2007

Railroad Innovator Award, presented by *Progressive Railroading*, 2009

Canadian International Executive of the Year, 2009

Chairman, Dynegy Inc., April 11–July 11, 2011

Chairman, National Horse Show Association of America, 2011–16 (Chairman Emeritus, 2017)

President and CEO, Canadian Pacific Railway Limited (CP), Calgary, Alberta, June 28, 2012–February 3, 2013 (Keith Creel appointed President on February 4, 2013)

CEO of Canadian Pacific Railway Limited, Calgary, June 28, 2012–January 31, 2017

Railroader of the Year, presented by *Railway Age*, 2015

CEO, CSX Corporation, Jacksonville, Florida, March 6–December 14, 2017

On medical leave from CSX Corporation, December 14–16, 2017

Died, December 16, 2017, Wellington, Florida

Hunter Harrison Award in Show Jumping, established posthumously by CP Palm Beach Masters, January 11, 2018

Inductee (posthumously), Show Jumping Hall of Fame, May 31, 2018

Director, various industrial boards: Dynegy, Wabash National, TTX

ACKNOWLEDGEMENTS

BOOKS REQUIRE NUTRIENTS from many sources. Certain texts proved to be enormously helpful: *The Pig That Flew* by Harry Bruce, *The Last Spike* by Pierre Berton, *Steve Jobs* by Walter Isaacson, and of course the two railroading manuals written by Hunter Harrison and published by CN; all of these and others are listed in the bibliography. News accounts, magazine articles, regulatory filings, videos, and other documents were of equal importance; they too are cited.

Books also require many hands. Interviews with Harrison and the people who knew him were the grist for this book. The words of the main character himself and those who lived and worked with him made this project a writer's treasure. More than seventy-five people were interviewed (some multiple times), culminating in almost three hundred and fifty hours of conversation, about half of that with Hunter Harrison. Most spoke on the record; some on the condition of anonymity. I am grateful to all who participated. Beyond those interviewed, others helped by confirming facts or providing leads.

Special thanks begin with the Harrison family. Jeannie Harrison was selfless in her assistance. She gave her time, candid thoughts, and access to endless scrapbooks and photographs, not to mention her hospitality. Libby Julo and Cayce Harrison—along with their husbands Earl and Quentin—also enthusiastically aided my quest, as did Morgan and Mackenzie Julo. Although Hunter Julo and Harrison Rhodes Judge were not interviewed, I have to believe that they were with the book in spirit.

Of course, Hunter Harrison deserves singular mention. He trusted me with his life story. During the many hours we spent together, we spoke, ate, and argued, occasionally at high volume. This occurred at all hours, often in the evening and on weekends. When he died, it was a shock (although not entirely a surprise) because I had been with him just days beforehand. I will feel an everlasting ache that he did not live long enough to read the book. I would like to think he would respect it, although I have no doubt he would dispute certain things, for that was his nature. I suspect we would have had another high-decibel discussion about various passages, and then he would have gruffly said, "Okay, that's fair. What's next?"

Harrison's sister Mary Couey graciously spent time on the phone telling me about her brother's childhood, their parents, and family life in Memphis. At Harrison's side for so many years, Mark Wallace was supportive of this project from the get-go. I thank him for his decency, patience, insight, and good humor. At Canadian Pacific, Keith Creel, Andy Reardon, Laird Pitz, Nadeem Velani, Peter Edwards, Tony Marquis, and my former colleague Marty Cej were generous with their time and recollections. Paul Hilal and Bill Ackman were also eager to assist. They were forthcoming and helpful, and I thank them for their contributions. A number of Harrison's other former colleagues also stepped up—among them Paul Tellier and Michael Sabia, both giants in their own rights and huge helps to me. Jim Gray, a fixture in corporate Canada for decades, lent me his prized CN Hunter Camp DVDs so I could watch the event in its entirety, some twenty hours. Marie-Clarke Davies helped scour for documents, checked facts, and provided perceptive suggestions after reading an embryonic draft of the manuscript. My thanks as well to Jim Keohane and Wendy Leaney Gray, who took the time to read a more advanced version for me.

Trena White and her team at Page Two guided the book through the publishing process. It meant the world that Amanda Lewis, the editor of the book, was so enthused about the story and "got" Hunter. I can't thank her enough. Project manager Rony Ganon made the trains run on time (excuse the pun), and Peter Cocking and Taysia Louie, the design team, produced a rock-'em-sock-'em cover and photo layout. Jenny Govier deftly copyedited the manuscript and Heather Wood was a sharp-eyed proofreader. Annemarie Tempelman-Kluit, the marketing director, cheerfully organized the campaign to sell the book, no small task in today's hyper-competitive media landscape, while Sheila Kay and Media Connect's Kristin Clifford and Adrienne Fontaine figured out how to get me ink and airtime. My agent, Rick Broadhead, and lawyers, Gigi Morin and Alison Woodbury—wise advisors—were invaluable in their assistance and support.

As always, my wife, Lynne Heller, was there every step of the way with her love and encouragement. It's impossible to quantify that, but this volume wouldn't exist without it. Books are also a product of human endeavor. As a result, they have flaws, and surely this one will not be an exception; those rest with me.

I've compiled a list of many others who helped. If I've left anyone out, please forgive my oversight. Thanks to Valencia Floyd, Cheryl Parks, Stephanie Blanchette, David McLean, Ed Lumley, Charlie Baillie, Ned Kelly, Brian Welch, Rebecca MacDonald, Rob Ritchie, Gerald Grinstein, Paul Guthrie, Buzz Hargrove, Ken Lewenza, Wes Hall, J.P. Ouellet, Sameh Fahmy, Cindy Sanborn, Gordon Trafton, Gil Lamphere, Alex Lynch, Paul Haggis, Sue Rathe, Phil Westine, Lyle Reed, Don Wood, Tom Matthews, Brian Sieve, Sandra Gentile, Isabelle Courville, John Baird, Matthew Paull, McLain Ward, Jeff Ward, Jim Valentine, Bill Green, Mike Cory, Diane Harrison, Bill Fox, John Kay, Erin Kay, Tom Caldwell, the Right Honourable Paul Martin, David Ferryman, Nathan Goldman, Jeff Ellis, Jeremy Berry, Leslie Higgins, Diana Sorfleet, Lauren Lieberman, Jim Stanton, Lily Lopez, Christian Rec, Susan Nicholson, Monica Pizzuto, Herbie Brown, Matt Rose, Rance Randle, Torrance Lesure, Myron Baker, Robert Poisson, Maxine Leverett, Robin Ferracone, Kristine Owram, David Willcott, Kevin Edwards, Wick Moorman, Jeremy Jacobs, Mike Zafirovski, Jim McNerney, Michael Larson, Noah Zivitz, Grant Ellis, Tyler Best, and J. Larry Carey.

BIBLIOGRAPHY

BOOKS

Berton, Pierre. *The Last Spike: The Great Railway 1881–1885*. Toronto: Anchor Canada, 1971.

Bruce, Harry. *The Pig That Flew: The Battle to Privatize Canadian National*. Vancouver: Douglas & McIntyre, 1997.

Collins, Jim. *Good to Great: Why Some Companies Make the Leap . . . and Others Don't*. New York: HarperCollins, 2001.

Del Vecchio, Mike. *Pictorial History of America's Railroads: 150 Year of Railroading*. Osceola, WI: MBI Publishing Company, 1998.

Gwyn, Richard. *The Man Who Made Us: The Life and Times of John A. Macdonald, Volume One: 1815–1867*. Toronto: Vintage Canada, 2007.

———. *Nation Maker: Sir John A. Macdonald: His Life, Our Times, Volume Two: 1867–1891*. Toronto: Vintage Canada, 2011.

Halberstam, David. *The Fifties*. New York: Random House, 1996.

Harrison, E. Hunter. *Change, Leadership, Mud and Why: How We Work and Why, Volume II*. Montreal: Canadian National Railway, 2008.

———. *How We Work and Why: Running a Precision Railroad, Volume I*. Montreal: Canadian National Railway Company, 2005.

Honey, Michael K. *Going Down Jericho Road: The Memphis Strike, Martin Luther King's Last Campaign*. New York: W.W. Norton & Company, 2011.

Isaacson, Walter. *Steve Jobs*. New York: Simon & Schuster, 2011.

Johnson, Judy, Les Dakens, Peter Edwards, and Ned Morse. *SwitchPoints: Culture Change on the Fast Track to Business Success*. Hoboken, NJ: John Wiley & Sons, 2008.

Maguire, Kathleen, with Elizabeth McNulty. *Chicago Then and Now*. London: Salamander Books, 2015.

McLean, David, with Patricia Finn. *A Road Taken: My Journey from a CN Station House to the CN Boardroom.* Vancouver: Greystone Books, 2014.

Richard, Christine S. *Confidence Game: How Hedge Fund Manager Bill Ackman Called Wall Street's Bluff.* Hoboken, NJ: John Wiley & Sons, 2010.

Standiford, Les. *Last Train to Paradise: Henry Flagler and the Spectacular Rise and Fall of the Railway That Crossed an Ocean.* New York: Broadway Books, 2002.

ARTICLES

Atkins, Eric. "Canadian Pacific: The Cost of Success (The Turmoil behind the Turnaround)." *Globe and Mail,* March 4, 2017.

———. "CP Overhauls Firing Policy to Improve Labour Relations." *Globe and Mail,* March 24, 2017.

———. "CSX Complaints Gather Steam." *Globe and Mail,* September 4, 2017.

———. "CSX's Hunter Harrison Eager to Talk Revamp with U.S. Regulator." *Globe and Mail,* September 7, 2017.

———. "Former CP Head Harrison to Join CSX as Chief Executive." *Globe and Mail,* March 7, 2017.

———. "'I Can Make My Own Decisions': Creel Looks to Make His Mark on Canadian Pacific." *Globe and Mail,* May 23, 2017.

Atkins, Eric, and Janet McFarland. "Harrison to Exit CP with $52-Million; Non-compete Pact Silent on CSX." *Globe and Mail,* January 24, 2017.

Bakx, Kyle. "CP Rail Encourages Office Workers to Learn How to Drive Trains." *CBC News,* February 2, 2015.

———. "CP Rail Shifts Focus from Acquisitions to Fixing Labour Strife." *CBC News,* May 10, 2017.

Barr, Alistair. "Activists Win Four Seats on CSX Board." *MarketWatch,* July 16, 2008.

Beatty, Dr. Carol A. "Hunter Harrison and the Transformation of Canadian National Railway: A Case Study of the Five Ps of Cultural Change." Queen's University Industrial Relations Centre, 2016.

Bebchuk, Lucian A., Alon Brav, Wei Jiang, and Thomas Keusch. "Dancing with Activists." *Columbia Business School Research Paper* No. 17-44 (June 2017).

Benoit, David. "Meet Paul Hilal, the Activist Investor Taking on CSX." *Wall Street Journal,* January 19, 2017.

Benoit, David, and Jacquie McNish. "Outgoing Canadian Pacific CEO and Activist Investor to Target CSX." *Wall Street Journal,* January 18, 2017.

Benoit, David, Jacquie McNish, and Paul Ziobro. "CSX Seeks Shareholder Input on Activist Investor's Request." *Wall Street Journal,* February 14, 2017.

Bloomberg News. "Bill Ackman Joins the Fray after Norfolk Southern Rejects Canadian Pacific's Latest Bid." December 8, 2015.

———. "Canadian Pacific Railway Ltd. CEO Hunter Harrison Says Proxy Fight Likely in Norfolk Southern Corp. Bid." December 14, 2015.

Boyer, Peter L. "Letter from Burbank: Jay Leno's Hard Bargain." *New Yorker*, November 9, 1992.

Business News Network. "Hunter Harrison, 2012 Newsmaker of the Year." December 20, 2012.

Canadian Business. "Ex-CP CEO Says He's Rooting for Current Boss Fred Green in Proxy Fight." February 20, 2012.

Canadian Press. "Canadian Pacific Launches CEO Search." May 17, 2012.

———. "CP Rail Wins Say-on-Pay Vote at Shareholders Meeting." May 10, 2017.

Carey, Nick. "Union Pacific Will Do All in Its Power to Stop Rail Mergers: CEO." Reuters, January 13, 2016.

———. "U.S. Military: CP, Norfolk Southern Merger Could Affect Defense." Reuters, April 7, 2016.

Caro, Robert A. "The Orator of the Dawn: With One Speech Hubert Humphrey Made Himself a National Figure. He Wanted to Be President. So Did Lyndon Johnson." *New Yorker*, March 4, 2002.

Caulfield, Brian. "The Public Twists and Turns of the Steve Jobs Health Saga." *Forbes*, January 17, 2011.

CBC News. "CN Fined $1.4 Million for 2005 Lake Wabamun Derailment." May 25, 2009.

———. "Faulty Track Caused Derailment, Oil Spill in Lake Wabamun: TSB." October 25, 2007.

Chicago Tribune. "CEO Compensation in the Top 100." May 11, 1997.

Collins, Jim. "The 10 Greatest CEOs of All Time." *Fortune*, July 21, 2003.

Cormick, Greg. "CN: Safer, Faster, Smarter." *Railway Age*, August 2004.

Coyle, Jim. "Intercolonial Railway: Engineering an Act of Union." *Toronto Star*, April 15, 2017.

Crown, Judith. "Illinois Central Keeps Chugging." *Crain's Chicago Business*, February 17, 1997.

Davies, Charles. "Riding High." *National Post Business Magazine*, July 2003.

DeCloet, Derek. "Hard-Ass of the Year." *Globe and Mail*, November 30, 2007.

———. "Hunter Harrison: Former CEO, Canadian National Railway." *Report on Business Magazine*, October 2011.

Deveau, Scott. "Bill Ackman Has His Day and His Way at CP Rail Annual Meeting." *Financial Post*, May 17, 2012.

———. "CN to Suspend Benefits for Former CEO Hunter Harrison." *Financial Post*, January 23, 2012.

———. "CP Blasted by Proxy Advisor ISS." *Financial Post*, May 3, 2012.

———. "CP Rail Shakeup Could Precede Shareholder Meeting." *Financial Post*, March 13, 2012.

———. "Get Ready to Deal with Fear: CP Rail Chief Harrison Fires Back at Union Critics Over Safety Concerns." *Financial Post*, May 22, 2013.

———. "Hunter Harrison Appointed CP Rail CEO." *Financial Post*, June 29, 2012.

———. "Looking for a Big Finish." *Financial Post*, January 5, 2009.

———. "Rivals CP Rail and CN Rail Forge Executive Poaching Accord." *Financial Post*, February 4, 2013.

Deveau, Scott, Frederic Tomesco, and Thomas Black. "Norfolk Southern Will Woo Shareholders to Block Ackman, CP Bid: Sources." *Bloomberg News*, December 11, 2015.

Dow Jones. "Illinois Central CEO: Search for Successor to End Soon." February 3, 1993.

Economist. "All Aboard: Can a Railway Legend Deliver at America's CSX?" March 11, 2017.

Erman, Boyd. "Ackman Fires Back at CP: The Full Letter." *Globe and Mail*, January 3, 2012.

———. "Back Off: The Full CP Letter to Ackman." *Globe and Mail*, January 3, 2012.

Esterl, Mike. "FedEx Opposes Merger of Canadian Pacific and Norfolk Southern." *Wall Street Journal*, March 3, 2016.

Foran, Pat. "CN: A Culture of Precision." *Progressive Railroading*, July 2004.

———. "CN's Hunter Harrison is the Recipient of *Progressive Railroading*'s 'Railroad Innovator' Award." *Progressive Railroading*, September 2009.

———. "Postcard from Hunter Camp." *Progressive Railroading*, March 2007.

———. "The Real Innovation Deal." *Progressive Railroading*, September 2009.

Frailey, Fred. "Hunter's Way or the Highway." *Trains Magazine*, August 2009.

———. "Interview with Hunter Harrison." *Trains Magazine*, February 26, 2009.

Franklin, Stephen. "As CEO Pay Soars, Debate Picks Up." *Chicago Tribune*, May 3, 1998.

Globe and Mail. "Board Games 2011 Corporate Governance Rankings." November 25, 2011.

Goldstein, Matthew. "William Ackman Sells Pershing Fund's Stake in Valeant." *New York Times*, March 13, 2017.

Green, Howard. "Another Tidbit from the CP Rail Saga." Business News Network (website), March 28, 2012.

Gurdis, Elizabeth. "Cramer Remix: One Stock That Could Benefit Big from the US Oil Glut." *Mad Money with Jim Cramer*. CNBC, June 13, 2017. www.cnbc.com/2017/06/13/cramer-remix-one-stock-that-could-benefit-big-from-the-us-oil-glut.html.

Hack, Greg. "Landon Rowland, Kansas City Southern CEO and Civic Leader, Dies at 78." *Kansas City Star*, December 28, 2015

Harrison, E. Hunter. "Putting the Operating Ratio in Perspective." *Railway Age*, June 1996.

Hatch, Tony. "Hunter Harrison, Mantle Ridge, CSX: What's Next?" *Progressive Railroading*, February 7, 2017.

Hayes, Thomas C. "Taking Control at Burlington." *New York Times*, April 16, 1982.

Flaherty, Michael. "Proxy Advisor ISS Recommends CSX Shareholders Vote for $84 Million CEO Reimbursement." Reuters, May 22, 2017.

Jake, Sasha. "CSX's New Engineer Could Work Wonders; Sell the Shares Anyway." *Wall Street Journal*, January 19, 2017.

Jang, Brent. "As Harrison Takes CP's Top Job, Ackman's Coup Is Complete." *Globe and Mail*, June 29, 2012.

Jang, Brent, and Jacquie McNish. "CN Suspends Hunter Harrison's Pension Payments." *Globe and Mail*, January 23, 2012.

Jinks, Beth, Manuel Baigorri, Katherine Burton, and Katia Porzecanski. "How to Lose $4 Billion: Bill Ackman's Long Ride Down on Valeant." *Bloomberg News*, March 15, 2017.

Johnson, Eric M. "CSX Chief Executive Attributes Service Disruptions to Employee Push-Back." Reuters, August 1, 2017.

———. "CSX Sticks with Plan to Cut Jobs, Trains." Reuters, March 1, 2018.

———. "CSX's Harrison Bashes Trade Groups over Rail Complaints." Reuters, August 17, 2017.

Kaufman, Lawrence H. "Illinois Central Confirms It Will Buy KC Southern." JOC.com, July 19, 1994.

———. "The Quintessential Operating Executive." *Railway Age*, February 2008.

Kelly, Bruce E. "CP's Next Move: A Bid for CSX Does Not Suggest that All of CP's Potential Lies Eastward." *Railway Age*, January 2015.

Kessler, Andy. "When to Sell? Look at the HQ." *Wall Street Journal*, April 10, 2017.

Kolhatkar, Sheelah. "Shorting a Rainbow: The Hedge Fund that Tried to Sink Herbalife." *New Yorker*, March 6, 2017.

La Roche, Julia. "Bill Ackman's Lieutenant Is Leaving Pershing Square to Pursue New Venture." *Business Insider*, January 27, 2016.

Lilwall, Scott, and Emily Fitzpatrick. "Wabamun Lake Oil Spill: A Decade Later, Disaster Still Fresh in Residents' Minds." *CBC News*, August 3, 2015.

Lopez, Edwin. "Executive of the Year: E. Hunter Harrison." *SupplyChainDive*, December 4, 2017.

Lowe, Dave, and John Sharkey. "Illinois Central's Single Track Project: Working as a Team to Achieve Results." William W. Hay Railroad Engineering Seminar, University of Illinois at Urbana-Champaign, December 18, 2009.

Lu, Vanessa. "CP Rail Proxy Fight: Hunter Harrison Fights Back at CN in Court Filing." *Toronto Star*, March 13, 2012.

———. "CP Rail to Eliminate 4,500 Positions by 2016." *Toronto Star*, December 4, 2012.

———. "CP Rail to Fight Order to Hire Back Engineer Who Used Cocaine." *Toronto Star*, July 17, 2014.

Lye, Chandra. "Experts Give Wabamun Lake Clean Bill of Health." *CTV Edmonton*, August 3, 2014.

MacDougall, Andrew. "Six Lessons Learned from the CP Rail Proxy Battle." *Osler*, July 9, 2012.

Macur, Juliet. "Some People Can't Help but Hate Tom Brady." *New York Times*, February 6, 2017.

Marcec, Dan. "CEO Tenure Rates" (citing study by Equilar Inc.). Harvard Law School Forum of Corporate Governance and Financial Regulation (website), February 12, 2018. corpgov.law.harvard.edu/2018/02/12/ceo-tenure-rates.

Marowits, Ross. "CP Rail's New Bid for Norfolk Southern Rejected." Canadian Press, December 8, 2015.

———. "Fossil Fuels Are 'Probably Dead,' Says Canadian Pacific Railway CEO Hunter Harrison." Canadian Press, March 9, 2016.

Martial, Allison. "New CP Rail Boss Harrison Shifted Culture at CN." Reuters, June 29, 2012.

Mathis, Karen Brune. "CSX's Road to Efficiency: More Cuts." *Jacksonville Daily Record*, March 28, 2017.

Mattoli, Dana, Jacquie McNish, and Dana Cimilluca. "Canadian Pacific Approached CSX about a Takeover in January." Dow Jones, March 1, 2016.

———. "CSX Rebuffed $20 Billion Canadian Pacific Merger Offer." *Wall Street Journal*, March 1, 2016.

McArthur, Keith. "CN Man Sticks to His Schedule." *Globe and Mail*, January 9, 2002.

McClearn, Matthew. "Forward, Fast: Hunter Harrison's CP Transformation." *Canadian Business*, April 23, 2013.

McFarland, Janet. "The High Cost of Change: Executive Compensation 2012." *Globe and Mail*, May 27, 2013.

———. "Investors Vent over Executive Compensation with Say-On-Pay Votes." *Globe and Mail*, May 4, 2016.

McIntosh, Andrew. "CPR Warns of Another Lac-Mégantic if Forced to Rehire Coke-Abusing Engineer." *QMI Agency*, August 16, 2014.

McKenna, Barrie. "CP Rail Strike Ends as Two Sides Agree to Arbitration." *Globe and Mail*, February 16, 2015.

McKenzie, Kevin. "IC Chief Comes Home to Visit Memphis." *Commercial Appeal*, 1993.

———. "Memphian Lists IC Growth, Labor, Cost-Cutting Goals." *Commercial Appeal*, February 20, 1993.

McNish, Jacquie. "CP's Hunter Harrison: 'There Is a New Sheriff in Town.'" *Globe and Mail*, December 7, 2012.

———. "*ROB Magazine*'s CEO of the Year: Bill Ackman." *Globe and Mail*, November 29, 2012.

McNish, Jacquie, and David Benoit. "CSX Agrees to Hire Hunter Harrison as CEO." *Wall Street Journal*, March 6, 2017.

———. "CSX, Railroad Veteran Hunter Harrison Discuss Three-Year CEO Contract." *Wall Street Journal*, February 10, 2017.

McNish, Jacquie, and Brent Jang. "Ackman's Slate Wins ISS Support." *Globe and Mail*, May 3, 2012.

———. "The CP Battle Begins." *Globe and Mail*, January 10, 2012.

———. "CP Demands Ackman Retract 'Outrageous' Comments." *Globe and Mail*, April 27, 2012.

———. "CP Directors Offer Compromise with Activist Investor." *Globe and Mail*, May 2, 2012.

———. "CPPIB Backs Pershing Square in CP Proxy Row." *Globe and Mail*, May 11, 2012.

———. "CP's Activist Investor Eyes Former CN CEO Hunter Harrison." *Globe and Mail*, December 30, 2011.

McNish, Jacquie, and Joann S. Lublin. "Hunter Harrison 'Disappointed' CSX Board and Activist Partner Unable to Reach Settlement." *Wall Street Journal*, February 16, 2017.

McNish, Jacquie, Paul Ziobro, and David Benoit. "CSX Investors Cheered by Former Rail Rival's Sudden Switch." *Wall Street Journal*, January 19, 2017.

Melin, Anders, and Frederic Tomesco. "Is a CEO Worth $200 Million? Shareholders at Rail Giant Think So." *Bloomberg News*, March 6, 2017.

Meyer, Gregory. "CSX Shareholders Approve $84 Million Payout for New CEO." *Financial Times*, June 5, 2017.

Modern Railroads. "The Aggressive, Innovative and Non-traditional Burlington Northern." November 1986.

Morgan, Geoffrey. "Hell on Rails." *Alberta Venture*, March 2013.

Murray, Tom. "Worst to First in 10 Years." *Trains Magazine*, November 2002.

New York Times. "Hedge Fund Dumps Stake in CSX." April 28, 2009.

———. "R.B. Sanborn, 52, Conrail Chief." February 13, 1989.

———. "TCI Starts Proxy Fight at CSX." December 19, 2007.

Orr, Kathy. "On the Right Track: CEO Says Outlook Is Positive for Illinois Central." *Daily Southtown*, October 8, 1995.

Owram, Kristine. "CSX Corp Chief Warns of 'Severe Service Disruptions' from Rail Consolidation." *Financial Post*, October 15, 2014.

———. "The Other Side of Hunter Harrison's CP Legacy: White Collar–Workers Driving Trains." *Financial Post*, February 16, 2017.

———. "Welcome to Chokepoint, USA: Rail Chaos Reigns in Chicago." *Financial Post*, 2014.

———. "Why Hunter Harrison's Status as a 'Legend' Remains Untarnished by the CP Rail–Norfolk Southern Merger Failure." *Financial Post*, April 15, 2016.

Peters, Stephanie. "Hunter's Jumpers: Hunter Harrison Moves to the Next Phase as His Daughter and Son-in-Law Manage Double H Farm." *Equestrian Quarterly*, Winter 2012.

Picker, Leslie. "Norfolk Southern Rejects $28 Billion Bid from Canadian Pacific." *New York Times*, December 4, 2015.

Podmolik, Mary Ellen. "IC Considering Sale: Negotiating with Canadian National on $2.4 Billion Deal." *Chicago Sun-Times*, February 6, 1998.

———. "Illinois Central Sold: Joins Canadian National in $3 Billion Rail Merger." *Chicago Sun-Times*, February 1998.

Politi, Daniel. "A Tense Exchange between Joe Biden and Billionaire Hedge Fund Manager Bill Ackman." Slate.com, June 24, 2017.

Progressive Railroading. "Harrison Takes Helm as Canadian Pacific's CEO; CN Intends to Continue Pursuing Legal Action Against Harrison." June 29, 2012.

Randell, Brian. "Family of CSX CEO Harrison Pays $14 Million to Buy Out Partner on Equestrian Property." *South Florida Business Journal*, November 1, 2017.

Reuters. "Canada Pension Plan Fund Backs Bill Ackman in CP Rail Proxy Fight." May 11, 2012.

———. "CN Accused of Building Fear Culture." March 8, 2008.

Riga, Andy. "Cocaine Use by Train Engineers Seen as Disability." *Montreal Gazette*, July 28, 2014.

Risher, Wayne. *Commercial Appeal*, October 7, 2011.

Sease, Douglas R. "CSX Reorganizes for Efficiency." *Jacksonville Business Journal*, November 17, 2003.

Siler, Julia Flynn. "Illinois Central Agrees to Prospect Merger." *New York Times*, March 11, 1989.

Smith, Eric. "CN's Harrison Yard Elevates Railroad, Memphis." *Memphis Daily News*, September 28, 2009.

Snyder, Jesse. "The No Bullshit Legacy of Hunter Harrison." *Alberta Venture*, September 2016.

Solomon, Steven Davidoff. "How Ackman Won in the Fight over Canadian Pacific." *New York Times*, May 17, 2012.

Stapleton, Shannon. "War of Words: The E-mails that Touched Off a Battle at CP." *Globe and Mail*, January 16, 2012.

Stephens, Bill. "Hunter Harrison and James Foote Meet Again." *Trains Magazine*, October 26, 2017.

Stewart, Sinclair, Jacquie McNish, and Andrew Willis. "CPR Confirms Brookfield Overture." *Globe and Mail*, July 18, 2007.

Toller, Carol, and Tim Kildare. "Worst Case Scenario." *Report on Business Magazine*, December 2017.

Tomesco, Frederic. "Bill Ackman, the Activist Who Sparked CP Rail's Turn-
   around, Quits Board after Pershing Square Sells Stake." *Bloomberg News*,
   September 7, 2016.
Tomesco, Frederic, and Scott Deveau. "CSX Near Deal to Name Harrison CEO as
   Soon as Next Week." *Bloomberg News*, March 3, 2017.
Toronto Star. "Meet CP Rail's New Board." May 17, 2012.
———. "Timeline of CP Rail's Proxy Battle." May 17, 2012.
Tully, Shawn. "Can a 72-Year-Old Railroad Legend Do It Again With CSX?"
   Fortune, January 21, 2017.
———. "How United's Oscar Munoz Bounced Back after a Heart Transplant."
   Fortune, November 18, 2016.
———. "The Last Railroad Tycoon." *Fortune*, September 1, 2017.
Valentine, James. "Dinner with the Dean of Railroading." Morgan Stanley
   Research Report, September 20, 2005.
Vancouver Sun. "CN President Plans to Cut 430 Workers from BC Rail."
   December 26, 2003.
Vantuono, William C. "CN Shows the Way Again." *Railway Age*, February 2008.
———. "Railroader of the Year: E. Hunter Harrison, the Master of Scheduled
   Railroading." *Railway Age*, January 2002.
———. "Railroader of the Year: Hunter Harrison, Canadian Pacific." *Railway
   Age*, January 2015.
Warwaruk, Eric. "The Americanization of CN." *Canadian Dimension* 38, no. 3
   (May/June 2004).
Warwick-Ching, Lucy. "Cascade Investment, Bill Gates' Wealth Manager."
   Financial Times, October 21, 2015.
Waters, David. "The Sixth Way." *Commercial Appeal*, June 4, 2011.
Watson, Thomas. "CN's Harrison Ready to Rule the Rails." Column for Brotherhood
   of Locomotive Engineers and Trainmen, posted on *Canadian Business* (website),
   May 8, 2003.
———. "Tough as Rails." *Canadian Business*, December 10, 2001.
———. "You Win Some: Inside Three Megadeals that Paid Off Big Time." *Canadian
   Business*, February 16–29, 2004.
Wright, Robert. "Ackman Pressures Norfolk Southern Board on CP Rail Deal."
   Financial Times, December 16, 2015.
———. "Bill Ackman Calls on Norfolk Southern to Accept CP's Revised Bid."
   Financial Times, December 8, 2015.
———. "TCI Quits Fight for CSX with Share Sale." *Financial Times*, April 27, 2009.
Ziemba, Stanley. "Illinois Central, Kansas City Southern Call Off Deal." *Chicago
   Tribune*, October 25, 1994.
Ziobro, Paul. "CSX, Shippers Clash Over Service Problems." *Wall Street Journal*,
   October 11, 2017.

————. "Trains in Vain: Epic CSX Traffic Jam Snarls Deliveries, from Coal to Fries." *Wall Street Journal*, August 22, 2017.

Ziobro, Paul, Jacquie McNish, and David George-Cosh. "Railroad Veteran's Turnaround Strategy Faces Hurdles in U.S." *Wall Street Journal*, February 9, 2017.

OTHER DOCUMENTS

Buffett, Warren E. Berkshire Hathaway Annual Shareholder letter, February 25, 2017.

Canadian National Railway Management Information Circulars, 1999–2010.

Canadian National Railway SEC Filing, Form 6-K, December 13, 2002.

Canadian Pacific. "CP Addresses the Financial Community." December 8, 2015.

————. "CP Addresses the Financial Community." December 16, 2015.

————. "White Paper on Consolidation." April 2016.

Canadian Pacific Railway Annual Report, 2001 (following spin-off from Canadian Pacific Limited).

Canadian Pacific Railway Management Proxy Statements, 2012–17.

Canadian Railway Office of Arbitration & Dispute Resolution, Case no. 4328. Heard in Montreal, July 10, 2014. Concerning Canadian Pacific Railway and Teamster Canada Rail Conference. Dispute: Appeal of the Dismissal of Locomotive Engineer A.

Chicago History Exhibit, John Hancock Tower, Chicago, Illinois.

CSX Corporation Annual Report (10-K), for fiscal year ended December 31, 2017 (filed February 7, 2018).

CSX Corporation Proxy Statement, 2017.

Encyclopedia of Chicago. "IC Industries Inc."

Illinois Central Corp. 10-K, 1998 (filed March 26, 1999).

Illinois Central Corp. 10-K, 1997 (filed March 17, 1998).

Illinois Central Corp. 10-K, 1996 (filed March 21, 1997).

Illinois Central Corp. Pre 14A (filed February 2, 1995).

Illinois Central Corp. Pre 14A (filed March 2, 1994).

ISS Proxy Advisory Services Canada. "Canadian Pacific Railway Limited." May 3, 2012.

Lake Wabamun Residents Committee. *The Lake Wabamun Disaster: A Catalyst for Change.* Report to the Railway Safety Act Review Advisory Panel. August 31, 2007.

Mantle Ridge Letter to CSX. *Activist Stocks*, February 17, 2017.

Norfolk Southern Corporation Preliminary Proxy Statement in Connection with Contested Solicitations, 2016.

Norfolk Southern Corporation Schedule 14A Information, 2016 Annual Meeting of Shareholders of Norfolk Southern Corporation, Proxy Statement of Canadian Pacific Railway Limited, March 29, 2016.

Ontario Teachers' Pension Plan Annual Reports, 2011–13.

Pershing Square Capital Management, L.P. SEC Filing, Form 13-D, October 28, 2011.

Railway Safety Act Review Secretariat. *Stronger Ties: A Shared Commitment to Railway Safety, Review of the Railway Safety Act*. Ottawa: Minister of Transport, 2007.

Reference for Business. "History of Whitman Corporation." www.referenceforbusiness.com/history2/27/Whitman-Corporation.html.

Regulatory filings and news releases by CN, CP, and CSX.

Tender Offer Statement, Illinois Central (subject company). Canadian National Railway Company and Blackhawk Merger Sub, Inc. (bidders). SEC Filing, 14D1. February 12, 1998.

Transportation Safety Board of Canada. "Lac-Mégantic Runaway Train and Derailment Investigation Summary." Ottawa: Minister of Public Works and Government Services Canada, 2014.

————. "Railway Investigation Report, R05E0059. Derailment. Canadian National Freight Train M30351-03 Mile 49.4, Edson Subdivision, Wabamun, Alberta. 03 August 2005." Ottawa: Minister of Public Works and Government Services Canada, 2007.

United States Department of Defense. "Letter to the Surface Transportation Board from Department of the Army, Military Surface Deployment and Distribution Command, April 7, 2016, re: Department of Defense Reply regarding Canadian Pacific Railway Limited—Petition for Expedited Declaratory Order." April 7, 2016.

United States Department of Justice. "Reply of the United States Department of Justice before the Surface Transportation Board re: Canadian Pacific Railway Limited— Petition for Expedited Declaratory Order." April 8, 2016.

United States District Court, Northern District of Illinois, Eastern Division. Canadian National Railway Company, Plaintiff, v. E. Hunter Harrison, Defendant. January 23, 2012.

United States District Court, Northern District of Illinois, Eastern Division. Canadian National Railway Company, Plaintiff, v. E. Hunter Harrison, Defendant. E. Hunter Harrison, Counter-Plaintiff, v. Canadian National Railway Company, Counter-Defendant. March 9, 2012. Case No. 1:12-CV-00493.

United States District Court, Northern District of Illinois, Eastern Division. Canadian National Railway Company, Plaintiff, v. E. Hunter Harrison, Defendant. E. Hunter Harrison, Counter-Plaintiff, v. Canadian National Railway Company, Counter-Defendant. December 21, 2012. Case No. 1:12-CV-00493.

United States District Court, Northern District of Illinois, Eastern Division. Canadian National Railway Company, Plaintiff, v. E. Hunter Harrison, Defendant. E. Hunter Harrison, Soo Line Railroad Co. d/b/a Canadian Pacific Railway Limited, and Canadian Pacific Railway Limited, Counter-Plaintiffs, v. Canadian National Railway Company, Counter-Defendant. Agreed Order of Dismissal, February 7, 2013. Case No. 1:12-CV-00493.

FILMS AND VIDEOS

Ackman, Bill. Interview by Howard Green. *Headline with Howard Green*. Business News Network, February 6, 2012 (recorded February 5, 2012).

———. Interview by Howard Green. *Headline with Howard Green*. Business News Network, April 23, 2012.

CN Hunter Camp (video), 2005.

Harrison, Hunter. Interview by Howard Green. *Headline with Howard Green*. Business News Network, November 12, 2009.

———. Interview by Howard Green. *Headline with Howard Green*. Business News Network, February 6, 2012 (recorded February 5, 2012).

———. Interview by Howard Green. *Headline with Howard Green*. Business News Network, March 13, 2012.

———. Interview by Howard Green. *Headline with Howard Green*. Business News Network, May 27, 2013.

———. Interview by Howard Green. *Headline with Howard Green*. Business News Network, September 17, 2013.

———. Interview by Howard Green. *Headline with Howard Green*. Business News Network, February 26, 2014.

———. Interview by Frances Horodelski. Business News Network, March 3, 2015.

———. Interview by Frances Horodelski. Business News Network, March 8, 2016.

———. Interview by Amber Kanwar. Business News Network, April 20, 2016.

———. Interview by Tyler Mathisen on being named Morningstar CEO of the Year. *Nightly Business Report*. CNBC, January 15, 2014.

———. Interview by Erik Schatzker. Bloomberg, December 14, 2015.

———. Interview by Erik Schatzker. Bloomberg, March 10, 2016.

———. Interview by William C. Vantuono on being named *Railway Age* Railroader of the Year. January 8, 2015. www.youtube.com/watch?v=5em1OYubF2s.

———. Railroader of the Year acceptance speech, 2015.

Mad Money with Jim Cramer. CNBC, Spring 2017.

Marin, Edward L., dir. *Canadian Pacific*. 20th Century Fox, 1949.

INDEX

ABOUT THE AUTHOR

HOWARD GREEN was a broadcast journalist for thirty-three years, best known as founding anchor at Canada's Business News Network, where he hosted the flagship interview program, *Headline with Howard Green*. During his almost fifteen years at BNN, he conducted more than 14,000 interviews, many with leading CEOs and the biggest names in business and politics, including Sir Richard Branson, Federal Reserve chairman Alan Greenspan, and former British prime minister Tony Blair. Prior to that, Green spent eighteen years as a correspondent, producer, and director making programs for a variety of networks, including the Canadian Broadcasting Corporation and PBS. Green is a two-time Emmy nominee and winner of Canada's top television prize for his documentary work, and his films have been broadcast worldwide. In 2013, Green became a bestselling author with the release of his first book, *Banking on America: How TD Bank Rose to the Top and Took on the USA*. His second book, *Distilled: A Memoir of Family, Seagram, Baseball and Philanthropy*, co-authored with Charles Bronfman, was also an instant *Globe and Mail* and *Toronto Star* bestseller and finalist for the National Business Book Award. Howard Green lives in Toronto.